— uses a Southwestern Engl herself

— especially with the land
— snakes
— desert
— especially w/ Laguna identity

The
Turquoise Ledge

ALSO BY LESLIE MARMON SILKO

Gardens in the Dunes (novel)

Yellow Woman and a Beauty of the Spirit (essays)

Sacred Water (autobiography)

Almanac of the Dead (novel)

Storyteller (short stories)

Ceremony (novel)

Laguna Woman (verse)

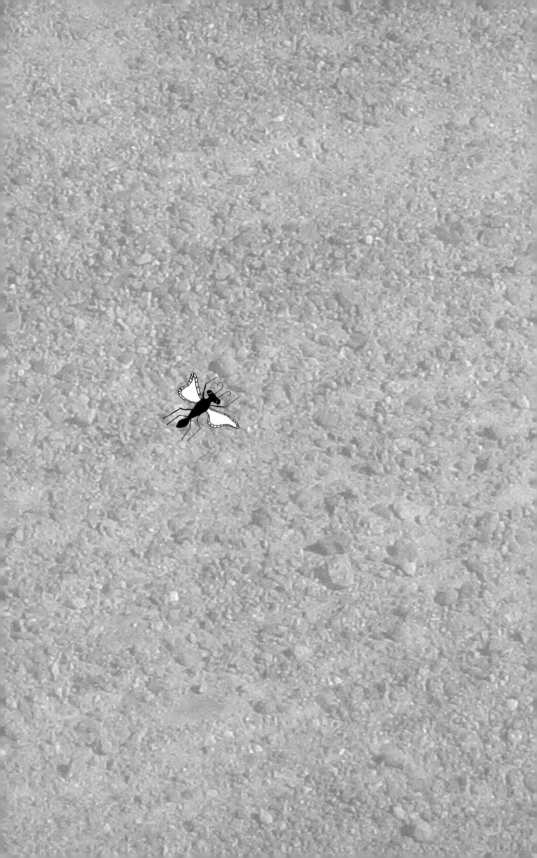

LESLIE MARMON SILKO

The Turquoise Ledge

VIKING

VIKING
Published by the Penguin Group
Penguin Group (USA) Inc., 375 Hudson Street, New York, New York 10014, U.S.A.
Penguin Group (Canada), 90 Eglinton Avenue East, Suite 700, Toronto, Ontario, Canada M4P 2Y3
(a division of Pearson Penguin Canada Inc.)
Penguin Books Ltd, 80 Strand, London WC2R 0RL, England
Penguin Ireland, 25 St. Stephen's Green, Dublin 2, Ireland (a division of Penguin Books Ltd)
Penguin Books Australia Ltd, 250 Camberwell Road, Camberwell, Victoria 3124, Australia
(a division of Pearson Australia Group Pty Ltd)
Penguin Books India Pvt Ltd, 11 Community Centre, Panchsheel Park,
New Delhi – 110 017, India
Penguin Group (NZ), 67 Apollo Drive, Rosedale, North Shore 0632, New Zealand
(a division of Pearson New Zealand Ltd)
Penguin Books (South Africa) (Pty) Ltd, 24 Sturdee Avenue, Rosebank,
Johannesburg 2196, South Africa

Penguin Books Ltd, Registered Offices: 80 Strand, London WC2R 0RL, England

First published in 2010 by Viking Penguin, a member of Penguin Group (USA) Inc.

1 3 5 7 9 10 8 6 4 2

Grateful acknowledgment is made for permission to reprint "Bee! I'm expecting you!" from *The Poems of Emily Dickinson*, Thomas H. Johnson, ed., Cambridge, Mass.: The Belknap Press of Harvard University Press, Copyright © 1951, 1955, 1979, 1983 by the President and Fellows of Harvard College. Reprinted by permission of the publishers and the Trustees of Amherst College.

LIBRARY OF CONGRESS CATALOGING IN PUBLICATION DATA
Silko, Leslie, 1948–
The turquoise ledge / Leslie Marmon Silko.
p. cm.
ISBN 978-0-670-02211-3
1. Silko, Leslie, 1948–   2. Women authors—20th century—Biography.
3. Authors, American—20th century—Biography.   I. Title.
PS3569.I44Z46 2010
813'.54   dc22
[B]
2010012128

Printed in the United States of America
Designed by Nancy Resnick

Penguin is committed to publishing works of quality and integrity.
In that spirit, we are proud to offer this book to our readers;
however, the story, the experiences, and the words
are the author's alone.

To Mei Berssenbrugge,
and to Linda Niemann,
wonderful writers and much-loved friends;
and to Bill Orzen—
Old flames burn brightest.

ACKNOWLEDGMENTS

Many thanks to Simon J. Ortiz, great poet and guest editor, and to all the people at *The Kenyon Review* for the lovely color images of Lord Chapulin and the story of his portrait in the special issue devoted to work by North American Indigenous Authors, Winter 2010.

Mil gracias to the Matias family, Teresa, Alfonso, and their sons, and to the wonderful staff at Teresa's Mosaic Cafe who fed me while I worked on this book. Their red chile chicken enchiladas and "cadillac" margaritas were essential to the writing of this book.

CONTENTS

The
Turquoise Ledge

PREFACE

I was born in 1948, the year of the supernova in the Mixed Spiral galaxy. My friend Joy Harjo, poet and astrologer, charted a triple triune for the afternoon of March 5, 1948 in Albuquerque, but dark planets rule my First House.

1948 is the Year of the Rat. We rats seldom make lasting friendships. We let the correspondence lapse and don't return phone calls.

A great deal of what I call "memories" are bits and pieces I recall vividly; but the process we call "memory," even recent memory, involves imagination. We learn to ignore the discrepancies between our memory of an event and a sister's memory. We can't be certain of anything.

Fortunately my subconscious remembers everything I need. Whatever I can't recall, later comes back to me as I write fiction. I make myself a fictional character so I can write about myself. Only a few proper names are included because it wasn't my intention to write about others but instead to construct a self-portrait.

PART ONE

Ancestors

CHAPTER 1

My friend Bill Orzen taught me to speed walk on flat ground in town, but I prefer the hills to the city, so I adapted the speed walk to the steep rough terrain. The walks took me back into the Tucson Mountains to the old trails where I rode my horses thirty years ago when I first moved here. The trails are narrow footpaths made by the ancient tribal people who lived in the Tucson Mountains for thousands of years; later on prospectors used the old trails and made new trails to their mining claims.

The trail I took on my walks passed the Thunderbird and Gila Monster mines—old diggings—they were never actual mines—the former is a shallow cave in the hillside and the other is a twenty foot vertical shaft where two big white barn owls live and once emerged as I rode by on horseback—truly startling and astonishing.

On foot I can see the ant palaces, some in solid rock, others with starburst circles of stones they've mined and somehow moved up from below. The star pattern reminded me of the Star Being images incised into sandstone thousands of years ago.

Eventually the trail descends and crosses the big arroyo and continues; but here I turn and follow the big arroyo back home. The sandy bottom of the arroyo is criss-crossed with bird and animal tracks that make the trail that humans have used for thousands of years. In rough steep terrain arroyos may provide the only access to an area so the arroyos are "rights of way" for wildlife and humans on foot.

At first I didn't pay much attention to the stones in the arroyo because I was focused on my walking—I was new to the notion of a speed walk through the desert. In the arroyo the deep drifts of fine white sand had a gravity of their own that sucked my feet down. So in those early months of learning how to walk over rough desert terrain at a fast pace I had all I could do to keep moving. I wasn't thinking about rocks in the arroyo.

I learned not to lift my feet in and out of the deep sand but instead to slide my feet through the top layer of sand very rapidly, to shuffle them back and forth so they wouldn't have a chance to sink farther into the deep sand.

Slowly it got easier and I started to notice the pebbles and rocks in the fine white sand, and the animal tracks and signs of coyote and bob-cat in the arroyo. I began to find small rocks and pebbles streaked with turquoise. Over the years I'd picked up some of these turquoise rocks but I wasn't as interested in the stones as I am now. I needed almost daily contact with the turquoise rocks on my walks to develop my interest.

Turquoise doesn't originate deep in the Earth as many precious minerals and gems do. It forms when certain chemical reactions take place during the weathering of surface minerals. Water is a necessary component of the formation of turquoise—no wonder indigenous people of the deserts connected turquoise with water and rain—it wasn't just the color of blue or green—turquoise meant water had been there.

The surface minerals necessary for the formation of turquoise are:
Copper, aluminum and phosphates.
Turquoise is a hydrous hydrate of copper.
Hydrate of copper indicates water in the latticework of the turquoise molecule.
Iron can substitute for aluminum and results in a color variation toward green.
In my research I learned the turquoise stones I'd found were technically not turquoise but chrysocolla which is a minor copper ore,

a hydrated copper silicate restricted to a shallow depth of less than twenty meters. Volcanic disturbance is required to make the cracks and fissures that allow water to reach the aluminum and iron ores in feldspars. Turquoise, malachite and chrysocolla are often found with one another so they all were called "turquoise" in the old days. Some turquoise was harder and shinier while some was chalky and soft. "Chalky turquoise" was the term for chrysocolla. It is not as easy as one might think to tell the difference between the two without chemical analysis in a laboratory.

I prefer the lovely sound of the word "turquoise" and even "malachite" to the sound of "chrysocolla." Chrysocolla sounds like the name of a soft drink—"Chrissy Cola." Turquoise comes from the sixteenth century French word for "Turkish."

So I will use the word "turquoise."

After a walk I would make a few notes about what I'd seen and where. The next time I walked I wouldn't be able to locate any of the places I'd noted on the earlier walk. The ant palaces I'd seen the previous day would have vanished.

If gravity is distributed in this Universe unevenly, then there are places here on Earth where the gravity is weaker or stronger, where even light may speed up or slow down. At a certain walking speed, my eyes received light images from a parallel plane. Parallel planes or worlds may be visible briefly at certain points in this world from time to time. Thus the discrepancies between my recollections and notes immediately after a walk and what I actually find when I attempt to locate these places again.

The idea was that the exercise and open air would help release my mind into a less self-conscious state where I could better perceive the delicacy of the light and the dawn moisture in the breeze. How sweet the air smells and how luxurious it feels to move through this yellow dawn light. The idea of the fast pace was a cardiovascular workout, but also the pace of the walks helped me edit the experience of the walks to the essentials.

As I walked along, I began to imagine a great ledge of turquoise temporarily buried under the sand and rocks. To find so many pieces of turquoise in the millions of tons of arroyo sand pebbles and rocks meant the turquoise ledge must be large. Or is there more than one ledge of turquoise?

The distribution of the pieces of the turquoise ledge may reveal its location to be somewhere below the place where the main road crosses the big arroyo. I don't think the ledge occurs higher in the Tucson Mountains.

My speculations and guesses proved to be wrong. I walked up the arroyo higher into the mountains far above the main road crossing and I found pieces of rock with turquoise streaks. I even found a small turquoise rock near the place the cottonwood used to grow higher in the mountains.

CHAPTER 2

When I was twelve, Great Grandma A'mooh's baby brother, Robert Anaya, gave me a ring of oval green and brown turquoise in an old Navajo silver setting. He was blind by then and he used to cry from happiness as he embraced us children. We always stopped at his house in Paguate on our way deer hunting so he could bless us, and he prayed for us, for our safety and success as we hunted. I cherished this ring from Uncle Robert Anaya, and I wore it every day.

When I was fourteen or fifteen, I was training a quarter horse filly. Every day after school I went to her corral to work with her so the saddle blankets and the saddle didn't frighten her. I noticed the stone in the ring was a bit loose and I knew I should take it off as a precaution, but one day while I was working with the filly, the stone fell out in the deep dirt of the corral. The silver setting and ring remained on my finger. I searched and searched the dirt in the corral but never found the green turquoise stone.

Recently I recalled some special quality in a small rectangular piece of turquoise I'd found awhile back. I looked around my house for this piece of turquoise. I remembered putting it in a "safe place" so safe now I can't find it. I vividly recalled the piece because it was naturally rectangular shaped and polished smooth by the sand in the arroyo.

But after that an obsession began to insinuate itself into my brain. Even after I found three pieces of turquoise larger and as nicely polished as the small rectangular piece, still I searched the house for the lost piece. What is it about us human beings that we can't let go of lost things?

The other morning I took a slow walk and found as much turquoise as I had found in a week of fast walks. I've trained my eyes to spot the smallest bit of blue or blue green as I scan the ground from side to side and up ahead. I will be delighted to take each turquoise pebble or rock and describe it in detail.

Today I found a small piece of turquoise on the trail as it passes the Thunderbird Mine. Two or more turquoise ledges may exist higher in the mountains.

Now that I have twenty or thirty pieces of the turquoise ledge, and many of them are much finer than the small rectangular stone, I can feel the obsession with the lost stone begin to recede in my consciousness.

I make a point of collecting trash I spy as I walk along: shards of broken bottles, a piece of mud flap with "4 wheel" on it, and pieces of electrical wire coated in red and yellow plastic.

This morning I spied four or five shards of broken glass that I picked up, but no turquoise. Was it because I thought there'd be no more turquoise that for two days I found none?

At a point in the arroyo I passed many times before, I glanced down and there was a large piece of turquoise stone in plain view. How odd, I thought, because it was a rock the size of my fist yet I'd never noticed it, and I'd walked the trail only the day before and I distinctly remembered walking past that very spot. I was sure I had not overlooked this turquoise rock. How did the rock get here? Flash floods down the arroyo stirred up the gravel and sand and often revealed new treasures, but there had been no rain at all for more than a month. This was the first time, but not the last that turquoise rocks mysteriously appeared overnight on the trail.

I don't limit myself to turquoise rocks. I keep a watch out for any sort of colorful or odd pebble or stone, and for bits of driftwood in the big arroyo. The Tucson Mountains were part of a volcanic ridge that exploded millions of years ago. Great fiery clouds welded ash and breccias of the basalt, quartzite and limestone that formed from the vast oceans that came and went from time to time. The great heat melted the quartz into chalcedony and jasper that sometimes bear hairline fractures from the shock of the volcanic explosions.

The footpaths through the Tucson Mountains are ancient. Humans have lived in these hills and arroyos for thousands of years. The palo verde and mesquite trees give great quantities of beans in June and the saguaro fruit and prickly pear ripened at the same time; the small game and birds were easy to hunt. For the ancient people, these hills and arroyos held everything they might need for survival.

In the arroyo I find pieces of light gray and pale orange quartzite with smooth surfaces and interesting rectangular shapes that might be the result of erosion by the water and sand in the arroyo or might be evidence that a human hand worked the stone.

A few years ago while I was walking along the edge of the ridge near the east boundary of my property, under a large old palo verde I noticed a large light-colored stone that stood out against the darker basalt. I looked more closely and saw the center of the stone had been carved out to form a cavity; and then I thought "Of course!" The grinding stone with the concave space prevented the hard dry beans from ricocheting and scattering all over when the stone mortar struck them. Previously I'd walked right past these grinding stones without realizing what they were because I was accustomed to grinding stones made for corn which are nearly flat.

These grinding stones were fundamental to survival on the mesquite and palo verde seeds or "beans" that the trees bear in June. The beans, though plentiful and nutritious, were indigestible unless they were ground into flour first then cooked in tortillas. Without a good grinding stone, precious beans would be wasted along with the energy and hard work it took to gather them. For a woman, her grinding stones were her partners in feeding and caring for her family. The stones were handed down from generation to generation. No wonder the grinding stones sometimes talked, and gave their owner warnings about those who might harm her or her family.

The ancestors left the stones under the trees because year after year, they returned there to harvest the mesquite and palo verde beans. It was inconceivable that anyone would steal or remove the grinding stones because they were so heavy, and only useful right there for the hard seeds.

Once I realized what they were, I kept my eye out for the grinding stones and the next one I found was under a large foothills palo verde that was hundreds of years old. After that I made it a practice to look beneath the oldest trees for grinding stones, and I usually wasn't disappointed.

Grinding stones are like other objects that humans make and use every day; they take on a presence of their own. When I see a stone that has been worked by human hands I bring it to the house so it will have a home again.

Up here late at night in November sometimes in the wind I've heard the voices of women singing their grinding songs. After dark I avoid looking out the living room windows on the west side of my old ranch house because I've seen as many as a dozen figures walk past in a group.

In my kitchen there is a window that looks into the hall and laundry area but at one time the window looked outdoors. Four or five times in the thirty years I've lived here, out of the corner of my eye I've gotten glimpses through that window of a woman and a man in the laundry area. I never see their faces clearly but they appear to be young adults, dressed simply, the woman in a gingham dress, the man in jeans and a shirt.

CHAPTER 3

In the rain mists that shimmer across the shoulders of the mountain in the west wind I can make out the tall graceful forms of the shi-wah nah, the cloud beings. I was amazed the first time I saw them crossing the Tucson Mountains.

Once when the rain clouds were hurrying east over the Tucson Mountains, I watched them from my front yard. They were dark with moisture and I wished they'd give us rain, but I could tell by their speed that we'd get no rain—maybe the taller mountains across the valley would get rain. Still the clouds were very lovely—I could smell their sweet moisture and felt the coolness as I watched them move past. Behind the main group of clouds, came others and I noticed one small cloud trailing them—its belly was fat and dark blue but its edges were sunlit silver—"Ah what a beauty you are," I said out loud, "just look at you!"

Then the most amazing thing happened: the small cloud left the path the other clouds followed and it came right over and rained down gently on us before resuming its journey behind the others.

Once I told this story at a Hopi school at lunchtime. Afterwards one of the teachers told me this: a year or so after her seven year old son died, she was outside her house when a small rain cloud stopped above her and rained a few drops before moving on. It was her son. Beloved family members and the ancestors show their love for us when they return as clouds that bring precious precipitation.

On book tour in Albany I met a young woman who'd grown up on a nearby farm. We were talking about horses as she drove me from the airport. Recently her beloved horse had died. The day after he was buried, she went down to the pasture in the evening to bring in the other horses and when she called them, off in the woods she heard the distinctive whinny of her beloved horse.

At the moment my dear old Arabian horse died, his stable mate suddenly galloped around the corral whinnying frantically and looking intently toward the south, as if he was trying to follow although he could plainly see his stable mate lying still on the ground.

After death, it may take some days for the spirit to bid farewell to this world and to the loved ones they want to reassure; so they visit us as birds or other wild creatures to let us know they are in a good place not far away.

The old folks used to keep a dish on the table and passed it around so everyone might put a pinch of food from their plates into the dish. That was to feed all their beloved family members who had passed to the other world. At the end of the meal, the contents of the dish were burned. Once when I was a small child I visited the neighbor as she cooked fried bread outdoors, and I remember how surprised I was when she flipped the first piece of fried bread from the hot oil into the hot coals and ashes. But then I realized that she'd done it to feed the spirits.

Within days of his death, my friend James Wright, the poet, made communication with me through the visit one evening of a small burrowing owl that refused to be frightened or startled by me. James especially loved owls, and he'd written about the elf owls in a poem about the Sonoran Desert. He and his wife, Annie, were scheduled to come to Tucson that April for James to read at the University of Arizona Poetry Center, but of course that was never to be.

Four or five days after my old friend Sheila died in 2004 a small grackle appeared right before dawn while all the other birds were still quiet. The species doesn't usually venture into the desert and I'd not seen one up here before. The bird made raucous teasing squawks as it did a wild dance of joy on the top of the electric pole next to my house. I recognized right away it was old Sheila joyously on her way. I never again saw a short-tail grackle up here.

One day around noon in early 2007, an unusually large cactus wren came to the big prickly pear cactus next to my living room window and perched on a cactus pad where wrens and other birds don't usually land. The wren looked through the window at me and tilted its head back and forth until I paid attention to it. It continued to hop back and forth on the prickly pear quite gaily as it saw me watch it. I turned to Bill and I said, "See that cactus wren? That's strange behavior. I've never seen a bird look through the window before. Someone I know died." Later that day my father called with the news my dear cousin Lana had died.

So it seems that after the passing of a friend or loved one, a few days or a week after they go, they manifest their loving energy: the wind chimes tinkle in the twilight though there is no breeze; the chimney of the oil lantern rattles by itself; the electric fan blades make an unusual sound—the realm of the spirit beings and the ancestors contact us from time to time.

Around the Arctic Circle, the Inuit people believe family and ancestral spirits get reborn again in a few generations. Howard Rock who was Inuit published the first Eskimo newspaper, the *Tundra Times*. He wrote a beautiful memoir of his childhood, and he published excerpts from it in the newspaper.

He recalled the time when he was a small child and his parents took him ice fishing, and he caught more fish than any of the adults. Howard was only five years old, so everyone noticed right away this was unusual, and then someone addressed Howard as "Grandmother," because his late grandmother always used to catch more fish than everyone else when they went ice fishing. That was how they recognized that her spirit had been reborn into the little boy named Howard.

A few times I've had dreams in which I visited beloved family members. Once I visited my great grandfather Robert G. Marmon, who died many years before I was born. My father loved him a great deal and talked about him while I was growing up and of course, Grandma A'mooh told me about him so I felt we knew each other somehow.

Twice in my dreams I visited with Grandma A'mooh. Both times she hugged me close to her as she did when I was a little girl; when I awoke her familiar scent was still with me. But after only a few moments that memory of her scent when she held me faded into my dream consciousness.

CHAPTER 4

Human beings have lived along the Rio San José in north central New Mexico continuously for the past eighteen thousand years. Not far from Laguna, to the southeast, near State Road 6, the river descends into a gorge, and it was here in shallow caves and cliff overhangs that archeologists found hearths used thousands of years ago by the indigenous hunters who chipped elegant leaf-shaped spear and arrow points to hunt the bison and elk that grazed on the plain. Archeologists called the culture San José man, a counterpart of Folsom man, whose spear points were found in eastern New Mexico, near the town of Folsom.

When I think of the Pueblo people, I think of sandstone—sandstone rainwater cisterns, and sandstone cliff houses; sandstone was the preferred building material at Chaco Canyon and at Mesa Verde, and in the pueblos when I was growing up. Sandstone is a sedimentary rock formed chiefly by quartz particles in a cement of calcite. The calcite cement is often white but some is also yellow, red or brown depending on the iron content in the calcite. Sandstone formations ring the fossil remnants of the great inland seas of the Jurassic Age, which left behind Lake Bonneville and its survivor, the Great Salt Lake in Utah. Southern Utah, western Colorado, northern Arizona and New Mexico are crossed by the same formations of yellow, orange and red sandstone the geologists call by such exotic names as Kaibab, Chinle, Entrada, Carmel, Navajo and Wingate.

The Pueblo people preferred to live along rivers like the Rio San José, the Rio Puerco, and of course, the Rio Grande. If they did not settle by a river, they sought mesas or hilltops with expanses of light yellow or ivory sandstone, the wind-deposited cross bedded dunes laid down eons ago in the Mesozoic, compressed and petrified by overlying sediments that later eroded away. The sandstone was fine-grained and hard enough to resist crumbling under the mason's basalt hammer, but soft enough to carve hand and footholds on the faces of cliffs. The people sought the sandstone formations because pools of rainwater collected in natural basins and cisterns in the petrified Jurassic dunes. The same formations contained long vertical seams that formed fissures in the sandstone where fossil water, artesian springs cold as ice, seeped and dripped down to form shallow pools. So it is not remarkable that the Pueblo people settled on or near the sandstone formations.

As a child I used to watch my great grandma A'mooh kneel on the floor of her kitchen to grind green chili with garlic cloves on the curved rectangular stone of fine-grained black lava. The people preferred the lava stones for grinding because stones made from sandstone sometimes left a residue of fine grit in the food.

Aunt Susie said when she was a child, the women of the household and the neighbors did the grinding together, and as they worked they sang songs. The songs changed their task from hard work to pleasure as they lost themselves in the sounds and the words. Maybe the grinding songs kept the clanswomen from gossiping too much. The songs belonged to particular clans and the women didn't sing the songs of other clans.

It was a grinding song that caused Coyote's disastrous plunge from a high cliff of yellow sandstone. Coyote wanted to learn the grinding song the cedarbirds sang while they were grinding cedar berries.

The cedarbirds dared not refuse Coyote's demand to grind with them and learn the song, but as soon as they could, the cedarbirds planned their escape. They told Coyote they had to fly to the top of the high sandstone mesa to drink from a water hole. Coyote demanded to go along so the cedarbirds each donated a feather and they glued the feathers to Coyote's legs with pine pitch. By flapping his legs very hard Coyote was able to fly in low circles that gradually took him higher, while the birds flew off to the mesa top.

The birds were finished drinking when Coyote finally managed to fly up to the mesa top. While Coyote was drinking he noticed the heat of the sun had made the pitch soft and the feathers were falling off his legs. He realized he wouldn't be able to fly and would be stranded on top of the cliff. He tried to threaten the cedarbirds to force them to help him, but they flew away.

Old Spider Woman heard Coyote's cries for help and came to his rescue. She told him to get into her magic basket and she would lower him down from the mesa top. There was only one thing he must not do while she was lowering him: he must not look up. But Coyote could not resist taking a peek and the basket he was riding in plunged to the ground far below and Coyote was smashed to pieces on the rocks. All this because Coyote wanted to learn the cedarbird ladies' grinding song.

The coarse blue corn flour ground between lava grinding stones made a thick tortilla with amazing flavor—far better than the thin tortillas from machine-ground blue corn. Our neighbors used to take orders from everyone in Laguna and the following day they delivered the most delicious big red chili enchiladas made with these stone-ground blue corn tortillas.

Aunt Susie told me about the special sandstone griddles required to make the delicacy called piki bread. The cook has to work fast; she pours a corn meal batter onto the hot griddle all the while quickly smearing the batter with her bare hand into a film over the griddle so it forms continuous paper-thin sheets that fold around one another.

If the griddle stone is too coarse, the batter sticks and the flaky sheets of corn batter are ruined. So the rectangular slabs of hard fine-grained sandstone were essential for making the piki. Griddles made with other stone would not do, and the people at Paguate village where my great grandmother came from possessed the best source of griddle stones. During droughts or other hard times, the people used to carry the griddle stones in backpacks and walk for four or five days to reach Jemez Pueblo where they traded them for beans and corn to take back to Paguate.

The Anasazi, the ancient Pueblo people, were haunted by memories of terrible famines when the weather or other conditions failed them. Even now the Western Pueblos and the Hopi tell stories about droughts and famines that struck their villages, and forced the people to take refuge at other pueblos to avoid starvation. Sometimes small children and infants were adopted by childless people in other pueblos so the babies might survive.

On the high desert plateau of north central New Mexico, the Anasazi had to pursue food sources relentlessly, gathering seeds, roots, berries and birds' eggs, hunting small rodents and snaring birds. Hunters stalked deer and elk in the mountains and the antelope and bison on the grassy plains that stretched away to the south and to the east.

Below the mesa and hilltop villages, in the sandy soil at the mouths of arroyos and other small drainages, the people carried on dry farming of corn, beans, melons, amaranth and greens. The deep layers of fine sand trapped and held the runoff down where the roots of the bean and corn seedlings suckled and grew. These deposits of fine sand were rich in nutrients gathered as rain washed the sand from the mesas. Unlike soils of clay, the deep sand deposits captured rainwater almost immediately so little precious water was lost to flooding or evaporation.

The most ingenious engineering was done on the floodplains where small stones were arranged in slender curved half-moons, spaced so the swift muddy runoff from sudden cloudbursts was slowed by the small stone catch-dams and the runoff sank into the deep sand then spread nicely to water the fields of corn and beans nearby.

The Pueblo people lived in the Laguna-Acoma area for thousands of years before the Europeans invaded, but the Spanish record-keepers made no mention of Laguna Pueblo, only Acoma. It was at Acoma Pueblo that the Spaniards chopped off one hand and one foot of every captured Acoma man or boy over the age of seven, in retaliation for an Acoma victory over the Spanish troops in 1598.

Because of their barbarity toward all the Indian tribes, the Spaniards were later killed or driven out of the country all the way to El Paso in the Great Pueblo Revolt of 1680. Even the Apaches and Navajos set aside differences with one another and with the Pueblos to join them in the action to expel the invaders.

In 1692 the Spaniards returned. The Indian alliances that produced the Great Revolt were no longer maintained and the Pueblo resistance failed. Those in the pueblos around Santa Fe who did resist the return of the invaders were killed and their families sent to Mexico as slaves or removed and resettled to Laguna. But the Kawaikameh, the Laguna people, had been living there by the small lake on the Rio San José for thousands of years already when the rebels from the northern pueblos were brought there. Thus the Spaniards erroneously stated Laguna Pueblo wasn't established until 1698. The error about the date of the founding of Laguna Pueblo was repeated in later histories. The Laguna Pueblo people didn't bother to correct the error because it made no difference to their reckoning of the world.

CHAPTER 5

From my earliest days, animals and beings of the natural world occupied as much of my consciousness as human beings did. Around humans often I sensed an uncomfortable feeling below the surface, one that left me with unease and anxiety to please everyone. So early on I preferred to play alone, or to be with cats, dogs or horses for companionship, not human beings.

Over time I realized the politics of the Marmons in the pueblo was part of this, but there was more. Another part of the unease I felt as a child may have come from what happened before I was conceived. I found this out when I was in my early twenties from my grandma Jessie, my mother's mother.

Grandma Jessie said my mother gave away a baby and immediately conceived me, perhaps as a way to try to forget the baby boy she couldn't keep. Of course she never forgot the baby boy and grieved all her life. She'd already arranged the adoption before she met my father. My father wanted to raise the child as his, but my mother believed in the prevailing notion of the time—that in such situations, adoption was best. For my mother adoption was the worst, and the pain helped keep her drinking all her life.

My mother never talked about it until she was in her sixties, and her old flame, the father of the baby boy, located her in Gallup. They tried to contact their son through a national organization for adoptees. She told me they filed their names and information with the organization but no one ever replied. The old flame rekindled for a while then sputtered out. My mother never again mentioned the old flame or the boy she gave up for adoption.

Sometimes I think about him, the boy, my lost half brother. He haunted my mother, and by extension, he haunted my sisters and me. Somewhere I have notes from when I tried to calculate the approximate time of his birth. First I count back from my birthday, March 5, 1948. (March 5th was my mother's birthday too.) Then I count back nine months more; she and my father went to Denver for the birth. I think about the Viet Nam War and all the young men who died there. Maybe that's what happened to my brother I never knew; maybe that's why he never made contact with my mother or his father.

My sister Wendy liked to dress dolls and play with little dishes. I wanted to have four legs and be able to run free in the hills as a deer or as a horse. For a long time I wished I wasn't a human being. Whenever I ran, I pretended I was a deer or a wild horse.

I talked to myself, and made up stories about myself and imaginary animals and people. I did the talking for each character. I was always "myself" as I made up the story, but I felt different from the little girl I became around the adults or other children. I preferred to play by myself. I was annoyed when other children or adults interrupted my imaginary worlds.

I seldom played with dolls or toy dishes because I was interested in the world outside the house. During my first four years, my playmates were two large dogs, a yellow dog, Bozo, and Blackie. My mother told me Blackie was the only one with me when I was about four months old and lightning struck the house during a summer storm. My parents and grandparents were working in my grandfather's store a short distance away.

I remember following the two dogs around the yard while they ignored me and carried on with their dog business—which was to attend and sometimes to eat from their large collection of buried bones. They made visits to the places the bones were buried to make sure none were stolen or exposed. When the bones were ready to eat, I used to watch the dogs dig enthusiastically, their noses smudged with dirt, and how they savored the rotting morsels they recovered from the ground. The dogs and I could not leave the yard, but it was a large enclosure about a quarter of an acre in size and included shade trees, outbuildings and storage areas for old lumber.

I was happy to play by myself. As I got a little older I liked to venture out of the yard. At first I went a short distance to some stacks of sandstone that were salvaged from a collapsed structure and intended for a house that was never built. A stray mother cat had hidden her kittens there in the crevices between the stones. I used to sit patiently on the sandy ground by the stacks of stone, to wait for the cat. She was yellow-striped, her yellow a little darker than the sandstone. I called her "Coonie." She was skittish but sometimes allowed me to pet her. When her kittens were old enough to begin to emerge, I was disappointed at how shy and wild they were. I had to wait a very long time and sit very still before the kittens would peek out from the rocks. When I was finally able to grab hold of one it hissed and scratched me until I let it go and it fled to the safety of the rocks. I never tried to catch one again.

Before my sister Wendy was born my parents moved out of my grandparents' place to the old house across the road where my father was born. I saw an old photograph of Old Laguna from the 1870s, and the only building below the village was that old house we grew up in. The mud and stone structure was older than my great grandfather's adobe house or the old train depot building of frame stucco across the road where Grandpa Hank and Grandma Lillie had turned the old train lobby into a living room and bedroom.

Until I started kindergarten when I was five, I spent most of my time trying to escape the yard to get to the village where the older kids were, the kids who stopped to talk to me at the fence on their way home after school. They told me about all sorts of wonderful things I could not see because the Marmons kept their little children in yards, corralled like goats.

I was the goat that climbed over the fence and took off. Marcelina Thompson, our neighbor, found me walking by her house and knew my parents didn't want me loose. So Marcelina took me home; I cried and fought her all the way. I still remember what compelled me to climb over the fence: the kids told me there were dancers who ate wood as part of their dance, and I wanted to see this. I was three.

One Christmas when I was in the second grade, my classmate Evangeline drew my name at school, and she gave me a lovely silver bracelet and ring with a honey brown stone. It seemed like such a generous gift at the time. Years later my mother told me that before Grandpa Hank met Grandma Lillie, Grandpa Hank had been married in the traditional way to a beautiful young Laguna woman who was related to Evangeline, but she died with Grandpa Hank's child during the birth.

Sometimes I felt Grandma Lillie was overshadowed by something. Was it the dead woman and child?

When adults talked, I listened while the other children went off to play. I realize now I was moved by the undercurrents of tension I sensed between the Pueblo and non-Pueblo members of my extended family. From a young age I was fascinated with how the different sides of the family talked about the other. I always felt such anguish when one side of the family said something mean about the other branches of the family. I understood all of them in their ways, and I loved all of them and felt they loved me in their ways. For a long time I wondered why they did not see themselves as I did and love each other. Of course I was a young child then and did not yet understand the injustice that fueled the undercurrents between the Marmons, the other family branches, and the rest of the Pueblo.

By the fifth grade I began to understand how the inequalities and injustice generated an impersonal anger, which sometimes got aimed at me because my paternal great grandfather was a white man. But I also knew that to other white men my great grandfather was a "squaw man" who set himself apart from other white men when he married my great grandmother.

During the time my father served as Laguna Tribal Treasurer in the middle 1950s the Pueblo of Laguna Tribe filed a lawsuit in the U.S. Court of Federal Claims. I remember when they took depositions for the case at the Federal Court in Albuquerque. My father carried piles of manila folders with him to the hearing. Millions of acres of Laguna Pueblo land had been taken by the Federal Government in the early 1900s for national forest and public land.

The Pueblo hired archeologists and anthropologists to testify to Laguna's ancient, continuous occupancy and use of the land at issue. After all the intrusions, theft and trouble that anthropologists had previously caused at Laguna, finally the people got some satisfaction out of anthropology.

The stories and accounts of the old folks were important evidence in the lawsuit. The elderly Laguna people traveled one hundred miles round trip day after day to testify in the Laguna language in Federal Court. Some of them used to come to our house to ride with my father to Albuquerque; they were apprehensive about testifying in Federal Court but they were also brave because they wanted the land back.

Years later a decision came down from the Court of Federal Claims. Laguna Pueblo got back none of their precious land; instead the tribe was paid twenty-five cents per acre although the fair market value of the land in 1967 was hundreds of dollars per acre.

What had lasting impact on me was that the old folks told their stories in their own words, in the Laguna language, and that together they stood the test in a high court of an alien culture. Maybe this is where I got the notion that if I could tell the story clearly enough then all that was taken, including the land, might be returned.

When I was a child, the Bureau of Indian Affairs day school at Laguna only had kindergarten through the fourth grade. For the fifth grade, we Laguna children had to leave our families to attend Indian boarding schools, or start riding the bus to school for hours every day.

I started writing when I was in the fifth grade because the transfer to Manzano Day School in Albuquerque was so difficult. The Bureau of Indian Affairs teachers had not bothered to teach us the times tables. I was mortified at how far behind I was at my new school.

The fifth grade teacher was Mrs. Cooper who came from England as a war bride. She was very patient and understanding about my deficiencies in arithmetic. Soon after school began, she assigned our class to take the week's spelling list and use each of the words on the list at least once in a story we had to make up. I can still remember how delighted I was with the assignment. I loved to make up stories to tell my younger sisters and cousins.

The story came to me effortlessly, and in no time I was finished. But when I glanced around the classroom I saw the other students had difficulty making up a story. Here was something I could do that the others could not do so easily.

All my life at Laguna I was surrounded by people who loved to tell stories because it was through the spoken word and human memory that for thousands of years the Pueblo people had recorded and maintained their entire culture. The stories I loved to hear were part of my early training; from these early years of listening my imagination raced off to make up my own stories. Making up stories was second nature to me.

I made an important discovery too: while I was writing the story, I was no longer in the classroom, I was no longer the girl in fifth grade who hadn't heard of the times tables. I was transported to the place the story was located; I wasn't a character in the story, but I knew the direction the story was headed and I followed along and wrote down what I saw happening. I loved it and I still love it, even as I type this sentence. At Laguna the notion of "a story" covers the widest possible range: historical accounts, village gossip, sacred migration stories, hummah-hah stories that included Coyote and the other animals and supernatural beings, deer hunting stories, even car wreck stories, were all included in the oral narrative tradition. Stories are valuable repositories for details and information of use to future generations; details and information are easier to remember when there is a story associated with them. Stories even served as maps because a person who was lost in the mountains in a snowstorm might see an odd rock formation and remember a story that described the strange rock formation in detail including its location.

My great grandma A'mooh, Aunt Susie and Aunt Alice, the women who spent the most time answering my questions and telling me stories, were also women who pored over books on their kitchen tables after their families were fed. They were proud to be women of the book as well as women of the spoken word because they had obtained their book knowledge the hardest, loneliest way: in long years of exile under overcast skies at the Indian boarding school in Carlisle, Pennsylvania.

To these women, books were precious, and because of their love of books I grew up surrounded by books. They placed the highest possible value on education because the Pueblo people have always believed that knowledge from all sources, including books, is necessary for survival.

From these women, my father learned to love books. He belonged to book clubs and I remember the big deal over the publication of the unexpurgated edition of *Lady Chatterley's Lover* and *Tropic of Cancer*, both of which he got.

He was always telling me that I should be a writer because writers can live anywhere they want and do their work. He had a vivid childlike imagination. He must have talked to me a great deal about writing in the years before I went to school. My father's passion and true calling was photography but he was a fine storyteller and writer himself, and always had a story to go with each photograph he made.

I will always remember the day two white tourists visited our school and asked each of us children what we wanted to be when we grew up. My turn came and I told them I wanted to be a "playwright." I was in the second grade. I never forgot this because the tourists reacted with such disbelief, but I knew a playwright made up stories.

Because I was of mixed ancestry, the older people in the community looked out for me; they tried to teach me things I might not learn at home so I wouldn't blunder into sacred areas in and around Laguna village. Rarely, it was with a scolding, but most often I was taught with kindness.

Back then everyone watched out for other people's children, and adults were expected to mind other people's children and send them home if they saw them in danger.

CHAPTER 6

Grandma Lillie, my father's mother, was born in Los Lunas, south of Albuquerque; she was a mix of Mexican, German and English and one quarter Texas Indian—she wasn't sure which tribe. Great Grandpa Zachary Stagner, Grandma Lillie's father, ran away from his Texas family when he was fourteen, and had no contact with them again. Our cousin Joanne after much research learned that Great Grandpa Stagner's mother was a Texas Indian named Rhoda Touchstone who died in Sweetwater, Texas.

I used to wonder why he ran away from home at fourteen. Was it because his father, Stagner the German, administered terrible whippings? Someone on Grandma Lillie's side of the family had begun the practice of whipping young children. The Laguna Pueblo people, who never hit their children, were horrified at the terrible whippings my father gave my sisters and me when we were small.

Grandma Lillie was a beautiful young woman, but she must not have felt or realized her beauty. I remember all the black and white Kodak snapshots in the Hopi basket with the grasshopper man pattern. Many of the photographs showed Grandma Lillie, when she was young, with Grandpa Hank but also with her younger sisters. There were snapshots of Grandpa Hank often posed beside fast cars. He wore stylish suits and was very handsome.

Sometime in the late 1950s (was it one of the times she thought

Grandpa Hank was having an affair?) Grandma Lillie took the Hopi basket full of snapshots and a pair of sharp scissors and carefully cut out her face from every photograph. If she appeared in snapshots with other people, the faces of the others were intact; only her face was neatly excised. The faceless images were very strange; without the face, the upright figure with the remaining top of the head and hair looked like a corpse.

Recently I learned something more about Grandma Lillie's mother's people, our Los Lunas relatives and their connection with the whipping of young children. All these years I thought I knew the whole story but I was wrong.

Long before I knew anything about the Indian slave trade in New Mexico, I'd heard Grandma Lillie's stories about old Juana, the Navajo captive who lived with them and cared for them when they were children. One Memorial Day when I was twelve or thirteen, Grandma Lillie asked me to go with her to take flowers to old Juana's grave. She told me Juana died around 1920 when she was more than one hundred years old. We filled clean coffee cans with water; then we cut some roses and lilacs from Grandma A'mooh's yard because those were the only fresh flowers to be found.

Grandma Lillie drove us to the south side of Laguna village and then down the old dirt road near the old bridge across the river. A low wall of black lava rock was partially buried in the pale gray river sand that covered an ancient floodplain; in the corners of the wall, dry weeds, scraps of paper and debris formed drifts. The graves were from the time when the Laguna people didn't use carved gravestones but flat pieces of sandstone or slate or black lava stones. I seem to remember the remains of a few wooden crosses scattered about.

She hadn't brought flowers to Juana in a while, but then that year, for some reason, she decided to do it. Grandma Lillie took a little while to get her bearings among the piles of stones and small dunes of sand that shifted in the graveyard with every wind. Then she located the five dark lava stones the size of cantaloupes that marked Juana's grave. I helped Grandma Lillie clear away the tumbleweeds tangled with other debris, and she talked about old Juana while we worked.

Juana had been captured by Mexican slave-catchers when she was just a little girl. Years later when Lincoln freed the slaves, it was already too late for poor Juana—thirty years or more had passed and she no longer spoke the Navajo language, and she did not know where she had been stolen from. Grandma Lillie gave me the impression Juana came to work for their family when she was an adult after Lincoln's proclamation because she had no place to go.

Grandma Lillie said Juana was the one who really mothered them, not Great Grandma Helen. In her eighties, old Juana raised my grandma Lillie and all her sisters and brothers because Great Grandma Helen followed the practices of the wealthy Mexican women at the time, which meant she took to her bedroom as soon as she was pregnant, and did not leave her bedroom again until two months after the birth. Grandma Lillie had eleven sisters and brothers and two who did not survive—so Great Grandma Helen seldom left her bedroom. It was Juana who cared for them while their mother awaited another birth. Juana bathed them and fed them, Juana rocked them and held them when they were sick or scared, not their mother. Juana was in her eighties by the time Grandma Lillie was born.

I remember my great grandma Helen vividly; she always wore a long black cardigan over her dress, and she rolled her own cigarettes from a bag of tobacco as she gossiped in Spanish with my grandma and her sisters Lorena and Marie. I don't remember her greeting us or hugging us; she hardly seemed to notice us great grandchildren. She was so different from our beloved great grandma A'mooh that we children were a little afraid of her.

Great Grandma Helen was born to Josephine Romero whose mother was a Luna, one of the founding families of Los Lunas, New Mexico. The Romeros were another founding family. Josephine Romero had married a Whittington, the son of an English merchant who married a daughter of the Chavez family.

Grandma Lillie always called her grandmother Josephine Romero "Grandma Whip" because she wore a black braided leather belt around her waist which she could remove quickly to use as a whip for naughty children. My father remembers Grandma Whip too. He said they called her Grandma Whip because as children, whenever they visited her, the first thing she did when they came into the house was to warn them not to touch anything in her house by saying "Grandma whip! Grandma whip if you touch!"

The whippings that were part of child-rearing in Grandma Lillie's family included my father, and finally my sisters and me. The whippings were a legacy from Grandma Whip and her family.

In 2006, I was asked to write a foreword to a book about a *corrido* or ballad that was composed in 1882 in the Mexican community of Cubero, near Laguna. The *corrido* is about a Mexican woman, Placida Romero, whose husband was killed and she and her baby kidnapped by a band of Apache raiders.

It is likely the Apaches chose the Cubero area deliberately because Cubero had long been the site of slave markets. Placida Romero was taken back to Chihuahua by the Apache warriors where she was held for forty-nine days and so badly mistreated that the Apache women felt sorry for the Mexican woman and gave her clothing, food and even a burro to aid her escape.

Of course the ballad written afterward made no mention of the compassion and considerable bravery of the Apache women who helped Placida escape. That angered me because at the time they helped her escape, Apache women and children were being murdered by Mexicans and Americans alike for the bounty on their scalps. Yet the Apache women who helped Placida escape did not let the genocide destroy their human decency.

I wanted to put the incident into historical perspective: Placida Romero was a captive for forty-nine days and then she got to go home. Juana was a captive for almost a hundred years, and she never got to go home.

To prepare to write about the captives, I reread L. R. Bailey's scholarly work *Indian Slave Trade in the Southwest*, first published in 1964. Though

I'd read it before, I'd conveniently forgotten some of the more horrendous details. The Spanish governors of New Mexico encouraged and participated in the Indian slave trade; it was their way of keeping the Pueblos, Navajos and Apaches at war with one another so they would not unite against the Spaniards as they had in 1680.

After the fur trade collapsed, the rendezvous held at river crossings from Taos to Tucson became slave markets where Indian captives were traded for whiskey and gunpowder. The captives were mostly young children, primarily young girls because they were less likely to try to escape. At the slave markets, in drunken exhibitions, the slave traders raped the young Indian girls.

The Catholic Church participated in the slave trade by possessing young Indian "servants" for labor, and by baptizing the captives. Baptismal records show that from 1700 to 1780, eight hundred Apache children were baptized as "servants" to the households of Spaniards in New Mexico. At the Catholic Church at Laguna Pueblo baptismal records revealed that the Spanish rewarded the Pueblos who accompanied them on military actions against the Navajos with young captives.

More money could be made from one slave hunting expedition of two or three weeks than could be made in one year of subsistence farming or ranching in New Mexico. When the U.S. authorities took the New Mexico Territory from Mexico in 1846, the U.S. officials made attempts to stop the Indian slave trade, but the wealthy Mexican families resisted, and even the U.S. authorities kept Indian "servants."

When I reread Bailey's book I came across the account of a young Navajo woman released by U.S. soldiers from her captivity with a Mexican family in 1852. The young Navajo woman complained to the U.S. military officer that the Mexican family stripped her naked and whipped her every day. Whipping slaves, it seems, was a common perversion with the founding families of New Mexico.

I happened to mention to my father that I wanted to write about Juana but I wasn't really sure when or how she came to work for Grandma Lillie's family. That was when my father told me what Grandma Lillie never told me. My father told me so off-handedly it angered me; I could tell he was ashamed and the off-handed manner was his way to cover up his shame.

Four young Navajo sisters were captured by the Spanish slave hunters during the Spanish governor's 1823 military campaign against the Navajos in New Mexico. Juana, who was four or five, was the youngest. The four captives came into the possession of Grandma Whip's brother.

Did he buy the young sisters from a slave trader or were they loot he got for volunteering to accompany the Spanish troops on the assault? Did someone owe him a gambling debt and give him the little girls in payment or were they a bribe to curry his favor?

If Grandma Whip was quick to take off the leather belt to whip her small grandchildren, imagine what Grandma Whip's brother was like: he must have been the Devil himself with the whip on the little Navajo girls. After he whipped the young Navajo girls, what other perversions? Was he one of those slave dealers who participated in the drunken public rapes of young Indian girls at the slave markets? His abuse was unbearable, so the three older girls poisoned their torturer.

With the son of two prominent Los Lunas families dead at the hands of Indian "servants," the local authorities could not afford delay. Copycats had to be discouraged immediately. The three young Navajo girls were hanged at once; only the youngest, Juana, was spared. Did other wealthy families of Los Lunas send their Indian "servants" to watch the hangings that day as a precaution? Did they make little Juana watch her sisters die? Did Juana understand then her last links to her family and people died with her sisters and there would be no reunion for her?

From her poisoned brother, Grandma Whip inherited the only remaining Navajo child to be her "servant." Poor Juana came to be part of the strange cruel family of Grandma Whip and her husband the Mexican with the English surname.

Both my father and Grandma Lillie told me about the huge ring of keys Grandma Whip wore on the belt around her waist. Every door, every closet, every cabinet, cupboard and drawer in Grandma Whip's house was locked at all times. When they visited and needed sugar for their coffee, Grandma Whip had to search among dozens of keys before she unlocked the cupboard with the sugar bowl. Grandma Lillie said all the locks and keys were because Grandma Whip didn't want the servants to steal things, but maybe Grandma Whip wanted to make sure the rat poison stayed out of the sugar bowl.

CHAPTER 7

My mother's ancestors weren't as well known to her as my father's ancestors were to him. My mother's maternal great grandfather, Grandpa Wood, was born in what is now Kentucky during one of the violent removals of the Cherokees from their homelands in North Carolina and Georgia. It was his daughter, my mother's grandma Goddard, who taught my mother that the black snake in the cellar was their friend. The Cherokees revered snakes before Christianity arrived. So my mother taught me to respect but not to fear snakes.

In my second year at the University of New Mexico, money was scarce. My elder son Robert was a baby then, and my husband Dick Chapman was in graduate school. I had good grades but in those days all the scholarship money there went to male athletes. The only scholastic scholarship available was one offered by the Daughters of the Confederacy. The financial aid counselor suggested I find out if I had any relatives who fought for the Confederacy. I asked my mother and she told me the Leslies, her ancestors, fought for the Confederacy. I got the scholarship for my high grade point average; it was two hundred dollars split between two semesters.

The Leslie name goes back to Scotland and the Leslie clan. My mother said that her father, Grandpa Dan, had belonged to the Ku Klux Klan during the years he and Grandma Jessie lived in Georgia. My mother was very close to her father; they both wept easily and loved to drink. I remember Grandpa Dan with happiness until I got old enough to want to watch *Hopalong Cassidy* when Grandpa wanted to watch the Friday night boxing matches. The anger he directed at me that night so frightened me I did not feel the same about him ever again. Some years later when he died, I felt sorry for my mother's loss and her sadness, but I didn't feel sad; I was about six years old then.

Later on when I was in high school in the 1960s, I tried to track down Grandpa Wood, and our Cherokee relatives; not all the Cherokees went to Oklahoma—some of the Wood family hid out in the mountains near Asheville. But in those days the Cherokees were poor with no casino money, and few records were kept of those who had been born or who died during the removals.

Years before, when I was in grade school, our cousin Charlie Wood from western North Carolina worked for the Bureau of Indian Affairs as a community health worker at Laguna. He stayed at Laguna for a few years before he went back to North Carolina. We didn't really get to know him. I'm not sure why. I remember he came to our house for supper a few times, but mostly we saw him when he came into the store to pick up the mail.

Maybe it was the liquor around our house that kept our cousin Charlie away. Alcoholic drinks were and still are illegal at Laguna. As a BIA public health worker it would have been awkward for Charlie Wood because he was very conscientious. He might have lost his job.

Now I realize how the alcohol in our house determined who might or might not be invited in spontaneously. People who possessed alcohol might be reported to the village officers who had the power to punish those breaking the law. In those days there were no tribal police or tribal jail; the elected village officers took care of keeping the peace in their village.

My mother was a bright well-educated woman, and a great teacher, but she was also an alcoholic. She came from a small Montana coal mining village. She told me she started drinking in the seventh grade when she and some school chums stole the wine her father and the other coal miners planned to drink after the union meeting.

I never thought of my mother as an alcoholic because she seldom got drunk or impaired by drinking, except at picnics and parties, and Christmas Eve and New Year's Eve. I was used to seeing the dramatic, extreme alcoholism of the World War Two and Korean War veterans who were my cousins, so it was easier to fool myself about my mother's drinking. She didn't drink on the job and she never missed work, but after work and on weekends, my mother kept a coffee cup full of whiskey nearby.

Except for Grandma Jessie and her sisters, Aunt Sarah and Aunt Lucy, and my mother's brother, Uncle Jack, my mother's relatives were not only distant, they didn't seem as interesting as my father's relatives who were active presences in my life. Except for Aunt Lucy and her love for Cherokee Grandpa Wood, my mother's relatives weren't storytellers; and except for my mother's brother, Uncle Jack, they weren't colorful either.

Uncle Jack flew for the Navy in the Pacific in World War Two. Afterwards he was a crop duster in Fresno with great stories to tell about close calls and the crashes he walked away from. His children, my cousins John Leslie and Lana Leslie, were like brother and sister to my sisters and me while we grew up.

Every summer John and Lana spent eight weeks with us at Laguna. They always knew the latest music, dances and fashion because they were from California and were popular and cool—far ahead of the rest of the country. Their town had a big municipal swimming pool which was the focal point of their summer. So I was impressed that they preferred to spend their summers with us in New Mexico without a swimming pool, hiking in the hills, riding horses and helping my father sell fireworks for the Fourth of July.

We never got to go stay with John and Lana in California because the summer growing season was Uncle Jack's busiest time to crop dust, and much of it had to be done at night when the fields were deserted. He needed quiet during the day so he could sleep. After high school we no longer saw as much of our cousins because they went off to college while we got pregnant and got married in college which wasn't cool.

CHAPTER 8

I n the keynote address I gave to the American Indian Language Development Convention in Tucson in mid-June of 2007 I decided to look into the future to see what languages people here will speak five hundred years from now, and I realized everyone in the Southwest will speak Nahuatl, not Chinese, although Chinese will be the dominant language of finance and commerce world-wide, and everyone's second language. I won't go into the details of the decline of the English language here for lack of space.

> The resurgence of Nahuatl will arise out of the sheer numbers of speakers especially in Mexico City, with the largest population of Nahua speakers in the world. Of course a great many of the indigenous tribal languages of the Americas are related to Nahuatl so I include them as well.

But before I could write about five hundred years in the future, I had to go back to the past, my own past. Writing about why I don't speak the Laguna language was much more complicated than I imagined. My parents sent me to kindergarten at the Bureau of Indian Affairs day school near our house. The first day of kindergarten I learned about invisible lines: the old cattle guard full of sand at the entrance to the day school property had an invisible line down the middle. We children were warned: once we crossed this invisible line onto the school grounds talking Indian was forbidden. If we disobeyed we'd be sent to the principal's office for punishment. That was the first thing the teachers taught us children on the first day of kindergarten.

I paid close attention to the rules because my father was very strict about the behavior of my sisters and me. I was afraid to get sent to the principal's office for any reason because I feared my father's temper.

Mr. Trujillo was our principal and his wife was my kindergarten and first grade teacher. They both were Pueblo people: she was from Isleta Pueblo and he was from Laguna. They spoke the Pueblo languages, but they had attended BIA schools when they were children. They were taught to believe in the goal of the Bureau of Indian Affairs in the 1950s which was to break us children from talking Indian so we'd learn English and one day relocate off the reservation.

In kindergarten class, Mrs. Trujillo taught the five year olds to speak English. I was happy to be with children of my age but after a week she sent me to the first grade because I already spoke English. I felt uncomfortable because all the other children knew I was treated differently because I spoke English. Afterward some of my classmates teased me with Laguna words about being a show-off so I ran to the teacher to get them in trouble. My mother cautioned me not to be a tattle-tale and I stopped.

I learned how to get along. I picked up the Laguna expressions and phrases my classmates used: my grandpa Hank taught me to count to ten and passed on handy phrases to use at the store like how to say "there's no more": "zah-zee hadti." I might have learned more Laguna from my grandpa Hank if he had lived longer and if I hadn't been such a tomboy always outdoors exploring at the river or off in the hills on my horse.

Grandpa Hank worked in the store twelve hours a day, six and a half days a week. He was a quiet man. After work around seven, he and Grandma Lillie ate supper and then he rested in his armchair. Grandma told us kids not to bother him because he was tired. He read science and car magazines, and later when TV came he watched until he fell asleep in the chair.

But when Grandma Lillie went on vacation to see her sister in California, I used to cook for Grandpa Hank. He talked more then, and told me stories he'd heard as a child. This is the one Grandpa told me one day at lunchtime: there was a young Laguna hunter who always brought back game because he could travel farther. The young hunter's secret was that he carried with him a magical lunch in a small cloth sack. No matter how much the young hunter ate there was always more food in the sack.

My great grandma A'mooh and my grandpa Hank and all our extended family around us spoke Laguna. At the store, most of the people who shopped there spoke Laguna. Only my father could not speak Laguna. I was aware of this oddity before I went to school, and I asked more than once why he didn't know how to talk Indian. He said it was because the other children made fun of his accent when he spoke Laguna so he refused to learn to talk Indian; he only spoke a little as a courtesy to the old folks who spoke no English.

Now I wonder if it was more than just his schoolmates who gave him a bad time about speaking Laguna. I have the sense there was an adult family member, maybe one of Grandma Lillie's brothers, one of my father's uncles, who teased him about talking Indian. Somebody filled my father's head with a strange idea: if we learned to speak Laguna, we would speak English with a Laguna accent. Of course that notion was completely ridiculous.

My great grandfather Robert Gunn Marmon and his brother, Walter Gunn Marmon, came to Laguna from Kenton, Ohio to work as Government school teachers and surveyors. Walter arrived in 1868 and Robert followed in 1875. They both learned to speak the Laguna language and married Laguna women.

My grandpa Hank was fluent in Laguna and knew the older dialect that was disappearing. He also spoke some Hopi, some Zuni, and some of the Dine language as well as Spanish. At that time among the tribes of the Southwest, people routinely spoke three or four languages.

My great grandma A'mooh and my great aunts Alice Marmon Little and Susie Reyes Marmon grew up speaking the Laguna language, and all learned to speak English with that unmistakable "proper" accent which was taught at the Carlisle Indian School in the latter nineteenth century. Years later in Alaska I met a Haida elder who had attended Carlisle as a child and she spoke English with the same Carlisle accent—maybe it was more of a cadence—it's difficult to describe—it was an American accent but with a hint of Scotland, not England.

Why do people choose not to teach their children their mother tongues—something unthinkable under normal circumstances?

"Because the occupying powers have outlawed the indigenous language, to speak it is to be placed at a socio-economic disadvantage" (Marwan Hassan, *Velocities of Zero*). That's the short answer. The longer more complex answer for me begins like this:

I spent a great deal of time with my great grandmother A'mooh when I was a baby and small child. Very early I understood what she said to me in Indian. My name for her, A'mooh, came from the exclamation she made in Laguna each time she saw me. "A'mooh" is a term of endearment for a girl. She spoke Laguna to me when I was a baby and small child, but after I started kindergarten, she spoke only English to me.

I didn't recall this until I started preparing the keynote address and got to thinking about who might have taught me Laguna. Why did she stop talking Indian to me? She was the family matriarch, so I know nobody dared tell her to stop talking Indian to me, she made the decision herself. My great grandmother was a great believer in education and she must have been concerned about us children speaking English at school.

But there must have been something else at work too. My great grandmother was a staunch convert to the Presbyterian Church. She used to read to my sisters and me—Bible stories, and Brownie the Bear. She told us a great deal of local history and family history, but she would not tell us the hummah-hah stories, the traditional Laguna stories, because the hummah-hah stories reveal the Laguna spiritual outlook toward animals, plants and spirit beings, one which was at odds with the Presbyterian view of the world.

By not teaching us children to speak Laguna, my great grandmother made it less likely that we would find our way into the traditional Laguna religion and ceremonies. She was the lone Presbyterian in her house; her husband, my great grandfather from Ohio, was a Quaker, so he didn't go to the Presbyterian church. None of her children or grandchildren went to church either. So my great grandmother did what she thought was best for us great grandchildren. To no avail of course. My father started taking me to the ka'tsina dances at the village plaza before I could walk. I heard the hummah-hah stories from Aunt Alice and Aunt Susie. My sisters and I were never baptized in any church.

Grandma Lillie grew up at Los Lunas where they spoke both English and Spanish in the house. Why didn't she learn to talk Indian after she married Grandpa Hank? Was it because her family in Los Lunas was uneasy about her marriage outside the Church to a Laguna Pueblo man? For Grandma Lillie to learn to speak Laguna would have caused a stir among the wealthier Los Lunas relatives who fancied themselves too good to associate with Indians. After all, our Los Lunas relations had been merchants of everything at one time, including Indian slaves.

Grandma Lillie spoke Spanish to her mother, Great Grandma Helen, and to her Los Lunas relations, but she did not teach Spanish to my father or his brothers, just as Grandpa Hank did not teach my father and his brothers to speak Laguna.

Over the years, whenever I tried to learn a language, all the ghosts of the past reappeared—the anxiety and sense of guilt and inadequacy and the loss. Whenever I try to speak, I go into a slow panic and my hearing becomes scrambled by anxiety. Years ago when I taught at Diné College I tried to learn a few Diné greetings and phrases but I couldn't do it. How could I learn Diné when I never learned Laguna?

CHAPTER 9

I never felt alone or afraid up there in the hills. The hummah-hah stories described the conversations coyotes, crows and buzzards used to have with human beings. I was fascinated with the notion that long ago humans and animals used to freely converse. As I got older, I realized the clouds and winds and rivers also have their ways of communication; I became interested in what these entities had to say. My imagination became engaged in discovering what can be known without words.

Stories themselves have spirit and being, and they have a way of communicating on different levels. The story itself communicates with us regardless of what language it is told in. Of course stories are always funnier and more vivid when they are told in their original language by a good storyteller. But what I love about stories is they can survive and continue in some form or other resembling themselves regardless of how good or how bad the storyteller is, no matter what language they are told or written in. This is because the human brain favors stories or the narrative form as a primary means of organizing and relating human experience. Stories contain large amounts of valuable information even when the storyteller forgets or invents new details.

So I found myself left with English and some Spanish but only a meager number of words in the language of Ka'waik, the Beautiful Lake place. When I started to write short stories in creative writing class at the beginning of my second year at the University of New Mexico the challenge for me was to make English express or evoke the experiences of hearing the stories told when I was a child.

My sense of narrative structure, of how a story needs to be told, all this came to me from the stories Aunt Alice, Aunt Susie and Grandpa Hank told me. They carefully chose the English words that best evoked the stories as they heard them told in the Laguna language when they were children, before they learned English.

Linguistic diversity is integral to the cultural diversity that ensures some humans will survive in the event of one of the periodic global catastrophes. Local indigenous languages hold the keys to survival because they contain the nouns, the names of the plants, insects, birds and mammals important locally to human survival.

As important as the nouns are the verbs that denote the actions, the activities, the states of being or consciousness that are important to human survival locally. Indigenous languages contain this knowledge; the survival information is encoded in the grammar of the language.

A language determines whether or not you pay attention to an experience or object; if you have a term or syntactical construction that denotes a relationship or an experience, then you look out for it and are able to see it or hear it. My old friend, the artist Aaron Yava who left us some years ago, made a wonderful line drawing of an old man who walked in a distinctive manner, in which the muscles of his back seemed to work themselves independently as he walked along. Aaron wrote this was "chickish muggee"—someone who exercises his back as he walks along. I never forgot that term, and years later I did see a man walking like that, "chickish muggee," his back was moving this way and that way as he went along.

In a lecture I gave in 2008 at West Virginia University I happened to mention that five hundred years from now, throughout the Americas, Nahuatl and related Uto-Aztecan languages will be spoken, not Spanish or English or even Chinese. Later, CC at West Virginia U sent me an e-mail with this newspaper article: "The mayor of Mexico City, Marcelo Ebrard, wants all city employees to learn to speak the Aztec language, Nahuatl. A possible presidential candidate in 2012, Ebrard presented his government's development plan this week translated for the first time into Nahuatl. He calls it a first step toward establishing the use of Nahuatl in the government. Translators who speak Nahuatl already work in hospitals and courtrooms, but now desk workers will learn the basics of Nahuatl from classroom sessions and on-line courses."

I realize now that from the time I was very small, I focused my attention more on non-verbal communication between people, between animals and between other beings. I used to trail along behind my great grandmother without a word, absorbing from her all the waves of experience and being in shared proximity. I helped her pick "graahdunt," cilantro, from her garden; I helped her carry the coal bucket and I pulled the hose along while she watered the cosmos and hollyhocks. She and the others of her generation happily existed without concern for clocks, were never in a hurry, never impatient with anyone. There was always time for everything as long as the sun was up.

I learned the world of the clock and calendar when I started school, but I've never lost my sense of being alive without reference to clocks or calendars. My great grandmother didn't know exactly when she was born; none of her generation did. Calendar age wasn't important. Time was very much present time; even the way the old folks talked about the ancestors and their time was located in the present. Those who passed on to join our beloved ancestors at Cliff House remained close by; Cliff House wasn't far away.

I learned adults would tolerate my presence if I kept quiet and didn't touch things. I used to go looking for adults at work in their yards, chopping wood or hanging wet laundry on the clothesline. I watched Aunt Alice rake up trash and weeds down at the dump (so they didn't blow into her yard, she said). She had a mania for order and for saving things. Her yard was spotless, swept clean every day with a broom. Her house was in complete order, so she cleaned the dump.

Aunt Alice saved every penny, so she wasn't poor. She had a pension from years as a Government nurse. My mother was the postmaster at Laguna when the U.S. Treasury Department sent a postal inspector to find out what happened to all the checks they'd sent Alice Marmon Little; none of her pension checks had been cashed. The postal inspector discovered Aunt Alice had a big stack of turquoise blue U.S. Treasury checks she was saving. The inspector explained she should cash the checks and then save the money.

Aunt Alice searched the dump for things that still had some good or some use left in them. Right away I sensed the excitement of a sort of treasure hunt. I remember her finding a broken kettle with a hole in the bottom, and a frying pan with a broken handle, both of which she carried home and washed and saved. In the early twentieth century, in rural New Mexico, the people saved glass containers and tin cans; they straightened nails and hinges for reuse, and they kept piles of remnant 2×4s and pieces of galvanized steel roofing. At Laguna the people were accustomed to reusing stones from fallen down walls or buildings.

Aunt Alice saved everything. All of her wedding gifts had been opened but then were carefully repacked in their boxes, labeled and put in order on the shelves that reached from floor to ceiling in her back room. As a child I loved to go back into the cool dim room that smelled of adobe clay and cedar wood. Aunt Alice didn't have a flush toilet, but she had something far more fascinating: a commode. Behind a curtain hung from the ceiling up on a wooden platform was a big wooden chair with a skirt around the bottom of it to hide the slop jar that had to be carried to the outhouse and dumped followed by a scoop of old stove ashes.

After Aunt Alice died, Grandma Lillie went to help Uncle Mike go through her things and they found boxes neatly packed with catsup bottles that she'd washed, balls of string and pieces of used aluminum foil she saved.

Aunt Alice had no children. She was always very kind to us. She often babysat when my parents drove to Albuquerque in the evening to see a movie. Aunt Alice was at her best when she was telling us girls the old-time, hummah-hah stories. The stories about Kochininako, Yellow Woman, being abducted by strange men who turned out to be supernatural beings were Aunt Alice's favorites.

My mother thought Aunt Alice was sexually repressed and the racy Yellow Woman stories that she told were her outlet. (My mother thought this because Aunt Alice only saw her husband twice a year: for eight weeks in the summer, and for a week at Christmas. Uncle Mike who was Mescalero Apache worked on the Santa Fe Railroad and lived in Richmond, California. This seemed to suit each of them just fine. They were entirely devoted to one another.)

Aunt Alice was my grandpa Hank's first cousin; Alice's mother, Margaret, from Paguate village, was married to Walter Gunn Marmon. My grandfather recalled when he was a young boy, he and the other children were afraid to walk past the yard if they saw Alice's mother outdoors.

Margaret apparently suffered a nervous breakdown sometime before 1900. Aunt Alice would have been a young child at that time too. Grandpa Hank said Margaret used to scream at him and the other young children and threw rocks at them when they walked through the large yard and garden area the families of the two Marmon brothers shared.

My great grandmother, who seldom had anything negative to say about anyone, told my mother a strange story. John Gunn, not Walter Gunn Marmon, was Aunt Alice's biological father. John Gunn and Walter G. Marmon were first cousins, and John Gunn came to Laguna with Robert G. Marmon, my great grandfather, in 1875.

Great Grandma said Margaret had a saddle horse she liked to ride very fast around the Laguna-Acoma area. While Walter G. Marmon was gone on months-long survey and map-making excursions, his wife saddled up her horse and galloped off for liaisons with John Gunn.

Grandma A'mooh said Alice's mother became so sexually active with white men that some people got together and stopped her out in the hills where she was riding her horse. They confronted her about her behavior and then they partially scalped her.

For me this story never quite added up. My great grandma was a stern Presbyterian who never lied about anything. She was very fond of my mother so why would she tell her such a story if it was untrue? But Grandma A'mooh must have left something important out of the story. The violence of the confrontation points in the direction of something else.

Marital infidelity was not a crime among the Pueblos. Plenty of women had extra-marital affairs just as the men did. Not a few women had affairs with white men, even with the Catholic priests. If this bloody confrontation took place as my great grandmother said, it would have occurred before 1900 and might account for Margaret's odd behavior or breakdown which Grandpa Hank recalled.

Aunt Alice proudly displayed a large photograph of her father in his Union Army uniform, but she had no photographs of her mother. Even as a child I took note of this absence of photographs of Aunt Alice's mother. I imagined her as one of those old-time people who disliked cameras and hid her face rather than be photographed.

Later my great grandfather Robert G. Marmon moved his family to the two-story adobe house (with the cellar that flooded) across the railroad tracks from his brother's house. From time to time my great grandparents took in guests who got off the train to spend a few days sight-seeing in the Laguna-Acoma area. They kept a guest book that was signed by the likes of Edward Curtis, John D. Rockefeller and Franz Boaz.

By 1917, Margaret Marmon apparently had recovered because she worked as an informant about Laguna ceremonial practices with the Harvard-trained anthropologist Elsie Clews Parsons in 1917 and 1918. Parsons described her fieldwork thus:

> ". . . I lived not in the pueblo, but about three miles away in the house of Mr. E. F. Eckerman near the railway station. In this detachment there were both advantages and disadvantages. Observation of the general life of the pueblo was necessarily limited and my circle of acquaintances was

restricted. On the other hand, interrogation was unhand-icapped [sic] by embarrassing visitors and the disposition of the informants was rendered comparatively frank and responsive. My chief informants were the mother and the aunt of Mrs. Eckerman. . . ."

Parsons footnoted "the mother":

"Mrs. Marmon, a native born Laguna woman, was the widow of W. G. Marmon, one of the early white settlers in the westward movement. Mrs. Marmon remained unso-phisticated and uncontaminated by American shoddiness. She was a strong, gentle and very lovable person. She died in 1918."

In her "Notes on Ceremonialism at Laguna," published in Volume XIX of *Anthropological Papers of the American Museum of Natural History* in 1919, Parsons noted that all the Laguna people who worked as infor-mants for her the two previous summers had died—two by influenza, and one by lightning strike, but that no one at Laguna linked the deaths to their work with her. Parsons fooled herself if she believed this; such links would have been made at once because it was well known that anyone who dared to reveal ceremonial secrets risked severe reprisals from the supernatural world.

Parsons also commented that my great grandfather and his wife were "indifferent" to the traditional rituals and were of no use in her ethnological research.

The stories about her mother, Margaret, explain a great deal about Aunt Alice; she might have been eccentric, but I spent many happy hours with her. I internalized her peacefulness during our blissful silent meanderings among the old bottles and broken tea kettles at the abandoned dump by the river. Even now I wander the trails of the Tuc-son Mountains looking for odd pebbles and colorful rocks for hours on end in the same blissful consciousness I learned from my days with her. She taught me her love of solitude and self-reliance which have served me well.

As a child I spent hours alone with my dogs down at the river playing with the minnows and toads. After I got my first horse I was able to roam farther into the sandy hills and up to the sandstone canyons along the piñon-covered ridges where I saw no one for hours, and then maybe only a pick-up truck with someone from Laguna on their way to sheep camp with supplies.

CHAPTER 10

When I was five years old Aunt Alice came to babysit us early one morning while my parents went to hunt deer on Mount Taylor. I was crying because I wanted to go with my parents and they'd almost agreed to take me along, but then decided no.

To humor me that morning, Aunt Alice told my sisters and me the story about the Estrucuyu, the big headed monster, and Kochininako, Yellow Woman, who was a fine hunter even when she was a girl. Aunt Alice wanted me to know there had been a brave and clever girl who hunted rabbits to feed her sisters and mother but who also outwitted the Estrucuyu, and stalled the monster long enough for the Twin Brothers to arrive and slay him.

When Aunt Alice told the story about Kochininako cornered in the cave by the dreadful Estrucuyu, she took a great deal of care to describe how the monster demanded the poor girl remove her clothing, piece by piece. Later I understood how the Yellow Woman stories allowed her to express a facet of herself that otherwise was muted. When Aunt Alice got involved in telling a Yellow Woman story she got carried away into her secret self. I will always love her for the indomitable spirit she had, for her love of the old stories and the way she told them to us; and of course, I love her for her gentle eccentricities which I appreciate all the more now that I have a few of my own.

I was six years old the first time my father allowed me to walk with him on the deer hunt. I look back now in wonder: because my father was very serious about hunting and liked to bring home the biggest buck. My father and uncles and their friends were in a competition over that. To take along a six year old child to hunt deer seems to me now a bit unusual for a serious deer hunter like my father was. Yet my parents took me along on the hunt that November.

I was warned again and again about the rigors of deer hunting. My parents told me if I went, there was no turning back. I could not cry if I got tired of walking and I knew my father walked fast. I could not complain if I got cold or hungry. If I did not do everything they told me to do then at lunch break I would be left in the jeep back at camp. Yes, I promised, I would not be any trouble.

It had snowed on Mount Taylor and in the high mountains above Laguna the week before and the snowfall had only partially melted. I will always remember: I wore my black cowboy boots. I hated any shoes with laces and because the decision to allow me to go along came at the last minute, I had no other boots to wear except my black cowboy boots with thin cotton socks. The sky was bright blue and the sun was shining and melting the snow. I had walked only a short distance with my father that morning before my black cowboy boots were soaked with icy snow melt.

The first thing my father taught me that morning is how a hunter walks. Not too fast. Stop frequently to listen. Stop and listen the way a deer listens; then the deer will think he hears another deer or animal moving through the brush, not a human. He showed me how to step from rock to rock to avoid dry twigs or leaves that make noise.

I never told my father how wet and cold my feet were, but when we all met back at camp two hours later, my mother saw the soaking wet cowboy boots and realized my feet must have been cold all morning. Cowboy boots are for horseback riding, not hiking. The adults wore waterproof hiking boots.

During the lunch break I sat near the campfire to dry my cow-boy boots and warm my feet. At noon the sun was so warm we had to remove a layer of sweatshirts we wore under our jackets. Afterwards my mother asked if I was sure I wanted to walk again with my father while he hunted that afternoon. By then the sun had warmed the scrub-oak hills and much of the snow melted; it was a beautiful clear day. I told my mother I wanted to hunt.

After lunch my father and I made our way up the east side of a dome shaped lava hill, called a "cerro," that was fringed with scrub-oak thickets. At the top of the hill we stopped to rest; we still only whispered. My father sat on a big rock in the sun while I went off to the bushes to urinate. As I returned, my father stood up on the rock ledge with his back to me; he raised his rifle and aimed downhill and fired one shot.

When I reached my father he pointed down to some big flat boulders about fifty yards below; at first I couldn't see anything but my father kept saying he'd shot a big buck that was bedded down on a sunny ledge. Finally I located the wide rack of antlers; the buck's gray coat blended perfectly with the basalt ledge where he appeared to be sleeping, not dead. It seemed unbelievable that the big mule deer buck basked and dozed so close by but did not smell or hear us when we came up the hill behind him. The wind had blown in our favor that day, and carried our sounds and scents away from the buck.

My father approached cautiously because we still saw no blood or entry wound. Finally my father got close enough to see the buck was dead, but it still took us awhile to find the tiny entry hole between the deer's shoulder blades where the bullet entered and killed the buck instantly. My father loved animals and hated their suffering, so this one-shot kill made the occasion even better.

For a six year old on her first hunting trip with her father, this was a completely wonderful and amazing afternoon. It was my first visit to the high plateau country below the volcanic craters of Mount Taylor in the Cebolleta Mountains.

As I got older, I visited Mount Taylor many times to work on the L Bar Ranch at branding time to gather cattle on horseback. I recalled that mountain terrain vividly as I wrote my first novel, *Ceremony*, and my protagonist, Tayo, rode his horse up to Mount Taylor to find the spotted cattle.

Later my father traded our cousin Bill Pratt a pistol for a child-size .22 single shot rifle for me and my sisters. He taught us gun safety from the time we could crawl, and he went over the rules again and again. He took me to the dump down by the river and taught me to line up the sights on the rifle and to squeeze, not jerk, the trigger as we fired. After a few lessons I was allowed to take the rifle and a box of .22 shells to go shoot bottles or targets at the dump by myself.

My father and his brother got their .22 rifles when they were seven, so he felt I should have a .22 rifle when I was seven. There was never any question that I would do anything improper with the .22. He believed toy guns were bad because they led children to think guns were toys. He didn't like BB guns because they led children to think a gun shot wasn't lethal and this caused children to use BB guns carelessly and injure one another.

He allowed us to light firecrackers for the same reason, so we would know how to do it safely. We always were extremely cautious with the firecrackers because they might start a brush fire. Every Fourth of July my father ordered great quantities of them—Black Cats, lady fingers, cherry bombs, M-80s, sky rockets, aerial bombs, Roman candles, fountains, pop bottle rockets, "snakes," cracker balls and sparklers, of course.

My father regarded sparklers as a greater hazard than firecrackers because sparklers were said to be "safe," even for preschool children, despite the fact that they burn at very high temperatures and might easily blind a child.

There was something of the child still in my father. At Christmas he bought us girls rockets that flew on a fuel of baking soda and vinegar, sling shots, and flying saucers that launched with the pull of a string—all toys he wanted to play with too, though we girls found them exciting and interesting and great fun outdoors.

Some of my earliest memories are of my sisters and me posing for our picture under the hot lights of my father's photography studio. In the big empty room next to his darkroom and the bedroom which my two sisters and I shared, my father hung a roll of background paper and set up his reflectors and lights and made it his studio to take formal portraits.

He was serious about every photography assignment he took. Before a wedding or portrait session with an elder, he always did a test run of his equipment, the cameras and the film, to make sure nothing would go wrong, so he'd get the best possible results the first time. My father was meticulous about the light and the image of the person in the portrait; it took awhile the way he did it, so he didn't want to ask the older folks to go through all that more than once. He tried always to use natural light, especially with the elders, and if they couldn't go outdoors, my father seated them near a window or in a doorway.

But indoors in his studio there were floodlights so bright we girls could barely open our eyes without being blinded. We'd complain but he'd say "oh just a few more" and he wouldn't be deterred, he'd get completely lost in the process of working with the light. My father knew how he wanted the light and what he wanted to see through the lens. It wasn't too bad if we were dressed in our play clothes but sometimes for Christmas or Easter my mother sewed us beautiful dresses that took her weeks to make. We posed in our new dresses and shoes but they were stiff, the fabric chafed and the lights seemed even hotter then.

By the ways he dressed us and posed us for the annual Christmas card, you can see my father was intrigued by the 1950s style of black and white photography used in fashion and advertising, as well as the images featured in *Modern Photography* and other photography magazines he bought.

One time he had my mother dress us as gangsters in fedoras and trench coats much too big for us and he posed us around his circular poker table that had a pile of chips and cards. There were beer bottles on the table and my sister Gigi held a real cigar. I was about eight, my sister Wendy was six and Gigi was four years old. One year he managed to superimpose our images onto Christmas tree ornaments, and one of the older folks who saw the Christmas card was amazed by the image and asked my dad, "Wasn't it difficult to get the girls in there without them getting all scratched up?"

The best Christmas card was the one my father made from the portrait of my two sisters and me dressed in our "Indian clothes" at the old water hole near the original tribal council building. Our cousins Esther Johnson and Rachel Anaya at Paguate loaned us the mantas and my mother sewed us the gingham underdress the Laguna women wore with the mantas. As they helped us get dressed Esther and Rachel explained each article of clothing and how it was to be worn; they wrapped the sashes around us and the white buckskin leggings around our legs. In the old days the women helped dress one another every day; they were always in the company of other women so they thought nothing of it. They loaned us all the silver and turquoise bracelets and rings and necklaces. To be so carefully dressed in the old-time way was very special for the three of us.

The dressing and posing happened on Sunday afternoons or in the early evening because my father worked at my grandpa Hank's store six and a half days a week. But almost every night after supper, my father also worked in the darkroom from eight to eleven, sometimes later. My mother worked on her sewing in the front room.

I often sat in the darkroom watching my father make prints until bedtime at nine. I remember his delight in showing me the exposed paper in the red safe light, apparently blank paper until he slid it into the first tray of chemicals in the long shallow sink. He'd tell me to watch, and at first I couldn't see anything; again he'd tell me "Look! See!" He was as excited as I was as the images began to appear.

During the day when my father made grocery deliveries to homes in the village or when he went to the depot to pick up packages for the store, he always took a camera along. He once told me a true photographer is never without a camera. Sometimes he'd be asked to take a photograph of kids or an elder and right on the spot he did it because he always had cameras with him. He was very disciplined about his cameras. We kids had to ride in the back seat with all the bags of camera equipment. In this way even as children we saw how absolutely serious my father was about photography.

My mother was the more dependable and practical of my parents, even if she kept her coffee cup full of whiskey all morning. She graduated from the University of New Mexico and always made more money than my father; she taught at Grants High School for some years before my youngest sister, Gigi, was born. Later she was appointed postmaster at Laguna in the middle 1950s. The post office was located in a corner of my grandpa Hank's small general merchandise store across the road from our house. My mother paid the bills, and my father spent the money she earned on cameras and darkroom equipment and supplies; so there were tensions in the house over money. My grandfather paid my father in groceries and a little cash each month, with generous time-off to go take photographs nearly any time my father needed.

From the time we could walk she taught my sisters and me not to fear or harm snakes. Her respect for snakes was part of her strength. My mother was the one who taught me to appreciate all snakes, even rattlesnakes; she married my father who was a snake-killer, but she stubbornly persisted in her appreciation of snakes. She handled live snakes but the sight of a mouse sent my mother up on the table in hysteria. No wonder snakes were her friends.

She had learned the mouse phobia from her grandma Goddard the old Cherokee who kept a black snake in the cellar to protect them from mice that Grandma Goddard believed would run up their skirts and attack them. My mother and her brother spent summers in Kansas with Grandma Goddard. Grandma's father, Grandpa Wood, was born on one of the forced marches of the Cherokee Removal or the Trail of Tears, somewhere in Kentucky.

My mother owned a .257 Roberts deer rifle with a scope. If she had not hunted deer with my father and the others, I would not have been able to go along as I did when I was six. One year she shot a doe, but seemed to enjoy the hiking more than the shooting. She taught home economics and loved to cook and sew for us when she had time which was seldom because often after a day of teaching she had to help out at the store.

When I was in the third grade her aunt died and left her a piano. We girls loved to listen and watch her when she played, and I saw sadness in her eyes even when she played pop songs from World War Two. The Albuquerque airport had a good restaurant when I was a child and occasionally my parents took us girls along. One evening after dinner as we left the restaurant, boarding for a flight was called and inexplicably my mother became very emotional and choked back tears. I once saw her do that at a train station years later when I was in college.

My sister Wendy loved my mother a great deal and as a little child, Wendy tried to comfort her. Wendy stayed in the house with my mother and made the house her realm too, so my mother wasn't alone. As we got older, Wendy stayed home with her while Gigi and I went hiking with my father on Sunday afternoons.

My sisters and I felt very protective of our mother because we sensed she was troubled. My mother didn't scold us or whip us like my father did. She was afraid of him too just as we were when he was angry, although he never touched her. She always helped us with our homework and encouraged us at whatever we wanted to try. She was the one who said I should have a horse when I was eight years old. She helped me with the colt because my father was afraid of horses. The colt knew my father was afraid and kicked him the first day.

My mother loved to dance and have a good time. She loved to repeat jokes she heard. She was the life of the party. She was devoted to our dogs and cats, and once had a canary she loved. She was also very attached to her goldfish and liked her tarantula so much she set it free. I come by my love for creatures wild and tame from my mother.

I come by my knack for writing from my mother too. I only learned this in 2001 after she died. In one of her old albums I found a clipping from the Great Falls, Montana newspaper that announced that Mary Virginia Leslie, a sophomore at Stockett High School, had won first prize in the Montana State high school essay contest sponsored by the Montana Electric Power Company. The clipping makes no mention of the essay's topic, and my mother never talked about it.

For as long as my mother lived there, she was part of the Laguna

Pueblo community and had a great many friends. One year she was invited to participate in the Corn Dance at Christmas time; her friend Louise Lucas loaned her the manta dress and moccasins and belt, and helped her get dressed. My mother didn't talk about her Cherokee background but it was clearly part of her. Even after my parents were divorced my mother stayed on at Laguna because she felt so much a part of the community. At the post office she always helped people read and fill out Government forms and send letters to Government agencies. At income tax time she assisted people with the forms, and in gratitude they brought her all kinds of good food—mostly oven bread but sometimes big tamales or blue corn enchiladas.

CHAPTER 11

On April 2, 1966 I married Dick Chapman, who was in his first year of graduate school in archeology at the University of New Mexico. My mother and both my grandmothers encouraged me to go to school full time the fall semester of 1966 when I was pregnant with my elder son, Robert. She told me new babies slept a lot and I would have plenty of time to study. She was right.

The pregnancy took an unforeseen turn. Early one morning I began to hemorrhage and both Robert and I nearly died. Robert was born six weeks early and weighed only four pounds nine ounces. He developed breathing difficulties soon after he was born, and there were seventy-two hours when we did not know if he would survive. But ten days later he weighed five pounds and was able to come home. All he wanted to do was sleep.

My mother babysat for me when she wasn't at work, and she enlisted her friend, our neighbor on Amherst Street, to help too. My sister Wendy babysat Robert when she wasn't in class, and so did Dick Chapman. At night I held Robert in one arm and a textbook in the other, so I got nearly straight As that semester even with a husband in graduate school and a new baby. I was eighteen.

My mother's true calling was to teach, and for years she taught in the Gallup, New Mexico public schools. She first attempted retirement in 1983 when she left Gallup. She moved to Tucson to live with my sons and me but my mother missed the teaching and the contact with the students too much.

When she was teaching she did not drink; retirement was a dangerous situation for her. My house in the Tucson Mountains was isolated, and my mother needed to be near more people. So in 1984 my mother moved to Ketchikan, Alaska; the local community college quickly called her out of retirement to teach at the resource and learning center where she gave special tutoring in algebra and geometry to older students who wanted to attend college. Going back to teaching had the best possible effect on her life until she retired in 1995. She died in Ketchikan on July 11, 2001.

Dick Chapman, Robert's father, had been an English major at UNM as an undergraduate and he tipped me off about Katherine Simons, Edith Buchanan, Mary Jane Powers, George Arms, Hamlin Hill and Ernest Baughman—the best teachers in the English Department. It was Dick Chapman who suggested I take a creative writing course the semester after Robert was born because he thought it would be "an easy A" for me. I was thinking about law school then, so I might not have reconnected with fiction writing without his suggestion. On my own I found the fine poet and teacher Gene Frumkin, who encouraged me to keep writing my way, and had great book lists for his poetry classes.

Eleanor and Carl Chapman, Dick's parents, were staunch allies of mine; in a way they were my parents too. I was eighteen and my parents had just gotten divorced and there was no money for school. Eleanor and Carl helped out financially and encouraged me to stay in college after Robert was born. They helped us pay off the hospital bills because we hadn't counted on the expenses of a premature birth. Eleanor gave me all the baby clothes she saved when she had Dick and his brother, Steve. Beautiful embroidered gowns and hand-knit booties and sweaters and appliquéd blankets and quilts which Eleanor made. She was a wonderful artist who could draw or paint or make stuffed animals like the Cheshire Cat and Eeyore and Piglet which she sewed for Robert.

Eleanor made all the drawings and diagrams used in Carl Chapman's scholarly publications on the archeology and pre-history of the Missouri River Valley, including the Spiro mounds where Eleanor worked on the fragments of copper plates with the wonderful bird men figures. As she did the drawings and helped to reconstruct the missing parts of the plates, she theorized that the figures had been embossed on the copper with deer horn. Eleanor got herself a plate of thin copper and a deer horn and made replicas of the Spiro copper plates to show that this was how the images on the plates had originally been embossed.

Years after Dick and I were divorced, Eleanor and Carl and I remained close. Every Christmas Eleanor sent wonderful boxes of little thoughtful gifts, mostly handmade, not just for Robert and me, but for my younger son, Cazimir, and for his father, my second husband. Eleanor and Carl died in a car crash in 1987. I miss them very much.

CHAPTER 12

Grandma Lillie used to take me and my sisters for walks by the river to the ruins of the old water pump house by the artesian springs where Laguna got its water and where the railroad got water for the locomotive engines. I remember a small pool wreathed with watercress where the water bubbled up through the sand. When I knelt down and drank, it was delicious and so cool.

She used to tell us stories about things that happened in the places we hiked and about the times she took our dad and uncle hiking in the hills when they were our age. She used to tell us the adventures she had when she was a girl in Los Lunas.

Grandma Lillie liked to say she was a tomboy when she was growing up. One time she and her sister Marie found a nest of baby prairie dogs and they managed to get them into a gunny sack and home but their dad refused to let them keep them. As it was, one of the prairie dogs bit through the end of Marie's finger.

She'd ridden horses with Marie, and had fallen from a horse and cut her scalp on a rail of the tracks in Los Lunas. She always preferred to wear pants and only wore skirts when she went to Mass which was only twice a year on Christmas Eve and Palm Sunday. She was excommunicated when she married Grandpa Hank because he wasn't a Christian. She could fix motors, lamps and leaking pipes. She preferred mechanics to cooking. She knew how to work on the Model A Ford to keep it running. She was always busy. She liked nothing better than to clean and completely rearrange the tool shed, down to sorting the bolts, washers and nuts into coffee cans she saved for just such purposes.

Grandma Lillie always had a pile of old used lumber and posts, and scraps of tin roofing and wire; I have piles here at the ranch of just such items that someday I am sure to need for some important task.

Poor Grandma Lillie. She always feared I'd be killed in a horse accident. She'd grown up in the days when most people still used horses and wagons because only the wealthy had cars, so she knew bad accidents could happen with horses. She'd been thrown plenty of times herself when she was a girl.

From the time I can remember, I've been crazy about horses. I used to ride my mother's brooms. When I was eight, my father drove me to the big tribal corrals by the railroad tracks at Quirk, south of Paguate where the wild horses on Laguna Pueblo land were gathered and sold every two years. The Government Extension agent picked out a bay weanling colt and my father bought him for twelve dollars. The colt had a pretty head, big eyes and small ears, and the narrow chest and shoulders of the North African horses. I named him Joey because he jumped the fence around our yard like a kangaroo.

Once the excitement was over, I was a little disappointed because it would be at least eighteen months before he was old enough to ride. We kept him in the yard around the house for the first year and my sisters and I played with him and made him carry our dolls on his back so by the time he was old enough to ride, he didn't mind having blankets or a saddle on his back.

For a long time I rode him bareback because I didn't own a saddle but also because it was less weight for the colt to carry. The Montgomery Ward farm and ranch catalog sold saddles and I found the one I wanted. It cost sixty-five dollars. So I delivered Sunday papers until I had saved up the money. I can still remember the big box that came to the post office and the smell of new leather that filled the room when we opened it; the leather was stiff and shiny, a light tan color and embossed with rosettes; it squeaked whenever the saddle stirrups moved. I was accustomed to old saddles that were well-worn and the leather supple. I used saddle soap to soften the leather and to get rid of the squeaks. On Western saddles the stirrup leathers have to be broken in so the rider's foot and leg fit correctly.

My father's cousins Fred Marmon and Harry Marmon and their cowboy, Jack Kooka, teased me and said I should break in my new saddle the way the cowboys did it: they tossed the new saddle into the water trough then cinched the soggy saddle to their horse and rode on it all day.

I think the cowboys were probably right but I couldn't bear to throw my beautiful new saddle into the stock tank so I broke it in over months, the hard way.

I was eleven and had only been riding Joey about a year when something happened. Our cousin old Bill Pratt found me on the ground unconscious in the salt bushes not far from the pen where I kept Joey. Joey was very gentle and Bill found him nearby, so it didn't seem as if Joey had bolted or bucked. I landed on my head. I have no memory of what happened. I woke up on the couch at Bill's house. He sent one of his sisters to tell my parents. For the next three days I was barely conscious; I don't remember much—only how badly the muscles in my shoulders and neck hurt. I have no memory of what happened that day, of what went wrong. I remember St. Josephs Hospital and an x-ray of my skull. It was during summer vacation so I didn't miss any school.

This might be the reason that later on when I kept horses, Grandma Lillie was always worried about me getting killed on a horse.

In 1971 I was in law school and commuting to Albuquerque from New Laguna where my son Robert and I lived with John Silko. Back then at Laguna very few people had telephones and there were no private phone lines, only party lines. We were renting the old Gunn house at New Laguna where we had goats, many cats and dogs, and of course, horses.

One morning we were eating breakfast at New Laguna (having decided to ditch law school that day) when the door burst open and Grandma Lillie rushed in; when she saw me she said, "Leslie! They told me you were dead! Killed on your horse!" I was so surprised—all I could say was that I hadn't even ridden my horse for the past three days.

Grandma Lillie had been at my uncle's coin-operated laundry at Laguna when some women from Paguate village came rushing over to Grandma in tears at the news of my death. A moment later Fred Marmon, our cousin, who had always helped me with my horses, arrived because he'd heard the same rumor.

Later we figured out what had happened. Grandma Lillie had a party line. About two weeks before the rumor about me, Grandma received phone calls about one of her nieces in Albuquerque whose young daughter was dragged to death by her horse after she became entangled in the lead rope. Someone must have picked up the party line and overheard them talking about it. So the rumor spread from this misunderstood overheard phone conversation.

Years later when I was teaching at Diné College (known as Navajo Community College then) I ran into Robert Fernando from Mesita village near Laguna. He worked for the BIA at the Many Farms boarding school. He couldn't believe it was me because he'd heard that I had been killed; no one had bothered to tell him the rumor was false.

CHAPTER 13

The old folks used to admonish us to leave things as they are, not to disturb the natural world or her creatures because this would disrupt and endanger everything, including us humans. The hummah-hah stories from long ago related what was done the wrong way and what calamity to the humans followed.

The U.S. Federal Government by way of the Department of the Interior/Bureau of Indian Affairs forced the Laguna Pueblo people to allow Anaconda to blast open the Earth near Paguate for an open-pit uranium mine. The tribe tried to resist but the Cold War politics fed the frenzy for uranium for atomic bombs. In the early 1950s the above-ground testing at Jackass Flats in Nevada began.

The frontispiece of Carole Gallagher's book *American Ground Zero* is an Atomic Energy Commission map of the locations that got dusted with radioactive fallout during the U.S. nuclear tests in Nevada. From the map, which indicates heavier fallout with darker shading, it is clear the U.S. Government managed to nuke this country more completely than the USSR ever dreamed. All (lower) forty-eight states have locations where radioactive fallout from these tests was detected more than once, although Nevada, Utah, Colorado, northern Arizona and New Mexico got the heaviest contamination.

On this map, I found the Rio San Jose Valley where Laguna and Acoma Pueblos are located; it was clear the prevailing west winds followed the San Jose Valley so the clouds of radioactive particles from the Nevada atomic test site passed over us every time they "tested" a bomb. We were "down-winders" with all the other "expendable" people who became human guinea pigs.

Because I was born in 1948 I had a few years to grow before my body was subjected to the radioactive fallout. I've been blessed with good health thus far, but my younger sisters have not been as fortunate. They were two and four years younger than I was the first time the radioactive clouds from Nevada followed the San Jose River Valley east right over Laguna.

To add to the exposure from this radioactive fallout, once a year the Federal Government sent chest x-ray vans to Laguna to check for tuberculosis; to save a few pennies, we small children at the Bureau of Indian Affairs day school were given chest x-rays at a strength meant for adult body weight, not young children.

The Anaconda Company was not required to dispose of the radioactive tailings or store them safely to prevent contamination of the air or groundwater. For years the mountain-like piles of radioactive tailings remained there, blowing east toward Albuquerque, percolating radiation into the water table with every rain- and snowstorm. No plants ever grew on the tailings though sometimes around the base of the piles, a few hardy tumbleweeds appeared. A few years ago the tailings were finally buried beneath piles of clean dirt, and now the weeds grow there profusely.

Far more egregious abuses of the people by the U.S. Government during these years came to light during the Carter administration and in the 1990s when U.S. Energy Secretary Hazel O'Leary declassified millions of pages of "Top Secret" documents. A number of disturbing books were written based on the contents of the declassified papers. Handicapped children in boarding schools were secretly fed plutonium in their oatmeal, and poor black men in Alabama were secretly injected with plutonium "to see what would happen." The aftermath of Hiroshima and Nagasaki had already showed us what would happen; these demented secret experiments of the 1950s and 1960s are more evidence that anything may be done by U.S. Government agents as long as the two words "national security" are invoked.

While nothing like a true "gold rush," at first the search for uranium was big business in the early 1950s; the Cold War and the U.S. atomic bomb production needed more uranium. For a few years prospectors descended on the Southwest with their Geiger counters over one shoulder like a purse. As a child I remember my father calling me over to look at a box full of rocks a uranium prospector had in his jeep. They were beautiful—bright glowing colors of lemon yellow and lime green on yellow sandstone.

My father showed a prospector the rock collection he and his brothers and Grandma Lillie made from their hikes in the hills, and sure enough, one rock they'd carried home made the Geiger counter buzz. They picked up the piece of uranium so long ago no one remembered where they'd found it.

Carnotite is the vivid yellow or green powdery mineral that coats the sandstone where uranium chiefly occurs. It is a secondary mineral formed by the change of primary uranium-vanadium minerals through intense heat and exposure to water, possibly during volcanic activity. Pure carnotite contains about 53 percent uranium and 12 percent vanadium minerals. Carnotite is radioactive and easily soluble in acid and in acid rain.

My father took me along with him when I was in junior high school to one of the Kerr-McGee yellowcake mills at Ambrosia Lake, near Grants. He'd photographed the facility previously and was bringing the proof sheets to the mill manager. He thought it would be "educational" for me to go. I liked to see how things worked so I went.

We got a mini tour of the facility by the mill manager who took us to the shipping room where the fifty-five-gallon drums were weighed and sealed prior to shipment by truck or by train. The shipping drums were ordinary steel drums. The manager lifted the lid on one of the barrels to show us the pure yellowcake refined at the mill. Another open drum contained pitch-blende which occurs as small grains of black or brownish black or dark gray nodules of uraninite, uranium oxide in sandstones which often weathers into secondary uranium materials.

The yellowcake and pitch-blende were powdered so finely they resembled velvet; the yellow was so bright and the black so intense I had the impulse to touch them; of course I didn't. We stood eighteen inches away from the open drums but none of us wore a mask. Of course the U.S. Government kept secret the reports that proved the dangers of these materials, but they and Kerr-McGee didn't want the workers and people who lived around the mills and mines to become alarmed.

As it was, the Laguna and Acoma people refused to work underground. Whites and others from the Spanish-speaking villages in the area were hired to go underground in the shafts to mine. The Laguna and Acoma people refused to desecrate the Earth by entering her. Work in the open-pit mine was permitted, and for twenty years the Pueblo miners worked in the dust of the rich carnotite but wore no protective gear for their lungs or skin.

In the early 1960s, Anaconda discovered that Paguate village sat on top of sandstone with very rich deposits of uranium. The company proposed to relocate the entire village, to move every household into a brand new settlement with new modern houses and modern conveniences. The Tribal Council discussed the proposal for weeks, and many at Paguate are still angered that a number of Council members from other villages argued for the relocation of Paguate village. In the end sanity prevailed, and Paguate was not destroyed.

Instead the mining company sank deep shafts under the village to reach the rich ore. The huge open pit continued to grow, swallowing entire sandstone mesas in a few years' time, and the pit moved ever closer to Paguate village. The sounds of the mine resounded in the village night and day, three shifts of workers, seven days a week, fifty-two weeks a year.

During this time, in the early 1970s, seven young people, high school students at Paguate, apparently made a suicide pact. The students were in their junior year and were among the brightest and most popular at Laguna-Acoma High School. Their families were financially secure. They seemed to have a great deal to live for, but they chose otherwise.

I always wondered if it might have been the presence of the mine—I could hardly stand the sound for the hour or two I visited my cousins Rachel Anaya and Esther Johnson at Paguate in the seventies while the Jackpile Mine was in operation. These young people heard that terrible mechanical roar of compressors and generators without cease, around the clock, every day of the year; they heard their elders rant about the destruction the mine wrought, they heard the old ones cry whenever they recalled the lovely orchards of apples and apricots that once grew where the open-pit mine left nothing.

The suicide pact ran its course, and then in 1980 something amazing appeared at the mine. Two Jackpile Mine employees whose job it was to inspect the tailings piles for instability or erosion had found a strange object only thirty feet away from one of the mountainous piles of tailings. The two employees made the same round of inspections of the tailings twice each week. Sometime between their last inspection of the southwest edge of tailings, a twenty foot long sandstone formation in the shape of a giant snake appeared only a few yards from the base of a tailings pile. The sandstone formation looked as if it had been there forever—but it hadn't.

For hundreds of generations, this area had been familiar ground to the Paguate people who farmed and hunted the area every day, yet no one had ever seen the giant sandstone snake before. Traditional medicine people came from all directions and all the tribes to see the giant stone snake. What a wonder it was to find something so sacred and prophetic; it was as if Ma'shra'true'ee, the sacred messenger snake, had returned, but not to some pristine untouched corner of the land, but instead to the uranium tailings of the Jackpile Mine.

That day I visited the stone snake, only three loose strands of barbed wire enclosed the sandstone formation. Some scraps of chain link from the mine were loosely strung up on one side. The effort at fencing off the sandstone was to protect the giant snake from damage by grazing cattle or horses in the area. I saw scattered bits of shell, and mother of pearl with small pieces of coral and turquoise, left with pollen and corn meal to provide ceremonial food for the spirit of the giant snake.

A few years later Laguna Pueblo got the state highway relocated away from this area. Paguate Hill was notorious for car wrecks; now the highway swings east and then continues north, closer to the remains of the open-pit mine that ceased operation with a world glut of uranium thirty years ago.

Aunt Susie told me that a spring flows out of the basalt ledge on the west side of Paguate village. In times past the medicine people used to send their patients to soak in the spring water because it cured certain maladies. In their natural undisturbed state, the uranium-bearing minerals in the earth beneath Paguate village were healing mediums, not killers.

Some years ago the U.S. Public Health Service tested a sample of the water the Paguate villagers drank for as long as the people lived there. The water was from a spring under the village and was slightly radioactive. As a "down-winder" exposed to fallout (and yellowcake), I pin my hopes for good health on my genetic inheritance from my Paguate ancestors who over the centuries might have acquired a resistance to radiation.

My great grandma A'mooh who was born and reared at Paguate, and drank the radioactive spring water much of her life, lived past her ninety-eighth birthday. She told my mother that as a young woman she had survived an appendicitis without Western medicine. That seemed impossible without penicillin or antibiotics, so I wondered about the story until a few years ago.

Then I became a patient of Dr. Roberto Zamudio Millán who immigrated to the United States from Mexico in the 1960s. On my first visit I wanted him to know that I wasn't impressed with Western European medicine so I told him that my great grandmother had survived an appendicitis without doctors, hospitals or penicillin.

To my delight, Dr. Zamudio Millán responded to my story with another story. While he was in medical school he found a book written by a doctor who worked in a small town in the mountains of the State of Chihuahua in 1920. The people traveled considerable distances on foot to obtain medical care in the town, and in emergencies family members came for the doctor to take him to their house where a loved one lay ill.

So a family brought the doctor to their modest home in an Indian village high in the mountains to take a look at their old granny who was feverish and quite ill. The doctor told the old woman's family they had to get her down to the clinic hospital in town at once for surgery or she would die of a burst appendix. The old woman refused to go to the hospital. So the doctor returned to the town, and a few days later they came again and said she was very ill now and again the doctor went and again she refused the hospital.

A week or two went by and the doctor heard no more from the family of the old woman, and the doctor thought she was dead by now. Then the following week, the doctor saw two of the old woman's sons and when he cautiously inquired about her, certain she must have died, her sons said, "Oh she's just fine; strong as ever." They told the doctor that the fever went down and she asked for the bedpan. Then she told them she was hungry and wanted to eat.

A few weeks later the doctor went to the village. When the old woman saw the doctor she yelled at him, "You don't know anything! See, I'm still alive. I didn't need your hospital!"

Dr. Zamudio Millán said that in extremely rare cases, before the appendix ruptured, the body formed a membrane around the infected matter inside the appendix so it was encapsulated and then the large intestine passed it harmlessly. That was Dr. Zamudio Millán's explanation of how my great grandma survived appendicitis without doctors and antibiotics. He completely won me over with that story so I see him on those rare occasions when acupuncture and herbs don't work.

After John Silko and the boys and I returned to Laguna from Alaska in 1975, we lived with Grandma Lillie in her house with my father who'd moved back from Palm Springs. I needed a quiet place to write so I set up an office in my great grandma's old house. My great grandpa Marmon's work table with a drawer was there; he'd had it made out of the oak shipping crates he saved.

Only one room was habitable, Grandma A'mooh's old bedroom.

There was electricity for my typewriter. I loved it because I'd spent my happiest hours as a child with Grandma A'mooh there. Out the window the old swing was still there; the morning glories and bridal bush were gone but I replanted the morning glories and hollyhocks the first chance I got.

Later we fixed up Grandma A'mooh's old house and moved in. It was while we were living there in 1977 that I suffered a misdiagnosed ectopic pregnancy that almost killed me. Four different doctors called it the "flu," but every day I got weaker and shorter of breath. One night as I slept in Grandma A'mooh's old parlor, I had a dream that was not visual but aural. A voice said "A flu like this one could kill you." The voice I dreamed didn't sound like her voice but I knew it was her.

The morning after the dream, Grandma Lillie came to check on me. I was sitting at the kitchen table and I looked up at her as she walked in the door. She looked at me and she said, "Leslie, you're dying," and I said, "Grandma, I know."

I drove to Albuquerque to the doctor who thought I had the flu. I told him I was weaker; I told him I thought it might be something uterine, and he sent me to the specialist who ordered a sonogram that revealed the ruptured ectopic pregnancy.

The rupture had occurred on October second; the correct diagnosis was finally made on November second, All Souls' Day or Day of the Dead. By that time I had lost a great deal of blood, I was very weak, and the specialist told me I was a poor risk for surgery but without the surgery I'd die.

I was diagnosed late in the afternoon and wasn't able to get to a telephone until early evening. I was only able to call a few people to tell them about the emergency surgery, and these were people who lived out of state or a great distance from Albuquerque.

By the time I was admitted to the hospital and John Silko had driven the fifty miles back to Laguna to tell my father, grandmother and the boys, it was too late at night for him to return. I told John Silko to stay at Laguna with my father and Grandma Lillie to comfort the boys.

I learned a great deal the evening and night of November second as they hurried the blood transfusions I needed before surgery. The other bed in the hospital room was empty. My mother, my sister Wendy and my friend Mei-Mei all lived out of state or a hundred miles away, so they telephoned me.

I don't remember what we talked about that night. In my rational thoughts I understood there was a strong chance I'd die in surgery the next morning and this was my last night in this world. But in my irrational hopefulness (I was twenty-eight and Viking Press had published my first novel *Ceremony* only three months earlier) I felt I would survive, that I would live although the doctor saw it otherwise. As sick and weak as I was, I didn't feel I was dying though I was; probably we humans always die thinking we aren't dying.

Except for the telephone calls I was alone that night before the surgery. I brought along the sweater I was knitting for Cazimir who was five. I kept knitting that night even though I couldn't finish the sweater before the surgery. Somehow I felt I'd be able to finish the sweater— completely irrational under the circumstances.

The close call changed my consciousness of myself and my life in a fundamental way; it made me understand how short my time in this world might be. Later my friend Ishmael Reed said the reason I didn't die was because I had more books to write.

In some ways the person I'd been before November 3, 1977 did die that day. I woke from the surgery with a profound sense of responsibility for how I lived my life. I did have more books I wanted to write but not if I stayed where I was. My writing was a source of tension in the marriage, and the teaching and other duties stood in the way. So I moved to Tucson in early January of 1978, two months after the emergency surgery.

PART TWO

Rattlesnakes

CHAPTER 14

I came to live at this old ranch house in the Tucson Mountains, and before long the desert terrain and all its wonderful beings and even the weather won my heart.

So many of the plants and shrubs and the birds and snakes of the Sonoran desert were unfamiliar—I had a wonderful time reading and learning about them as I watched them outside my house. I knew it might be some time before I knew this desert well enough to write about it.

As the poet Ofelia Zepeda wrote, "Tucson is a linguistic alternative." She explains in one of her poems that the Tohono O'Odom word "Cuk Son" means "place by Black Mountains." "Cuk Do ag" means "Black Mountains," the name for the Tucson Mountains.

I rode horseback in those days. The view of the land from horseback is a high and wide expanse, good for distances but not so good for small things on the ground. I was able to spy deer antlers and desert tortoise shells from the high vantage of the saddle, and I'd stop the horse to pick them up. Occasionally I'd stop and dismount when I spied a turquoise rock or other interesting rocks, and walk alongside the horse to pick them up.

On horseback I traveled farther into the wilderness than I do now when I walk the trail. I haven't found any tortoise shells or antlers on the walks but I do see deer now and then, and on rare occasions live tortoises. In the past thirty years the bulldozers and urban sprawl of Tucson have destroyed hundreds of square miles of pristine desert habitat and left the desert tortoises in danger of extinction along with the Gila monster lizards and spotted owls.

The old ranch house and the sheds and outbuildings are home to pack rats and deer mice accompanied by the gopher snakes, racer snakes and rattlesnakes that eat them. So in the beginning, I got to know the snakes and pack rats because we were neighbors. I began to keep notes about my encounters.

Ca'cazni is the Comcaac or Seri name for rattlers. Onomatopoeia for the sound of the rattle—it begins to rattle with slow "ca-ca-" but breaks into a buzzing rattle, thus the "z" and "ne" sounds.

The Raramuri, the Tarahumara Indians of the Sierra Madre in Chihuahua, use rattlesnake venom to treat cancer tumors. Snake oil has many medicinal uses, and the pejorative meaning for fraud is because a snake oil salesman called Rattlesnake King Stanley, at the 1893 World's Columbian Exposition, was arrested for fraud. He claimed to have lived among the Hopi people and to have killed and processed hundreds of snakes. But the oil in the bottles contained no rattlesnake oil, only mineral oil, turpentine, red pepper and camphor.

Steep banks of violet blue cumulus drift over the southwest horizon, off the Gulf of California; later in the morning, the rattlesnakes come out in anticipation of the rain. The light is pearly blue and cool enough for the snakes to await the rain. They favor spots near sources of water or shade, so it is easy to anticipate where they may be. In my yard one rattlesnake sits next to a ceramic bowl and its twin curls up in the rainwater drainpipe nearby. They lie in wait for little birds and rodents.

When I first came to this old ranch house there were the remains of a mesquite log corral below the hill, and I later repaired it so I could keep a horse. A big black and white Western diamondback rattlesnake lived near the old corral; what interested me at once was its calm demeanor. No coiling or rattling when we met, the snake made me feel welcome here. He knew I was a friend of snakes. I was careful to watch for him around the hay barn where he got fat on pack rats. If I found the big snake in the shade of the corral fence when I was making repairs, he patiently tolerated a gentle lift in the bowl of the shovel to a more out of the way place in the shade.

I called him "Baby" as a joke because it was an unlikely name for a rattler four feet long and about five inches in diameter. He was a grandfather snake not a baby. He kept me company for my first two summers in Tucson, but after the summer of 1980 when I was away in New Mexico much of the time, he left. The black and white color of the snake was dazzling and unusual, and I always hoped I might see another rattler like him, but more than thirty years later, I have not. Maybe the old snake was a messenger of welcome and more supernatural than I realized at the time.

Other big rattlesnakes live near the old corral but these snakes are shades of light brown and beige, the usual colors for snakes in this area; the only black and white they had were the rings of stripes on their tails by the rattles. I found an Arizona black rattlesnake under a piece of plywood on my driveway, but he was small and completely black with no white markings. I haven't seen him again, but I always remember to watch out for him on the driveway, especially at night.

I was seven years old and still under the influence of my father the snake-killer, when I shot and killed a yearling rattler with my single shot .22 rifle. It was early September and the poor snake was looking for a place to hibernate when it coiled on the step to my grandparents' house. But I knew in a matter of minutes my ninety year old great grandmother would come from her house to spend the night and she would walk up those steps.

I still regret the summer after my divorce from John Silko in 1979 because I allowed the neighbor boys to kill the big dusty red rattler on the west side of the house. I tried to persuade the big rattlesnake to relocate by splashing buckets of cold water on him three times. My younger son Caz was seven at the time and I was afraid he'd get bitten. But after that day, I promised myself to protect the rattlesnakes.

Yet my ignorance and carelessness have killed a number of rattle-snakes. Ordinary chicken wire I discarded became the death snare for a fine three foot long rattler on the west slope of the hill below my house. The snake was able to get its head and neck through the oval open-ing but when the fatter part of it could not fit and the snake attempted to back out, the wire snagged its scales so it was trapped and died terribly.

I was able to save a big beautiful Sonoran gopher snake that became trapped while climbing through the chicken wire enclosure around the back patio. I got rid of all the chicken wire; hardware cloth with its tiny mesh is superior in every way to chicken wire and does far less harm to reptiles.

Monofilament nylon netting used to protect trees from birds is even worse than chicken wire for reptiles. The threads of monofilament nylon easily entangle a lizard's toes and feet and as it struggles to get free, its delicate scales only become more entangled.

The iridescent sky blue lizards that live on the roof and walls of my house are usually combative if they fall into human hands, but the fat sky blue lizard I found tangled in the nylon netting remained calm as I snipped away the netting with my kitchen shears. Somehow the liz-ard understood I meant no harm; similarly I've heard cowboys describe mule deer entangled in barbed wire that allowed the cowboys to cut them free without a struggle.

After I freed the sky lizard, I removed that wretched nylon bird netting from the patio and was about to drop it into the trash when I noticed horse damage on a young mesquite tree in my front yard, so carelessly I tossed the netting over the tree and forgot about it. A few months passed. Then early one morning just at dawn I heard my dogs barking like maniacs and when I went outside I found a big rattlesnake caught in that piece of bird netting.

The snake was terribly snagged with the nylon filaments cutting deeply into his body at the thickest point, about ten inches from his head which moved freely while his middle remained trapped. He was about thirty inches long and as big around as my wrist, but as soon as I called off the dogs, the snake stopped rattling. It was early July. The sun was rising and in only a few hours the trapped snake would die from the heat. I had to save his life but I didn't know how I was going to do it because I was alone and the nearest neighbor a half mile away. I didn't have much time. The sun was up and felt warmer by the minute.

The snake didn't want dogs near him but he didn't seem to mind me, not even when I squatted down and slowly and very carefully examined how badly he was trapped. It was bad. As the snake struggled to free itself, it had only pulled the netting tighter, until the filaments drew blood on the tender skin between the scales. I had to act fast. I ran indoors and found a pair of tin shears, about fifteen inches long, handles and blades included. No matter how I did it, I was going to have to put both hands within easy striking range of the head and upper body that was not entangled and moved freely. The big snake was calm so far, but I'd have to press the tips of the steel blades firmly against the snake's body in order to reach the nylon filaments jammed under the scales. What would the snake do then?

The sun was higher now, and I had no choice. I found a dry aloe stalk about twenty inches long with a forked end. Dry aloe stalks are hollow and flimsy and I knew the big snake could easily break the stalk, but force wasn't the point. The aloe stalk was there to give me the illusion of safety. Twice I gently tried to put the stalk's Y over the snake's neck to give me the illusion of control, but he became uneasy when the stalk actually touched him, so I withdrew it a few inches but held it between the snake and me. I hoped the snake could read my thoughts because I was determined to set him free before the sun killed him.

With my left hand I held the aloe stalk like a wand above his neck without touching him; somehow this made me feel safer although the stalk would have been completely useless if the snake suddenly doubled back to strike.

I watched the snake intently for his reaction as I slowly moved my right hand with the tin shears toward his belly scales entangled in the nylon filaments. He didn't seem to mind my proximity, so I took a deep breath, and focused entirely on the nylon threads cutting deep under the snake's scales; I didn't want to cut or harm the snake in any way. I slowly moved the tin shears down to the ensnared scales; I was so intently focused on freeing the snake from the netting the snake must have somehow understood. Because the snake allowed me to press the cold steel of the shears against his body. That touch was provocation enough that he might have reached back and struck me, but instead the snake remained calm, stretched out and motionless. Then a strange confidence came over me which I still can't explain. In my left hand, I held the forked aloe stalk above his neck without touching him; with the tin shears in my right hand I pushed the steel tips firmly against the snake's body to try to reach the nylon threads cutting into his skin. I managed to get a nylon thread in the shears and snip! The snake didn't react. I exhaled. Again I gently but firmly put the blades of the shears under another nylon thread and cut it. When he felt his fat midsection cut free, the big diamondback glided away gracefully and I felt blessed.

I didn't see the big snake again until late October. It was dark in my front yard. I was coming from the car on the driveway without a flashlight; near the mesquite tree I felt my foot leave the ground with the sickening sensation of live moving flesh under my foot and instantly I knew what I'd done. As I jumped as high as I ever have, away from the snake, I heard him rattle once softly and then he was gone.

My carelessness should have earned me a snakebite on the instep or ankle; maybe the big rattlesnake remembered that I once set him free. The snake knew I meant him no harm.

I know of a number of instances when people accidently (usually in the dark without a flashlight) stepped on rattlesnakes or even sat on a snake without a bite. An emergency room doctor told me that all the rattlesnake-bite victims he'd seen were people who were actively molesting the snakes—holding them or poking them with sticks.

CHAPTER 15

The drought began in 1985. The small cottonwood tree I planted in 1989 died in the summer of 1997. The tree depended on gray water from the kitchen sink but I did very little cooking and washing while I completed my novel *Gardens in the Dunes*.

The last good rains came in 1983 from a hurricane that came out of the Gulf of California. The rivers and arroyos that were usually dry suddenly filled with torrents of water that swept over their banks and washed away bridges and condominiums.

The approach of rain clouds on the horizon became an important occasion. I'd stop whatever I was doing, including writing, and sit outside to wait for the clouds, and hope they wouldn't pass us over.

In 1997 I started writing little notes about the sky, the clouds, and all us desert creatures anxious to have the rain. The first rain of any duration came stealthily around the tenth of May that year—no weather radar map showed any clouds even when I could see the clouds and the wind blew. I didn't look outside again for hours until I noticed the sky darkening. I left art magazines and a VCR outside in the yard as an unwitting offering to the rain; I brought the items indoors then worried that I'd offended the rain clouds. To leave valuable possessions outside indicates the wretched hopelessness felt after years of drought.

Clouds please take pity on us.

Ten days later the northeast sky is violet blue, the spin of the storm spiraled it north but now we may be in its path if it begins to spin southward.

But it didn't spin southward after all. No rain. The air is so dry even if rain did fall from the clouds in a gossamer veil of blue, it would evaporate before it reached the ground.

Here I abandoned the rain journal for a while. A superstitious person might say don't keep a rain journal because it won't rain if you do.

Even the chance for rain puts me in the mood to write about the approaching clouds; they are so lovely I want to sketch them in chalk too.

If I kept a heat journal I would have a great deal to write about every day.

Temperatures above 103 degrees overheat the ape brain and humans become slightly crazed. Minor traffic accidents increase in Tucson. Those of us with overheated monkey brains brook no delays at traffic lights or in supermarket check out lines.

Newcomers to Tucson's summer heat are amazed to find their car's rear view mirror lying on the front seat because the glue melts. Car windshields become solar furnaces capable of melting plastic objects left on the car dashboard, including cell phones, sunglasses, cameras, DVDs and credit cards. Dashboards themselves gradually crack and disintegrate. Car batteries suddenly explode. Transformers on electric power poles also explode in the heat.

During daylight hours the dash from the air conditioned supermarket to the car wilts all fresh produce or cut flowers, and defrosts frozen food; so the wise shopper waits until the night. So do the wise hunters.

Night. Heavenly delicious sweet night of the desert that calls all of us out to love her. The night is our comfort with her coolness and darkness. On wings, on feet, on our bellies, out we all come to glory in the night.

There are a few deserts on Earth that go without measurable rainfall or snow for years and years and not just six or seven months, as Tucson does. Places in the Taklimakan Desert on the old Silk Road, in the Atacama Desert in Chile, get less rain than Tucson does. Places in Iraq and Arabia get hotter than Tucson; even Phoenix and Las Vegas get hotter than Tucson.

Over time the monkey brain adjusts to the temperatures above one hundred two Fahrenheit, but there are compensations which must be made.

Long before there was any such thing as daylight savings time, the people of the desert Southwest got out of bed long before dawn—at midnight if the moon was up—to work in their cornfields until daylight. By noon the people would be asleep. The Englishmen saw this and accused the people of laziness; but to work in the heat at high noon as the old gringos did was madness.

Tucson nights in the summer approach a perfection of temperature between the night air and that of the human body. The air is faintly perfumed by the reina de la noche, the Queen of the Night, an indigenous variety of the night-blooming Cereus cactus that bears blossoms of astonishing beauty which last only one night.

The light of the moon on the desert causes subtle motion to become perceptible as the giant saguaros move in the wind along the ridge. It all happens with the light; what we see, what the human brain registers—what we call "reality"—is all light.

CHAPTER 16

One hundred five degrees Fahrenheit on this late June day but I see clouds, high thin cirrus clouds that give me hope; the level of humidity in the air is rising as moist air flows from the Gulf of California and the Sierra Madre.

Then two days of prayers and deer dances are offered by the Yoeme and the Tohono O'Odom people in honor of San Juan to call in the rain clouds. Today one hundred two degrees Fahrenheit. By afternoon a light rain falls.

Off come the leaves of the mesquites and palo verde, and my datura plants too. Down the hill a little whirlwind swirls in the chicken yard. In eight minutes or less it's passed and then the second wave comes with big raindrops for two or three minutes and it's over.

Sometimes in the rain or at sundown one may catch glimpses of ancient scenes of grandeur—cities of gold in cliffs of sandstone mesas in remote valleys beyond the black volcanic peaks.

It's mid-July now and yesterday when it was bright and hot, I was picking ripe figs and noticed the odd branch actually brushed the ground now, pulled down by the two fat black figs ready to pick. My attention was focused on the two ripe figs and how to reach them in the shade by the wall. I was about to blindly push past the fig branches and around the pots of tomatoes to pick the figs when something caused me to look more closely at the shady ground where I intended to step:

almost invisible on the ground under the ripe black figs was a large, beige-colored rattlesnake in a low profile coil.

This snake lives under the back step and knows my morning routine in the garden of red clay pots. She doesn't bother to rattle because she trusts me, as do the blue-bellied sky lizards who wait for me with the hose to wash out scores of caramel-colored cockroaches.

The rattlesnake that lives in the front yard was determined to come inside the front room last autumn. He would come and press his nose against the glass by the front door. Indoors, the dogs, Tigger and Thelma, could see the snake and went wild with concern. The snake stayed awhile then left.

Finally one evening the snake came while the dogs were away. The dogs left the broken screen door wide open. Persistence paid off for the snake, and he found a way to get inside the house.

The dogs soon returned and smelled at once what happened. They tracked the snake in the front room and cornered him by the front door and barked furiously until I came out with a dust mop and gently guided the snake out the front door.

The dogs were devastated by the breach of their sanctuary and ever after they came in the front door with a certain hesitation because the snake got inside once and might do it again.

Some years before this, I came in from the front room where my studio is located now, and I heard a loud rattling from the direction of the kitchen. Right away I could tell by the sound this was not the rattler that lived underneath the kitchen floor, the one that used to rattle whenever I stepped near the refrigerator door. No, the sound wasn't coming from under any floor, the buzzing rattle sound was coming directly from my kitchen.

The merry Feng Shui remodeler never bothered to fix the holes in the wall behind the stove and the refrigerator; a small spotted Sonora skunk used to come out into the kitchen from under the stove in the winter, so it was inevitable that one day a snake would follow the same route. The big red rattlesnake looked at me and at the kitchen in bewilderment. I opened the side door and used the broom to guide the snake outside. When she felt the outdoor air on her face she accelerated and was gone.

A large light-colored Western diamondback rattlesnake lived under the house, under the kitchen floor when I moved into the house. At first she didn't recognize my footsteps and used to rattle loudly under the kitchen floor where I stood. I jumped every time she rattled then gradually she stopped rattling because she got used to me. I suspected that she was the source of the half dozen baby rattlesnakes that appeared on the living room floor in 1989.

My father and his wife, Kathy, came for a visit. I had gone grocery shopping but I'd left the door unlocked for them and they made themselves comfortable on the couch in the living room. My stepmother was almost nine months pregnant with my youngest half brother, Leland. They were watching TV waiting for me to get back when Milo the cat alerted them to the six newborn baby rattlesnakes wiggling on the old brick floor next to the fireplace where there were small holes in the plaster. My father and Milo promptly killed five of the newborn snakes; their tiny mangled remains greeted us by the front door when Gus and I returned with the groceries.

While my father recounted the bravery of Milo and himself, Gus spotted the lone surviving baby rattler under the couch where my pregnant stepmother sat only moments before. Oddly, only a few weeks earlier, Gus had talked about wanting to get a baby rattlesnake; yeah, nice idea, I said at the time because I thought it would be impossible for Gus to get a baby rattlesnake.

The mother rattlesnake must have given birth to them under the dining room floor near the back side of the fireplace, right next to the hole in the plaster that leads into the living room. Gus scooped up the tiny snake in a glass jar. The newborn snake was the diameter of a piece of spaghetti; coiled flat it was only the size of a quarter. Gus fed it live crickets from the pet store for two weeks and then the snake was ready to eat baby pinkie mice, and before long, it ate small mice. Gus named the snake Evo Atrox.

In the snake's first year it quickly grew to more than twelve inches in length and was big around as my ring finger. Like macaws and parrots, rattlesnakes have to grow fast to fool the predators or they won't survive infancy.

The second year, in September, the rattlesnake became restless and tried to get out of its cage. It wouldn't eat. The winter hibernation instinct perhaps.

The third year when Evo got restless I had a plan.

A few months earlier in the summer I'd discovered a terrible thing—a fine rattler got entangled in poultry netting and had died some days before. I removed the poultry netting, but I didn't forget the big snake that lived on the west side slope about seventy feet below the west door to the house.

That September, when Evo began to move restlessly, Gus and I decided to take Evo to the eco-niche vacated by the dead snake, and set him free. There was a big palo verde tree next to a pile of lava boulders with intriguing holes under them. A perfect home for a snake. For the first year while Evo transitioned, I planned to bring him white mice and to keep a bowl of water under the palo verde tree. We slid open the cage door and Evo glided out and went into the hole at the foot of the boulders under the palo verde tree. We felt proud of ourselves for returning the snake to the wild.

The next morning the dogs were barking on the west side of the house at eight a.m. and when I looked out the window on the west side of the house, I saw a rattlesnake that looked like Evo. But I thought it must be one of Evo's relatives that lived under the house.

About two hours later, the dogs were barking again on the west side, and when I opened the door, the rattlesnake was leaning against the door and flopped into the house. It was Evo. We retrieved the snake cage and water bowl from the site down the hillside and guided Evo into his cage where he's remained ever since.

CHAPTER 17

Search the Internet under the subject "rattlesnake" and you'll find the same proportion of snake-killers and snake-haters as there are snake-lovers and snake-appreciators. I downloaded the photographs of dozens of rattlesnakes stretched out and piled up on top of one another to cool off in the concrete culverts under the highway near Bakersfield, California. I was heartened to see so many big rattlesnakes together.

I was telling rattlesnake stories at a Lannan Foundation dinner one evening in Santa Fe. I talked about the people I knew who've stepped on or even sat on rattlesnakes without being bitten. My uncle Wafer, Dick Chapman, myself—we had all stepped on rattlesnakes without incident. One cold day when Linda Niemann was a brakeman on the Southern Pacific Railroad, she sat on a small rattler that was trying to warm itself on a rock, and it didn't bite.

J.E. who worked for the Lannan Foundation was seated at our table and said she had a rattlesnake story. It happened when she was nineteen and had just arrived in Tucson from Connecticut for her freshman year at the University of Arizona. She had no experience in the desert or in the West. A week after her arrival, she was invited to a big beer bust at a campground on the road to the Catalina Mountains. After dark the party-goers built a bonfire and everyone was having a jolly, noisy time. She had to urinate so she went a distance from the bonfire in the dark. She pulled down her jeans and panties and as she squatted her right heel came down on a big rattlesnake.

The snake buried its fangs deep into her heel. With her panties and jeans still down around her ankles, she ran back to the bonfire screaming for help with the big rattlesnake hanging onto her heel. No one saw whether she wore panties or pants—all eyes were on the snake as the people around the bonfire ran over one another in their haste to escape.

Fortunately someone had invited a cowboy from a ranch nearby to attend the beer bust. The cowboy wasn't afraid to help J.E. He told her to stand still while he went back to his truck. He returned with a shotgun and she said she thought "Oh no!—I've been bitten by a snake and now I'm about to get shot."

The cowboy thought the better of it and took the shotgun back to his truck. This time he brought back a hatchet. He chopped the snake's head from the body but the head would not come loose from her heel, and the cowboy had to chop the snake's jaws with the hatchet to get it off her heel.

Next the cowboy called out for whiskey and took two or three big swallows "for protection" while he sucked the venom from the wound. J.E. believes the cowboy saved her life that night because it took the ambulance more than an hour to arrive. As it was she spent a week in the hospital but sustained no permanent damage.

All the people and noise must have frightened the rattlesnake a great deal before J.E. came along, which may account for the severity of the bite.

If you go to a place where the rattlesnakes don't know you or places where humans attack snakes, then you must be much more careful. It is wise to cultivate a certain self-discipline that requires you to look before you step or reach. For me watering in the garden is the time I have to be cautious because the spray from the hose may cause a snake to move silently from a shady place behind a flowerpot behind me and if I step back without first looking, I might step on a snake.

The angle of the sun about a week before the first day of spring is their signal. The rattlesnakes begin to emerge. The big orange snake suns herself by the west door on a heap of cut flower debris; she only rattled the first day when she and I startled one another. When the pup sniffed the big rattler it allowed the puppy's nose to touch it without incident.

Later, on the west side of the house I looked out the window and saw two rattlesnakes dancing in a heap of stove ashes.

The big albino rattler under the fig tree is the same color as the limestone around the base of the clay pot. This year he got angry at the dogs on the other side of the fence because they kept barking and spoiled his hunting. Now he's sprawled under the fig tree with a big lump of dinner distending his belly, too full to be comfortable but also too full to flee. He's back in a day or two to sit next to the pale limestone under the fig tree to watch the drainpipe where rats keep their nurseries.

Later we found a yearling diamondback in the pigeon cage. He wasn't after pigeons because they are too big for him to swallow. So he tolerated many pigeons stepping all around him without striking one. He was waiting for a sparrow or small rodent to come inside the cage to pilfer feed.

Charlie herded him out of the cage and the snake hasn't been back. Was he the one who tried and failed to swallow pigeons last summer?

The snake by the fig tree is the same one that turns itself almost white when it sits in the sand outside the military macaw cage on the white sand. He shares that area with a small snake with a black mask.

I once touched the dark masked snake when I was weeding my wild asters after sundown. I felt the snake shudder at my touch and draw away, but the snake didn't rattle. The snake had every right to bite me when I touched him but he sensed I meant no harm. I don't weed after dark anymore, and the snake didn't sit under the wild asters again.

The big snake that lives under the feed shed is a Western diamond-back of medium to dark brown, and no mask. She's the one that ate so much she couldn't fit the lump in her belly under the shed and had to lie there for a few hours until her meal digested a bit. At first glance I feared she might be dead until I gently touched her tail and she stuck her head out from under the shed to see what I was up to. Lately she sits by the rainwater outlet into the pool. She shares that spot with one or two other smaller snakes that look just like her. She has a sister as big as she who sits out by the small watering hole.

The fourth morning after July 11, 2001 when my mother died, I took my horse for a ride. I left the house before dawn to get saddled and ready for daybreak. The Catalina Mountains were heaped with blue rain clouds so the light of the rising sun was diffuse and luminous—a silver blue shimmered in the jade green of the jojoba and palo verde, and greasewood.

The horse took his time and picked his way through the rocks on the trail; when he stopped I thought he was malingering until I heard a faint rattle and saw a rattlesnake on the trail, motionless, half coiled and poised for full retreat. In the early morning light the snake was an amazing ethereal pale blue—rain cloud blue.

The horse walked another fifty feet and stopped again; there in the middle of the trail sat another pale blue rattler in a flat hunter's coil. The horse stopped soon enough so the snake did not rattle.

As a child I'd seen a grass green rattler and a rattler as black as local basalt, but I never expected a blue rattlesnake. The snake's scales are actually tiny hard feathers with a prismatic inner structure in which the color of a feather comes not from pigment but from light. Like the opal with shifting patterns of refraction that allow different hues of light to pass through, the snake's scales soak up the color of the surrounding light making them invisible to the human eye for minutes at a time.

Twin blue rattlesnakes—I thought of my mother at once—that's where she was now—her human form and energy changed and joined with the silver blue light of the morning. The twin rattlesnakes caught my attention; they were her message to me. Where she was now was in this world and nearby me, but not as she was.

On the seventh night after my mother's burial, the dog in the front room barked nonstop until we went out to see. The door outside was open so the dog could go out whenever she wished. I didn't turn on the light in the room because Charlie had the flashlight. He walked through the dark room and outdoors but as I followed I heard a snake rattle in the room with me.

When I turned on the lights I saw a small rattlesnake, no more than ten or twelve inches long, but I knew right away this was an adult; its body wasn't shaped like a baby snake. Its proportions were smaller than those of a diamondback; its head was small and its rattles were small so the sound wasn't nearly as loud.

What a beautiful rattler it was—instead of the familiar diamondback pattern this snake had a wide banded pattern in maroon brown on gray. The banded pattern and the snake's small size meant it was a banded rock rattler, a rare species. It was no coincidence that the mesquite bean pods on the ground and the pattern of the snake were indistinguishable from one another; the camouflage enables the snake to prey on the rodents that eat the pods.

I recalled the nights the dog insisted there was a snake indoors with her and I searched and found nothing; but since I was looking for a big diamondback I easily might have overlooked the small snake.

CHAPTER 18

I tried to keep working on the novel *Blue Sevens* in August, but it was difficult. On the eleventh of the month I thought of my mother.

I thought of her on the morning of September 11, 2001 as I was getting up; a few minutes later the planes hit the World Trade Center.

I lost my mother on July 11, and two months later, I lost my country.

I was not able to write about this period of my life for a long time, and then when I did, I chose to write fiction.

The Tucson TV weatherman said 2002 is the driest year since European record keeping began here. It is now early July and the ground is so dry that it shrinks, and the plastic pipe of the water line is cast up and out of the baked earth. Even the indigenous plants and trees begin to die off—the smallest, the oldest and the sickest die first.

The big rattlesnakes don't even bother to come out—no point in wasting energy when there's nothing there to eat—the rodents and birds are scarce. The smaller rattlers have to come out and take a chance; they don't have the reserves so they can't sit out the drought like the big snakes can.

I've had to perform two rattlesnake rescues this season. One of the three small snakes that live on the west side of the house managed to fall into the old ranch cistern which is half filled with dirt. He'd been trapped in there long enough to shed a skin. The rainwater kept him alive. On the cold nights of early spring the snake took shelter under a tin garbage can lid that was covered by a sheet of old plywood. I felt I had to free the snake but I wasn't sure how to do it yet. The snake appeared to be o.k. but hungry, so after sundown I carefully dropped the snake two live white mice intended for the indoor rattlesnake. The rattler in the cistern ate both mice at once.

Because the cistern belonged to me, I felt obligated to free the snake. I saw it try to climb the concrete walls so I gave it some 2×4s to climb out, but rattlers aren't agile climbers. I thought about putting the ladder down in the old cistern and going in after the snake with my parrot net. But I realized the ladder bumping around would only upset the snake. Instead I duct taped the handle of a dust mop to the handle of my parrot net to give me the length I needed so I could reach down into the cistern and gently scoop the rattler out.

At first the snake didn't want to go into the parrot net and tried to hide under the plywood. He didn't like the disturbance and coiled but didn't rattle—maybe because he recognized me from the west doorstep where we meet from time to time. I moved very slowly and gently with the parrot net made of soft fabric; I tried to carefully scoop the snake into the net but it was fearful and shrank away.

On my second attempt the snake made a half-hearted strike at the net but then he seemed to decide it wasn't going to kill him if it hadn't already; or he understood I meant no harm. He might have recognized my scent from the white mice I fed him earlier. The snake remained in his coil, but he was calm now and did not strike or move away from the net, and then he went into the net and I made a twist in the top so he couldn't escape. I lifted the snake in the net out of the cistern and left the net on the ground with the top open near the entrance to the snake den under my house. He stayed in the net for a while and later when I checked on him he was cautiously crawling out, headed for the snake pipe entrance under the house.

I had a pipe installed under the kitchen floor out the west wall of the house to allow the snakes to get in and out from under the house. One time during a remodeling project, the workmen accidentally buried the pipe entrance with construction dirt and debris. Later I noticed the blocked entrance but I forgot to get a shovel and fix it because it is on the west side of the house where I seldom go.

There was an alternate entry place for the snakes on the east side but during the summer I covered this entryway with a piece of window screen to keep the squirrels out from under my house. As the first cool weather arrived in October, right after dark I heard an eerie buzzing and rattling sound outside that I'd never heard before.

I went to the window and listened; I could make out the sound of seven or eight rattlesnakes all buzzing and rattling in unison on the west side of the house in front of the blocked snake pipe.

The next morning I got a phone call from my poet-astrologer friend, Joy Harjo. She said, "I don't know if you'll be able to make anything out of this—but I have a message for you. Last night I had a dream and in it, this giant rattlesnake kept following me; I recognized him as Grandfather Rattler. When I asked him what he wanted, he said he had a message for Leslie. Tell her she owes me a plug of tobacco and a screen." Joy asked if any of it made any sense. Yes, I told her, the message did make sense.

I owed the plug of tobacco to the snakes because I allowed the snake pipe entrance under the house to be blocked. The "screen" referred to the piece of window screen that blocked the east entrance under the house; but the word "screen" also referred to the large canvas painting I'd been working on.

Usually in the fall, I painted a snake image of some kind as I did in 1986 with the Stone Avenue mural which featured a giant messenger rattlesnake with human skulls in its belly. But I decided I should do something different, and I sketched a regal horned lizard on a piece of unstretched canvas eight feet long and four feet high. But the painting was a failure; I just couldn't seem to get into the right rhythm with the lizard.

After Joy's phone call, I went back to the canvas and painted out the horned lizard with white paint. I worked all November and December to paint a giant snake with blue macaw rain clouds above it and these words:

> Every Fall I painted a snake. This year when I painted a lizard instead, Old Grandfather Rattlesnake sent me a message in a dream.

When I was a child, the old-time people used to sprinkle corn meal and pollen in the circles the snakes made just as they used to sprinkle corn meal and pollen in the tracks of mountain lions.

The Western diamondbacks here are light colored to blend in with the pale volcanic ash that forms the thin topsoil in the Tucson Mountains. Herpetologists call the white snakes "albinistic" because they are white but are not true albinos. The albinistic rattlers have dark eyes and black and white stripes on their tails.

The big white rattler that lives in the back yard found an empty clay pot that was sitting upright next to the water tub where the wild creatures come to drink. Somehow the big white snake managed to crawl into the empty clay pot and arranged his bulk so that he could hide down with just his head peeping over the rim of the pot, where he could strike a dove drinking water from the tub. The dogs noticed him first. And a good thing they did. I probably would have stood right next to the snake in the pottery bowl and not even have seen it and then had a good scare when I did finally notice it.

I told the dogs to leave the snake alone, and they did; the snake stopped rattling as soon as the dogs backed off. The snake didn't rattle at me, most snakes here don't rattle at me, only at the dogs.

The snake hunkered back down in his bowl and went back to his hunt for small creatures that might yet come to the water tub; he didn't have a lot of time left before he lost the shade and had to retreat from the sun. Later I saw some dove feathers scattered near the pottery bowl so I think he got a meal out of his strategy.

The following morning I had a close encounter at six a.m. before the sun was quite over the mountain. I hadn't had my morning coffee when I went out to water my pots of ruellia and fig and lemon trees. I leaned down face first to turn the water valve to the hose, and it was only as I raised back up that I noticed the small snake sitting under the big night-blooming cactus. He was calm despite my being only twelve inches away from him.

Yesterday morning I saw the rust brown rattlesnake from a distance across the yard. The big snake had compacted itself against the rainspout to be less visible to the doves that come for water, and to avoid confrontations with dogs.

Once my pit bull tried to bite the brown rattler but the snake bit her first and got the dog by the nose and hung on; the dog shook her head and the snake let go and landed about ten feet away. Snakes are relatively delicate creatures but fortunately this was a big snake that was able to survive being thrown.

There are two nearly identical brown rattlers in back so I can't tell if this is the big brown snake from under the tool shed or the big snake that lives under the old timbers by the pool. Yes, this is why scientists torment snakes with tiny implanted radio transmitters—to identify them. Me? I prefer to muddle along with uncertainty and leave the creatures in peace. The transmitter microwaves interfere with the normal life of the snakes so the information gathered is flawed anyway.

The rattlesnakes that live under the house by the fireplace keep warm all winter so they don't hibernate. They smell the mild winter rain as it falls and have enough body warmth to come out and sit by the west door. The three of them sit in loose coils side by side, nearly touching; as the rain falls on their backs they gracefully sip the raindrops from their scales. One of them tipped its head delicately to one side so the raindrops rolled into its mouth.

I thought I was the only one with rattlesnakes in and under her house, but I was mistaken. My friends Vernon and Becky from Hopi came to a Water Blessing gathering in Tucson. Before the meeting I was talking with them in the hotel lobby and the subject of rattlesnakes in the house came up.

Becky said a rattlesnake lived in their house; it would hide in a pipe in the kitchen wall when it saw her. Vernon was surprised to hear this, and Becky said she didn't tell him because she only saw it twice. Most older houses have ways for the snakes to get in, usually holes made by small rodents and pack rats. I didn't get to hear how it got out but probably it used the same hole as it entered. Snakes don't get lost because they can follow their own scent trail and backtrack. The snake probably left after it had consumed all the small rodents in the house.

Vernon said the Hopi farmers copied the tight coil of the rattlers to make their garden plots. The farmers made deep circular depressions in the garden soil that were designed to catch and hold rainwater for the seeds planted in the center just the way the rattlers caught rain in their coils.

The followers of José Díaz Bolio and the cult of Ahau Kan in the Yucatán believe we live in a "Crotalus-centric" Universe in which Rattlesnake taught the Mayans architecture and how to build the great pyramids based upon the rattlesnake's coil.

CHAPTER 19

On the night before the seventeenth of September 2002 a cold wind blew out of the northwest. The next morning the dogs in back, Banana and Dolly, were barking madly because their yard had a rattler in it but it was a snake that came to hibernate, not one of the regular snakes from around the house. The snake was unfamiliar with the yard as it searched for the opening to the snake den under the house.

At hibernation time I see rattlesnakes I've never seen before: the reddish diamondback, the light masked snake, the dark masked snake, the albinistic snake, one by one they come to the entrance to the big snake den under my front yard. These are the snakes that spend the summer farther away from the house and aviaries, away from people, and return only in the late fall. The big reddish diamondback was pinned down by the dogs in the yard, so I brought the dogs indoors for ten minutes or so to allow the snake to get away.

The change in weather brought another snake after that one. The dogs barked with great agitation. I called them off and heard rattling from the direction of their dog house, and when I looked I saw a small light masked snake in the door of the dog house. The snake seemed to be exiting, and the odd thing was that just as I made eye contact with the snake, it immediately rushed toward me as if I reminded it of the garden area it intended to reach for safety. But no sooner than one snake was safe, I heard the dogs bark and another snake was trying to cross their area to reach the entrance to the snake den.

It's three days later and the red diamondback is caught between the parrot wire and the hardware cloth because it has a meal in a lump in its belly it needs to digest. The sun is on the snake so I hurried the dogs out of the way and went for the wire cutters. When I returned the snake had already escaped and its tail end was disappearing into its hole under the macaw aviary. The snake never rattled at me once the whole time it was trapped.

Mid-October now, and at night the temperature drops below seventy-five degrees. In the morning I find deep imprints of circles in the soft dirt, circles as precise as any circle drawn with a compass. The circles are so perfect one cannot help but notice them. Perfect circles in the dirt are usually man-made—the imprints of big round man-made objects—garden pots or spare tires.

I looked more closely and realized the deep imprint was left by a rattlesnake that nestled itself down a half inch in the dirt for warmth last night while it waited for a rodent to pass. I didn't see deep imprints earlier in the year while nights were in the nineties. The snakes left only faint imprints of themselves in the dust.

The circles are identical and I imagine the same snake made them each time he moved; he made another circle imprint when he coiled. Three of the five imprints were directly over small holes as if the snake blocked off one rodent hole to force the rodents to use the hole most convenient for the snake to strike.

It was my friend the writer Linda Niemann who discovered the cult of Ahau Kan inherited by the poet José Díaz Bolio. He wrote a book titled *The Geometry of the Maya and Their Rattlesnake Art*, in which he laid out evidence for an ancient belief system in which the rattlesnake Ahau Kan was the central figure. The Costa Rican rattlesnake *Crotalus durissus durissus* was the key figure. The poet claimed that the rattlesnakes taught human beings what Díaz Bolio termed "a Crotalus-centric" geometry and architecture in which the perfect circle was seen in the Moon and the Sun, and in the imprint of the rattlesnake in sand.

The Maya design of pyramids, each level resting on the previous in a concentric stacked pyramid form, was nearly identical to the morphology of the rattlesnake in its coil. That concentric pyramid form in stone, while very massive, also meant the pyramid did not easily fall down in an earthquake.

Díaz Bolio also pointed out that the number of dorsal scales of the Yucatán rattler is thirteen, which is one quarter of the solar cycle of fifty-two weeks. Maya glyphs for the Sun included images of the rattlesnake, represented by a coiled rattler with the "face of the Sun" just below the rattles on his tail.

Linda said the Maya experts, including Maya people themselves, accused Díaz Bolio of using poetic license to construct the geometry and architecture of the Maya around the rattlesnake. But I found his book very appealing because I have been a "Crotalus-centric" believer for years without realizing I belonged to the cult of Ahau Kan.

Evo, the indoor rattlesnake, was cranky and edgy this year, 2002; was it some negative energy I carried back with me from Mexico, from the town of Puerto Penasco, full of witchcraft? Or was it all the earth-smashing the neighbors did to remodel their house? When I fed him, Evo ignored the white mouse I offered him and half-heartedly sprang at me to show his irritation. I am always careful, but it was a good reminder.

I bought long tongs so I can reach in and get his water dish safely. When he was slow and docile, a few times I dared to reach in with my bare hands to remove the water dish, but no more, not after the mood he's been in.

I watched Evo's skin. It appeared lighter in color first, still beautiful, but then it looked faded, and the designs of his diamonds lost their clarity. The scales on the surface of his eyes became cloudy—a pale blue—as if he were blind.

The following day his eyes cleared, those scales molt first; his skin was dull and dusty looking, the outlines of his diamonds blurred. Evo went in the dark corner of his cage and sat in a loose coil. Even when

I filled his water bowl he didn't move to investigate. Only a day before he'd been animated and alert. Three days passed and Evo didn't move. He was waiting to molt. I watched him more closely than usual because as soon as he molted, he would want to eat. I had to go out of town and I wanted to feed him the rest of the mice before I left.

Maybe it was the arrival of the humidity with the rain that finally triggered the molt. He began by rubbing his nose on the porcelain water dish until the scales and skin of his nose loosened. The dampness on the inner surface of the skin adhered to the porcelain; the snake's reaction was to pull his nose away from the porcelain and as he did, the skin peeled back over his face and head inside out, like a sweater coming off, and he crawled away from the water dish and the skin peeled off him to leave behind a delicate translucent tube.

At Christmas a visitor arrived. He was a friend of a friend. He knocked at the west door and when he came in we greeted one another by the snake cage, which was covered with blankets. But the visitor was anxious and exhausted by the travel. He didn't come into the living room but instead stayed in the west porch conversing with my companion while I made dinner.

Before we could warn him or stop him, the visitor sat down on the top of the snake cage which he mistook for a couch. His weight caused the screen top of the cage to collapse. Fortunately Evo was in his winter doze, so the visitor was safe. I covered the damaged cage top with a piece of plywood and forgot about it until the warm weather came and it was time to feed mice to Evo again.

I never repaired the screen on Evo's cage after the visitor fell through. The other morning I took off the plywood in preparation to feed the rattlesnake a few white mice. Evo rose up suddenly through the broken screen—he is about twenty-eight inches tall when he does that; oddly my heart didn't skip a beat because I was standing well back from Evo's cage. Simple caution or some intuition?

Still his aggressive behavior left me feeling very cautious. I know he is very hungry. I bought him mice, but how do I get him to settle down enough to safely feed him?

Evo is so beautiful—a pale beige and pale brown, a kinsman to the near albino rattlesnakes in these black mountains. His big head is potentially lethal if I am not careful. Next time feed me sooner, is what he meant by rearing up in front of me.

Evo associates the light-colored or white clothes I wear in the summer with the white mice I feed him in the summer. Bright white means food and now when Evo sees me he gets very excited and jumps up like a pet dog. I've made a decoy mouse out of cotton balls I sewed together with a length of string to dangle outside the long glass snake cage to catch Evo's attention and to lure him to the far end from me. I wait until he watches the decoy before I slide open the lid and drop in the live mouse.

He only eats in the warmest months when the nights are in the eighties and the days over one hundred because heat aids the rattler's digestion, and helps activate the enzymes in the venom which also aids the snake's digestion.

The last time I fed Evo, without thinking I spoke aloud to him and said, "Now don't scare me. I want to feed you and give you fresh water." Speaking to him seemed to help or maybe he just wasn't as hungry as he'd been the time before but he remained calm and didn't move toward me.

At sundown as I walked toward the old corrals from the road, out of the corner of my eye motion caught my attention. About forty feet away, a rattlesnake three feet long was on the move through the desert—the most graceful of creatures, sinuous as flowing water, the snake gliding smoothly and silently as if it were floating a little above the ground between the jojoba bushes and palo verde by the old corral.

The biggest rattlesnake I ever saw was on a dirt road in the high grasslands east of Elgin. The grasslands are full of food and water is plentiful so a rattler can grow quite large. This snake was nearly five feet long and as big as my forearm. It crossed the road in front of the car, swift and sinuous, its head held high through the tall grass and sunflowers. As it headed west it seemed almost a golden apparition as the afternoon sunlight glittered off its scales.

Laurence Klauber the great rattlesnake expert wrote that a seven foot Eastern diamondback would be rare but possible. Any reports of rattlers over ten feet are myths, he writes. The extinct *Crotalus giganteus* reached twelve feet in length.

At the time of the coming of the Europeans to the Americas, giant rattlesnakes in excess of ten feet in length with the diameter of a man's thigh lived near springs and permanent sources of water. The indigenous people believed the springs belonged to the big snakes, and they revered the snakes as divine messengers and bringers of rain. Reports by the Spanish troops and the Catholic priests recount their diligence in hacking up these giant snakes or burning them alive in the name of Christianity.

But the Americas are vast. Great expanses of mountainous areas are virtually inaccessible even by helicopter. Many rural locations are only visited a few times a year by a handful of people. Rattlesnakes are wise beings, so it seems possible that in remote box canyons in mountains too steep and rough for humans to enter, a number of twelve foot long rattlesnakes have survived after all. Viva *Crotalus giganteus!*

CHAPTER 20

Late June now, and the heat penetrates the highest reaches of the atmosphere, burning away the gases and chemical pollutants above the city. As the heat expands the air molecules they are thinner and less buoyant, no longer able to carry the particles of dust. The heat boils the sky to a deep blue. No traces of clouds, only the deepening blue as the air becomes crystal clear. The angle of the Sun causes the light to have the luminescence of a blue flame. The Sun is seated in the north corner of Time.

The dry heat of the desert is sensuous. There is a perfect exchange between the dry air and the human body's moisture so there is no end or beginning of skin or air.

> The wind moves past the screen
> no sound
> the curtain billows back.
> This indeterminate Spring
> is dreaming
> older days outreach the Sun
> higher and beyond
> memory is metaphor
> not the thing itself

but enough it may fool us
listening for the green edge along the canyon
Never certain
when the next rain may come.

The endless afternoons of dry heat return—110 in the shade. The last of the yellow blossoms shrivel under the palo verde where the dry petals stir in a swirl of wind.

The tortoise leans his face against the gravel and mud of the arroyo's east bank. He is in his niche and he doesn't want to be seen. He felt the shock waves of the horses' hooves long before we arrived.

Here the seasons are rain and no rain. In a drought the desert is in perpetual autumn when things come to the end of growth and what was once alive turns yellow and then more pale.

When the temperature exceeds one hundred twelve degrees Fahrenheit, the air smells of wood and bark just before they burst into flame.

Twice since I came to this place, the ground here has caught fire. Oddly, both times this happened, the weather was cool. The first time it happened, I smelled what I thought were burning weeds. I searched for the source but could see nothing until I reached the old horse corral. There I was amazed to see many small threads of white smoke rising out of the bare, hard packed dry layers of dirt. A fire truck had to come spray the smoldering ground.

The second time, I looked out the living room window and saw curls of white smoke rising out of the bare dirt of the embankment on the west side of the house. I thought maybe a pack rat had carried a lit cigarette butt into its nest. But when we dug into the dirt of the embankment to stop the fire we found no rat nests—only smoldering pieces of scrap wood buried in the dirt. Apparently enzymes and organic compounds in the desert soil had a strange intense chemical reaction which caused the soil to ignite and burn the wood.

For the past two mornings a small rattler was coiled by the potted fig tree. Yesterday the little snake was on the shady side of the fig tree, but today it faced East. Not long after I came indoors I heard angry loud rattling that made the dogs bark. I went to see and there was nothing there to harass the snake, nothing to account for the little snake's furious rattling except for the Sun—the snake was rattling angrily at the Sun's heat that only got hotter and hotter as it rattled, until finally the snake fled into the drainpipe that goes underground.

I saved a small rattlesnake from the pit of the old cistern last year, but this time when I saw a small snake down there, I delayed because the weather wasn't hot yet, and I thought maybe the snake wanted to be there where little mice also live. Alas, when I went to check on the snake later, it was stretched out dead. In no time the hungry creatures of the desert happily consumed it.

It's July 6 and the wildfires in the Catalina Mountains have filled the entire valley with smoke. On the night of July 4, the flames came over the crest of the mountains and spread down toward the city, dwarfing the fireworks displays there. That was the night the rattlesnakes disappeared underground where six inches of dirt over your head will save you from wildfire.

Here are some of the practical measures people can take to safely live side by side with rattlesnakes in the Sonoran Desert. Look first before you reach into a flowerpot—they hold cool dampness and provide shady spaces for rattlesnakes to rest during the day. Always provide a water bowl far away from the dog's water bowl, far from the paths humans and pets take, and keep the water bowl full so the snakes never need to come close to your garden path or doorstep for water. Keep your pathways and walks open and well swept so you have a clear view at all times. Keep paths and steps well lit. Watch where you step—look behind yourself before you step backwards.

I have a sketch for a snake house for the garden made with five rectangular pieces of gray slate from south of Laguna, but any flat stones will do. This gives snakes shady sanctuary so they will feel secure. If you give the snakes a secluded cool area in the summer you will seldom see them elsewhere.

Over time the rattlesnakes will get to know you and your pets. They learn human and dog behavior and seem to understand the timing of our daily routines; they try to avoid encounters with us at all cost. A few times I've been very early or very late with my outdoor chores and I've surprised snakes that didn't expect me at that time of day.

The rattlesnakes that live in your garden or under your house will prevent unfamiliar rattlesnakes from moving too close until they learn how to get along with humans and dogs. Unfamiliar snakes are usually refugees from the real estate developers' bulldozers that scrape the desert bare and kill everything in their path. Understandably these uprooted snakes may be edgy, so back off and give them space; they will learn quickly that you mean no harm.

CHAPTER 21

A few months ago on a ridge near my house, a bulldozer destroyed the hives of the wild bees to clear a building site. The bees have lost their stores of food in the hive, and now they want me to feed them until their scouts locate a new site for their hive. Swarms of them crowded the hummingbird feeder near my porch so the hummingbirds couldn't get near. So I tried pouring sugar water into shallow saucers for the bees but a number of them had to be rescued from drowning. Then I tried a clean sponge in the sugar water, but the hummingbird feeder still works best to feed the bees.

It is mid-July now and the bees come for water and swarm above the bowls. The bees are attracted to sweat or wet clothing or wet hair, so I try to take care not to accidentally squeeze or crush them.

Bees understand kindness. They never try to sting me while I try to save one of them from drowning. I extend a leaf or twig and leave them to recover in a safe place. My dog Dolly eats the poor bees if I am not careful where I put them.

The wild bees know me after all these years. I remind them that I am a friend each year when they return. In the hardest part of the summer, the wild Sonora honeybees eat the green algae that grow around and on top of desert ponds. Years ago when I kept water hyacinths in the rainwater cistern pool, the wild bees ate the outer layer of the plants during the hottest and driest part of that summer. If you are lost and need water, follow the honeybees and they will take you to water or at least to damp earth.

For years the pack rats chewed on the 2×4 and 2×6 lumber in the kitchen floor and walls of this old ranch house. The pack rats found holes left by inept, careless remodelers and gnawed their way up through the floor into the kitchen cabinets, next to the electric range.

I patched the holes with squares of wood but the rats made short work of that; I even tried metal roof flashing but they chewed it like aluminum kitchen foil. Hardware cloth worked, so I was vigilant where I saw incursions by the rats. What I could not see, behind the electric range, was the wall with the opening down to the crawl space under my old ranch house.

Charlie was away a great deal of the time, and while he was gone, the pack rats gnawed through the old floor under the cabinets. Charlie offered to pay for the kitchen remodeling. No, I told him, I didn't want the disruption while I was working on the novel. I bought a stainless steel bread box to keep fresh fruit and other goodies safe from the rats.

The following winter the reddish-colored rattlesnake that lived under the house found its way through the holes and came hunting for rats in my kitchen. No one was home at the time so the snake went into the dining room and crawled under the red chaise longue. The snake waited until the house was dark and quiet and in the middle of the night it roamed around though it was always careful to return to its place under the chaise longue before daylight.

I sat on the chaise a time or two and thought I heard a faint rustle of sorts, but I wouldn't call it a "rattle."

I left the mastiffs alone indoors in the middle of the day and the rattlesnake came out from the red chaise longue and got into an altercation with them. When I got back from town, the mastiffs were nursing minor snakebites, and the red rattlesnake was hiding under a shelf on the kitchen floor. I put the dogs outside and the red rattler came out from its hiding place, ready to return to its place under the red chaise longue, but I opened the side door and encouraged it to go outside where it could get under the ranch house for the winter, not under the chaise longue.

A couple of pack rats soon took over the front room too—they were able to get indoors because the pit bull needed the front door left open. The dog was a great rat killer back then and she became so excited and obsessed with reaching the rat hiding behind it that she nearly chewed off one entire corner of a big wooden bookcase. Finally to save the other bookcases and furnishings in the front room from the frenzy of the pit bull, my son Robert shot the rat with a .22 target pistol.

The pack rats nested in the big copier machine I used to print my Flood Plain Press books in the front room. They chewed off all the plastic coating on the electrical wiring. Later Charlie dismantled the dead copier and chopped it into six inch pieces for easy disposal.

The pack rats are intelligent beings and are held in great esteem by the Tohono O'Odom and other desert tribes who depended on the creatures in times of drought and famine. The people used to loot the rats' nests for seeds and dried fruit and roots and for the baby rats as well. I once trapped a large female pack rat that had great presence as if she were the Great Mother Pack Rat. Charlie wanted to kill her but I set her free.

I carried her down the hill to release her in the hikers' parking lot; she scampered away to a shady bush. A few moments later, as I walked back to the house, right at my gate I looked down and saw a perfect arrowhead of gray basalt, elegant and refined, made by the ancient ones. I knew it was a gift for sparing old Pack Rat's life.

The pack rats in the attic know how to spring the traps we set for them by using scraps of wood. The sprung traps gave me an appreciation for their cleverness.

I call the big female pack rat that lives in my front yard "Ratty" after the character in *The Wind in the Willows*. I never bother her big rat complex in the middle of the front yard because it would disturb the rattlesnakes that live under the aloes and greasewood with Ratty.

In late August I returned from a visit to my sister in Wyoming to find the large rattlesnake that lived under the feed shed had been killed earlier that day. A roadrunner or owl tore her into three pieces, but then was interrupted and abandoned the big snake's remains.

The big snake had lived under the shed for fifteen years or more; she did have the odd habit of climbing small bushes and trees which left her vulnerable to birds of prey. A few hours later I went out to bury her and the three pieces of her were gone, taken for a meal by some creature, maybe her killer or a passing scavenger.

I found a turquoise bead on the lawn chair in the front yard under the mesquite tree. I saw the turquoise bead as a gift, a sign of the loving presences or energies always nearby and helping me. Later I realized it came off a piece of art I had made many years before, a gourd doll with a turquoise bead around her neck which I hung in the mesquite tree. Still it was a wonderful occurrence that the single turquoise bead should fall at that time from the gourd doll onto the center of my chair.

All day and all night, a heavy silvery blue mist enveloped the jade green desert, along with a gentle hurricane rain, warm and blue through the early morning light.

CHAPTER 22

Before I walked the hills, I rode over them on horseback. In the 1960s, the National Park Service ruled the Tucson Mountain mustangs were an "alien species" and a threat to the Saguaro National Park, despite the hundreds of years the wild horses had lived here. The park rangers managed to remove the stallion and most of the mares, but a few escaped.

By 1978 when I moved here, only three wild horses remained in the Tucson Mountains. They were nearly identical bay mares with white markings that covered their faces entirely and reminded me of clouds. They followed the same trails the deer and javelina used.

By the mid-1980s, there were only two wild mares left and they were showing age. After one died the other did not last long.

The Tucson Mountains are terribly rough going for horses but manageable for mules. In 1980 my quarter horse mare fell with me on the high steep trail near the top of Wasson Peak. I jumped off her as she fell but her hind hoof (steel shod of course) clipped me in the side of the head. Her hoof smashed into my straw cowboy hat which absorbed the blow and saved me.

As it was, I lost consciousness for an instant, and my head was bleeding. When I stood up, I saw the mare had fallen and rolled twenty feet down the mountainside and lay on her side, motionless. My heart sank. We were miles from help, miles from even a jeep trail. If the mare had broken her leg, she would have to lie for hours to suffer before we'd be able to do anything for her.

But when I reached her and examined her legs, I saw that except for one deep laceration, she had no broken bones. She was just frightened by the steep terrain and precarious footing, and felt safer lying flat on the ground. I reassured her she was o.k. and encouraged her to stand up. I walked her most of the way home, and by then she had recovered nicely while I had a pounding headache; so I rode the rest of the way.

Months later I returned to the site of the accident to retrieve my hat. I ended up keeping the hat for a long time. The stiffness of the straw made the blow glance off and probably saved my life or at least my brain. The whole side of the straw hat was caved in and there were bloodstains. I should have saved it forever but I threw it away in one of my rare house-cleaning frenzies.

Years later my good Arabian gelding Hudson Bay lost his footing on the Wasson Peak trail and began to fall. I jumped clear of him and watched in horror as he tumbled end over end. But he jumped up nimble as a cat without a scratch on him.

> Pansy moth
> yellow and brown.
> Last night you
>   landed on the moon
>   in the water.
>   This morning
>   you are floating
>   between the
>   water lily leaves.

It's St. Patrick's Day, 2004. The saint drove all the snakes out of Ireland; for "snakes" read "the indigenous religions of the British Isles" which held the snake to be sacred. I have ancestors among the Scots in the Leslie clan. "From the dark rock tower" is one translation I have seen for the name "Leslie."

While I was working on my novel *Gardens in the Dunes*, Bettina Munch, my German translator, gave me a book about the archeology of the "Old European" period, five thousand years ago, and the Paleo-lithic cultures of Macedonia, Hungary and Latvia. The Old Europeans left behind a number of ceramic and other archeological artifacts with snakes as the dominant figures. The Old Europeans regarded the ser-pent as a sacred Earth being. There is even a horned serpent figure on a ceramic bowl. Well into the twentieth century the rural people of East-ern Europe kept black snakes under their floors because they regarded them as family guardians as well as good luck charms.

The first snakes to come out from hibernation in the spring of 2005 were down by the old corrals—the big dark gray rattler that lives under the old saddle shed and the smaller lighter reddish snake that stays under the fallen saguaro behind the corrals. I wasn't expecting to see the reddish snake so I blurted out something as a greeting as I might to a person I met suddenly on the trail. The ugly sound of my human voice upset and frightened the reddish snake. The wild beings prefer silent communication with humans.

Around the middle of June I watched as the big reddish snake that lives under the house hugged the perimeter of the house to find its way from the west side of the ranch house. Tigger the old pit bull dog barked excitedly at the snake as it crossed the front yard. I called for her to come to me, and I brought her indoors. Meanwhile the snake then ran into the mastiffs on the east side of the house so I called them and all six came running. I locked them indoors with me to give the red rat-tlesnake time to move out of their area.

Snakes remember unpleasant encounters with humans and other predators and will try to avoid further encounters if at all possible.

Then I found a three and a half foot black masked rattler was inside Sandino and Bolee's aviary. The snake remained motionless until I turned my back to get the macaw feed, and then it was gone.

Later as I was watering the datura plants in the clay pots under the mesquite tree, I splashed a two and a half foot long brown diamond-back that I hadn't noticed at rest in the shade under the tree. The snake moved away but didn't rattle because it is one of the regulars in the front yard.

CHAPTER 23

Cirrus: a curl or spiral. Over mountains and pushed by high altitude winds, cirrus clouds form at twenty thousand feet; gauzy wisps of ice crystals form streamers and streaks composed of delicate white filaments or tenuous white patches and narrow bands that feather and swirl. I see them in the ancient black and white Pueblo pottery designs—the long parallel lines with hooks and convergences.

Gradually more cirrus clouds arrive and fill the sky so the Sun is visible as a shield of orange red with a rainbow around it.

Stratus: to spread out as with a blanket. Stratus clouds are low horizontal layers of light to dark gray water droplets that look like fog with little structure. Stratus clouds indicate saturation near the ground.

Cirrostratus are high thin hazy clouds that give a halo to the Sun and the Moon.

Stratocumulus clouds form white to gray layers with bands or rolls that hang low across the sky like strands of cotton. Light rain or snow may fall from them.

Cumulus: a heap or mass; a pile. Rising air that flows over mountains creates cumulus clouds. Small cumulus clouds are fair weather water-droplet clouds that are detached from each other, with sharp outlines, flat bottoms, and no taller than they are wide. The base is dark but the sunlit part is brilliant white. If there is lightning or thunder the cloud becomes a cumulonimbus. They can develop into rising forms of mounds or domes, rounded masses piled on each other swelling to become towering cumulus, from eight thousand to fifteen thousand feet high in the Southwest. In one of the ancient Pueblo stories, a wicked ka'tsina imprisoned the rain clouds in his house on a mountaintop and caused a terrible drought.

Nimbus means rain or mist.

Nimbostratus are dark gray to deep blue clouds formed from water droplets. They are rain and snow clouds that are deep and foggy with the falling precipitation; a dim light glows from within.

Cumulonimbus clouds have flat tops like anvils and voluptuous bottoms with edges that appear fuzzy from ice particles. They can roll into rows of swollen pouches that move in waves ahead of thunderstorm wind gusts.

The great heat of 2005 arrived in late June: thirty-nine consecutive days of temperatures above 100 degrees—mostly above 103 degrees.

Signs of a hot summer were written all over that earlier day on the fourteenth of March when it was already 103, and no one in Tucson had prepared their evaporative coolers yet. The heat never wavered—not even after late spring storms cooled the mountains of northern Arizona—the heat parked right over southern Arizona.

During those thirty-nine days, I spent my time caring for my eight dogs and fourteen parrots, to make sure they were kept cool and comfortable during the hottest part of the day—around four p.m.

I'd get up at dawn while the air was cooler to feed the parrots and dogs and give all of them fresh water. As soon as the heat would begin to descend, I'd bring all the dogs indoors with me; the six mastiffs fill two large rooms. They lie low in the air conditioned coolness, perfectly quiet and well-mannered lest they get evicted into the heat.

By one p.m. the temperature would be over 101 and it would be time to begin spraying the parrots so they'd be cooled as the water evaporated. By the time I finished these chores, I'd need a break.

When the break was over, it was time to wet down the parrots again. Now the big heat would descend as a blinding white hot curtain that cuts off the oxygen; I'd feel my stamina wane.

The water out of the hose was too hot to use at first, so I saved it by filling buckets and water bowls and after a while the water from the hose cooled enough for me to turn the hose on myself. I'd wet down my hat and all my clothes for evaporative cooling while I worked outside in temperatures above 101. In such intense heat, my soaking wet hat and clothes protected me.

Afterwards I would be too worn out to do much of anything but sit in the dim cool living room with the gray parrot and watch old movies on TV. My overheated brain wasn't much good for writing or anything else.

In the early days of the heat wave I didn't leave the property because of my concern for the parrots outdoors, and the dogs that stayed indoors with me. But finally I needed bread or dog food or parrot food and I'd venture out in the car after sundown.

The desert evenings are lovely even in the high nineties because the breeze moves across the hills and the air is dry. Rodents, reptiles, all refugees of the heat come out after sundown. After dark I managed to get my groceries to the car without them melting.

The desert hums with activity and the night calls of birds and owls; sometimes the coyotes sing out exaltations because they've caught something for dinner. Breezes stirred after dark and cooled everything.

I watched the planets and the stars and hoped for a message like the one I got in 1998 when the name for one of my characters came to me suddenly while I was sitting outside watching the stars. But before long I would be sleepy and go off to bed without a message.

On day nineteen of the heat wave Bill fled to his house in Albuquerque. I didn't like to watch him suffer in the heat, so it was good he left town. Of course it was over a hundred in Albuquerque and Santa Fe too, but Tucson was 110.

As the thirty-seventh or thirty-eighth day of the heat wave dawned, a voice in my head said "Tell me again—why exactly do I live here?"

PART THREE

Star Beings

CHAPTER 24

I originally wanted to be a visual artist, not a writer. But at the University of New Mexico I discovered the fine arts college was blind to all but European art with its fetish for "realism" and "perspective." I dropped the basic drawing class and majored in English but I never stopped drawing or painting with watercolor and tempera for my own pleasure. I learned to use acrylic paints in 1986 and 1987 when I painted the big mural of the giant snake on the side of the building on Stone Avenue in downtown Tucson.

In the fall of 2005 I decided it was now or never; I wanted to take a year away from writing just to paint. I wanted to improve as a painter—to be competent enough not to distract the viewer.

It was exciting to think about my illicit holiday from writing. I went to my sketchbooks full of parrot designs from old pottery and many versions of the Great Serpent I love to draw and paint.

But something from the reading I'd done earlier in 2005 suddenly came back to me. Many indigenous tribes in the Americas and Australia have ancestral stories about the stars that came to Earth. The Star Beings came to contact human beings; or perhaps we are their descendants.

I began to make sketches of old petroglyphs I recalled from my childhood and youth in Laguna when I roamed the sandstone mesas and cliffs where the petroglyphs could be seen. I searched carefully for the figures with the tell-tale white crosses that represent the planets and stars in these petroglyphs.

While I looked at a book of photographs of petroglyphs I began thinking. I decided the Star Beings must only visit Earth every seven or eight hundred years—or maybe they remain in a parallel world next to ours but cross over from time to time when the "membranes" of the parallel universes make contact.

The evidence of their presence lies in the petroglyph figures of the visitors which the human beings made afterward to record the visit and to pay homage and even to worship the Star Beings. Further evidence is painted on the frescoes of the kivas unearthed at Pottery Mound, Kauau and Awatovi.

In the early seventies I lived in Chinle near Canyon de Chelly and I had the opportunity to explore the narrow side canyons on horseback where the walls of the cliffs were covered with hundreds of petroglyphs. The Star Being figures are recorded there too. All these years I've carried their images in my memory.

As I sketched the petroglyph figures, I realized that the Star Beings wanted me to paint their portraits. They insisted I use the largest canvases possible and that their portraits must always be hung at a height that dwarfs the human viewers in order to intimidate them.

At first I painted in the kitchen under the tube skylight; I didn't wear glasses; one day I put on my drugstore reading glasses and was horrified to see how sloppy my painting was. I got new prescription eyeglasses and a good easel lamp as the days got shorter and the sunlight wasn't as bright. I left paint and brushes scattered over the kitchen table because I was alone and ate standing up at the counter between the stove and refrigerator. But when others are with me, this won't do; the kitchen is narrow and the framed canvas three feet wide and four feet tall.

Before Christmas of 2005 I moved into the room that once was a garage, now the old pit bull's room. The room was fine by day in the late fall to the early spring, but by March the days would be too hot to bear. The first painting of the Star Being was nearly finished as well as the sketch for the next one.

It was around ten in the morning and we were sunning ourselves in the front yard. The hummingbirds were jousting over the feeders I'd just filled. Sometimes I heard the clash of their tiny beaks. Great warriors. Huitzilopochtli, Hummingbird, the greatest of the Nahua deities.

Bill and I laughed as we watched the hummingbirds. Suddenly I heard and saw something to my left. A cloud of gray feathers and white down drifted to the ground, and a mourning dove picked herself up from the ground slightly stunned, and flew away. High in the mesquite tree above us, full of disdain for humans, the peregrine falcon shook off his loss and flew off to scout other prey. The dive into the top of the mesquite was a risky one—the peregrine might have shattered a wing.

At just the moment the falcon missed the dove, I was thinking about our friend Bert in Placitas in the snow, and how she might enjoy the warmth of the December sun in Tucson, and the hummingbird jousts in the front yard.

One evening from the living room I distinctly heard music, 1950s big band music in the distance. I headed for the front bathroom where I thought I might have forgot to switch off a small transistor radio I keep there. As I walked toward the sound of the music the volume remained constant but some of the notes sounded oddly "thin"; this triggered my intuition and instantly I realized it was ghost music.

As I reached the kitchen, suddenly the music merged into the electric hum of the refrigerator and the whirring sound of the ceiling fan. Ghosts love to inhabit electric fans—I don't know why unless it is something about the electromagnetic field a fan makes which draws the spirit energy entities to it or at least broadcasts their music.

I switched on the transistor radio and carried it from the bathroom; it played jazz. As I passed a table fan on the dining room table, voices of the spirits in the fan broke into the radio and I heard voices of the spirits in the jazz music from the radio. I stopped at once to listen.

I had difficulty making them out—were the voices happy, gathered for a party, or were they disgruntled and ready for a fight? Before I could get a sense of their mood, the voices stopped. I switched the radio on and off and listened but the ghost music was gone.

In late August I was invited to Mexico. I made an exception to my rule of no travel only painting during 2006 because I knew the Star Beings wanted me to go there to learn certain things I would need as I painted their portraits.

I received two invitations from the Arts Festival organizers in Ciudad Chihuahua. After my first visit in late August I liked the people and the town so much I returned to Ciudad Chihuahua a month later.

My first visit was to receive a writer's award from the governor of the State of Chihuahua; the second time was to participate in a celebration of the indigenous tribes of Chihuahua and Sonora and other parts of Mexico and the United States. I got to witness the main plaza of Ciudad Chihuahua, the state capital, filled with indigenous tribal people from all over Mexico. Barely one hundred years before, the Mexican Government had been at war with many of the tribes represented in the main plaza.

The first visit was the best because my gracious hosts took me away from town out into the countryside within sight of the grand Sierra Madre towering ahead of us. The altitude and terrain reminded me a great deal of New Mexico where I grew up, and immediately I felt I could live there or in another life I had lived there.

I got to meet prominent Mexican writers—a poet from Casas Grandes and a poet whose grandfather was Raramuri. The Raramuri poet said, "My grandfather rode with Pancho Villa" and the poet from Casas Grandes said, "My grandfather was killed by Pancho Villa"; we all laughed when she said this, but then she added that Pancho Villa hated her grandfather so much that he ordered his men to kill all her grandfather's dogs as well.

When I returned from Chihuahua I was thinking about the statue of Tlaloc outside the Anthropology Museum in Mexico City. Tlaloc is a Nahua rain deity, one of the nine Lords of Night, associated with the Star Beings. So I made some sketches and I got out a big canvas and primed it with stucco and prepared to paint Tlaloc's portrait. He is usually portrayed in blue or turquoise but I had read about a mural at the great Mayan ruins at Bonampak where Tlaloc was painted red. So I decided to paint him red but to give him a blue background.

I worked on Tlaloc's portrait this morning and within a few hours clouds began to appear in the south and the southwest, a bit unusual for mid-September. If I complete his portrait to his satisfaction, will it rain? Of course Tlaloc might just send hail and sleet in high winds or flash floods.

———

We had wonderful rains in the summer of 2006. The rattlesnakes got really fat because all the rain meant many baby rodents and birds. I recognized one of the rattlesnakes because it is almost an albino. It got huge. Last summer it was long but not so big and fat, and it was never upset to meet me in the yard; but this year for the first time when we met, he let me know he was nearby when I was forty feet away. The snake seems to know it is too big to easily hide anymore, so it has to scare predators away. I appreciated the polite warning while I was far off; the next time I saw him the mastiffs were barking at him through the fence and the snake flexed out its ribs and puffed itself up so it was one third again its size.

I shook the red plastic dustpan in the face of the small light-colored rattler who thinks she owns the front patio. But rather than back out the way she'd just come in she drew herself up furiously into a z shape and advanced on the invader to her patio. The red plastic infuriated her. I backed off and let her stay in the patio as long as she pleased.

CHAPTER 25

My idea was I would paint, not write, in 2006. But as I painted the portraits of the Star Beings I began to receive thought communications from them, often while I was sketching or painting one of them. I found myself jotting down short notes and messages that I later incorporated into this account.

The second Star Being portrait I painted was the figure of the Star Being rattlesnake on a lavender background. The old ancestors used a blue violet clay to make lovely lavenders and purples in sand paintings and frescoes.

I was painting the third Star Being portrait in March when the heat in my studio became unbearable. I covered the windows in layers of emergency blankets and old bed sheets and I cranked up two humidifiers in front of a big desk fan on high speed.

With the windows covered I couldn't see to paint anymore but I realized the Star Beings prefer the dim light. I bought an easel light. At night they want the windows uncovered to let in the moonlight and starlight so the titanium white in the portraits will glow.

The portraits of the Star Beings are a great success for me. I feel a close relationship with them because of the process of painting—each stroke of the paintbrush brought the form of the being a bit closer to its emergence in the world. Sometimes I felt the canvas on the frame shiver as I painted.

I began to record conversations I had with them as I painted.

One morning while I was completing a portrait of a Star Being as the Sun, I took a break outside on the front porch. After a while I noticed a large brown masked rattlesnake loosely coiled and relaxed in the shade under the mesquite tree. The delicate patterns on the scales of his face were shades of burnt umber and dark sienna brown. How perfectly the lines of the patterns followed the edges of the scales—I thought about the tiny smears my brush stroke left, requiring touch-ups.

The patterns of stripes and the dark brown mask around his eyes were powerful visual elements that caught my imagination at once. I sat on the porch and admired him, then suddenly I wanted to draw the pattern the mask and lines made on his face. I looked at the pencil lines as I copied the design on the snake's face. When my sketch was finished I realized I'd drawn the mask of another of the Star Beings, the Venus-eyed Rattlesnake. There is a cliff-painting of this incarnation of Tlaloc painted thousands of years ago by the paleo-Indians at the Hueco Tanks in Texas.

My portrait of the brown masked Tlaloc includes a headdress of dove feathers to acknowledge how much the snakes around here depend on the mourning dove and occasional white wing.

The Star Beings first contacted me years ago. I saw a Navajo war shield at a small museum, and I was strangely affected by it because there was a star map painted on the war shield—white stars painted on black—Venus was a cross near the top, the arc of the Milky Way and then the Pleiades, and Orion, and below them a crescent Moon cradled in darkness. I drew the star map from memory as best I could; I made a number of drawings in crayon, and in ink on black paper. The memory of the star map never left me, and I incorporated the map into the first novel I wrote.

Later on I bought two or three dump truck loads of washed sand to cover a large circular area on the hilltop next to my house. The big circle of white sand would stand out against the darker basalts and lavas that formed the hill. The Star Beings liked to use white sand against dark volcanic rock to mark their landing places. That's why they chose the great Pinacate mountain range near Puerto Penasco on the Gulf of California where dozens of prominent volcanic cinder cones rise above white sand washed inland by the sea.

Not long ago, late at night I heard loud thuds and bumps on the roof of my house right over my bedroom. A great horned owl? A bobcat that somehow leaped up?

It was something heavy, heavier than an owl, maybe heavier than a bobcat. I sat still in my bed and held my breath as the bumps and thuds continued. All I could think about was what happened one time before I was old enough to go to school.

I was playing outdoors when some older children stopped outside my house and pointed up at the roof very excitedly and shouted to me there was a Guumeyosh on the roof. I ran indoors to hide, terrified because I knew it was one of those ka'tsina beings that grabbed children and ate them alive.

The struggle on the roof above my bed continued and then suddenly whatever it was, stopped. I've seen great horned owls two feet tall, big around as the tops of the saguaros they perched on. The old-time people saw a resemblance between the face of the great horned owl, round and fuzzy, and the face of Venus, the warrior star being in a halo of bright fuzzy light. Great Horned Owl took scalps with his six inch talons, and so did Venus.

From the evidence in ancient Pueblo kiva frescoes and in the petroglyphs and pictographs of the Southwest and Mexico, before they return to this planet, the Star Beings customarily make contact with the dreams and imaginations of selected artists whose consciousness is open to them.

They chose me to make their portraits because they want images that are accessible to ordinary people, to the masses, not to some rarefied audience. Other artists are similarly taken over by the beings. In Santa Fe, my old friend Roberto found their images on his wall panels of copper and bronze.

The Star Beings don't care if I suffer ridicule because I'm not a professional painter.

Watching night after night I saw the size and brightness of Venus fluctuate dramatically, as if the planet changed according to whom it watched. When it watched us here, it got bigger and brighter to let us know it was watching.

Later Venus disappeared from the evening sky for months, so I almost forgot about it. Then one night in the living room just after sundown, I felt someone was nearby listening and watching my friend and me talk. At that moment, out the window above the western horizon, I saw Venus but so bright and large that at first I mistook it for a jet airplane.

While I'm sketching or working on the canvas, the Star Beings communicate with me, to let me know how they want to be portrayed.

The previous year, when my laptop's hard drive failed, I had wondered if the Star Beings had intervened electromagnetically to stop me from working on the book so I'd have to go back to painting their portraits.

I had run into financial difficulties at that time, and I thought I could sell four or five of the portraits just to get me through. Of course I would have immediately painted replacement portraits, even better than the ones I sold, but the Star Beings refused to allow this.

You want us to go out into the world to make money?

You go out into the world and make the money to keep us, and to paint more of our portraits.

I realized then the Star Beings didn't care about my financial situation, or that I was anxious and worried about money. This was after I sacrificed a year of my book project to serve these Star Beings.

Inexplicably, the Star Beings understand the meaning of capital letters in English and German, so I've been careful to capitalize. They appear to value the first or the oldest in a series above the most recent or the newest; this at a time when new software succeeds the old in a matter of weeks or even days.

The Star Beings find the human appetite for novelty stupid and pathetic and a threat to human survival because the flow of the new and the newer is not infinite and can easily be interrupted or stopped by natural causes, never mind terrorism or war. The first things, the earliest of things, Old Things, are in good supply all over the world, and there exists little chance of disruption, especially now that all attention is fixed on the newest things.

The Star Beings aren't vulnerable like humans. They don't lose anything.

The Star Beings have little knowledge of the human predicament, and no compassion.

The Star Beings return from time to time though it is not clear why. They appear to dislike humans so much; yet there are anthropomorphic features in their appearance—do they really look like this or are they merely simulating an appearance?

We are limited by our experiences here on Earth. Our imaginations fail us.

Do the Star Beings experience emotions? They seem angry at humans but this could be my own human misinterpretation. Maybe what they term "ordinary consciousness" we humans would term "angry." What then?

They are always returning to Earth. The upheavals here don't seem to matter to them. Do they care that humans slaughter one another? Maybe the slaughter is part of some dark purpose of the Star Beings.

The Star Beings don't care about understanding humans—much as humans are not interested in them and ascribe the worst characteristics to extraterrestrials.

Are all Star Beings alike in their disdain for humans?

I stopped painting their portraits for a while because I had to try to make some money. It was about this time that I understood why I'd recently bought not one but two Nahuatl-English dictionaries. Apparently, now the Star Beings expected me to write poetry in Nahuatl although I have no knowledge at all of the language.

I started with the a's—ayahuitl, ayahuitlin which means mist and descending ghost warriors, a shower of revenants. These are the same ghost warriors the Paiute prophet Wovoka summoned with the circle dances in the 1890s across Indian country.

ayahuitl ehau-ya means mist is rising
ayauhcozamalatl means mist bow or rainbow
ayauhcozmalotonameyoa means to shine like a rainbow

I thought I'd accidentally skipped to the c's—no, I didn't skip anything—there are no b's in Nahuatl.

citlalin means star
cicitlalmatiliztli means astronomy—along with the Maya
      and the Inca, the Nahua were great astronomers, and
      over the millennia they'd given other galaxies some
      thought
citlalloh means full of stars
cicitlalpuzacalili means space ship. It makes me happy to
      know that Nahuatl has a word for space ship
coacuechtli means snake rattle
coaizlactli means snake egg
coatl means snake or twin
coatlantli means incisor fang
cochini means sleeper
cochitta means dream
cochtemictli also means dream
cochtlatoa means walk in your sleep
cochtapiazohua means wet the bed
cochtotolca means snore

As the portraits of the Star Beings neared completion, I realized the images themselves were alive. Sometimes when I was painting one of them, the canvas frame would make peculiar noises when I wasn't touching it. The titanium white on their portraits glowed after dark. They watched me. I moved my laptop and my notes and copies of drafts of the book to their room because they promised to help me write this book.

In the beginning the converted two-car garage was more than large enough for my writing area and a painting area with an easel near the front windows. Now the Star Beings stood shoulder to shoulder and looked down on me. I painted their portraits as they directed me. They'd cause my hand to drop the paintbrush so paint splattered on the area I was working on. Whatever action I took—to use a rag to try to clean up the splatters of paint or to apply the new color I chose to repaint the area—the Star Beings controlled these actions and that was how they controlled my portrayal of them.

I kept making mistakes and had to keep reworking and repainting the image in the portrait. The Star Beings want definite lines with clean edges as on the Pueblo pottery, but not "realism." They want the style the fresco painters used on the walls of the kivas seven hundred years ago. None of that Impressionism for them!

I think the Star Beings chose me because as a child I'd seen the old petroglyphs and pictographs on sandstone cliffs near Laguna, and later on in canyons near Chinle. I'd seen star map petroglyphs without realizing what they were.

Now the Star Beings had a vantage point to see and hear what human beings were doing. Maybe they listened to the radio in my studio when it was on.

I sit in front of the portrait I'm painting, and only then am I able to write. Whatever I write is connected somehow to the Star Beings or to the particular Star Being I am working on at the time.

Not long ago, I realized the Star Beings wanted me to draw a star map of the Pleiades on black paper with metallic color crayons. I'm expected to draw other star maps of Orion and Scorpio while I finish the portraits.

The other day, I became weak and shaky although I'd had a bowl of Cheerios for breakfast. Was it the weeks of e-mails that went unread while I worked feverishly on the portraits or was it not working on the Star Beings' portrait for even a day?

A happy anticipation of working on the paintings each day reminded me of the happiness I felt writing novels. The joy I feel when I paint the beings is their gift to me.

I was painting one of them an ochre color, a light brown suited to a human skin tone although I knew the intent was not to present them as humans in masks and paint. My sense was that the Star Beings wanted handsome if fearsome portraits, painted in pleasing colors.

Later I was wondering which background color to use for the portrait of a terrible figure, dangling a human head from a string. Then as I stood at the bathroom sink flossing my teeth, out of the corner of my right eye, I caught a glimpse of a tall dark shadow figure. The message was to use paint as dark as the night. I finished him with a star map in white paint over his horns, face and chest. The lovely patterns of the constellations make the severed head appear even more forlorn.

In another of the portraits you can see right away the figure depicted is a troublemaker. When I first found the figure in a petroglyph it was clear he was dancing around, posturing and bragging. So of course he'd want to be portrayed just like that—with that ugly blue dick and big blue balls—to upset humans, to incite human envy and fear. As it turns out, a number of ancient petroglyphs portray beings with balls and dicks, sometimes erect, and they hold severed human heads. The calculation to cause human discomfort with the display of genitals in the state of arousal may be a rare instance of a joke or an insult from the Star Beings to humans. In general, however, the Star Beings seem oblivious to human discomfort, and most human concepts mean nothing to them.

One Star Being insisted on a necklace of the whitest shells with delicate cobalt blue figures of stars linked by bars of light. Another Star Being was not satisfied with the bloody skull he held, so I changed it to a freshly killed head with a clean face. A gentle cool rain from the Gulf said thanks to the painter for making the head of the enemy look presentable. Certain beings instructed humans on what must be done to call down the rain; apparently this involved an enemy's head.

They return to Earth every seven or eight hundred years from another region of the Milky Way. Or maybe it is a parallel world. To prepare for their return, they send dreams and visions to artists of all kinds all over the planet so they will begin to make images of the Star Beings. In this way the poor slow-witted humans might be somewhat prepared for the reappearance of the Star Beings.

It is a natural tendency of humans to interpret the large mouths of the Star Beings as "smiling" and "inviting" or "friendly"—we all want to believe that because these beings project such power. But the mouths are big, and not so much smiling as showing their sharp incisors.

I was so enthralled by Comet Hale-Bopp in 1996 that I watched it for hours on end outside my west door. It was the single most beautiful and seductive visitor to this solar system in my lifetime. I felt an odd affection for the comet and looked forward to gazing at it night after night. I lived alone here. The comet was my evening companion. As the comet began to recede I experienced a strange desire to go along, to never let the comet's beauty out of my sight.

When I heard the news report I understood how it happened that the Heaven's Gate cult members committed suicide to board the giant space ship they believed was hidden behind the comet.

CHAPTER 26

The unique geology of the Tucson Mountains makes the place a rock hound's paradise. There are a number of anomalous formations and rocks that indicate metamorphic activity, but geologists still argue over exactly what happened.

Some sort of volcanic activity took place that formed a number of round dark hills of basalt and prominent ridges or hogbacks of basalt. The rounded dark hills or cerros are not volcanic cones but rather the remains of volcanic structures; some geologists argue that leaks in faults allowed the molten rock to extrude and form the cerros and hogbacks. Other geologists think the great explosion of a giant volcano left behind only the volcanic ridges that form the Tucson, Tortolita and Rincon Mountains.

When I walk the big arroyo I pass a large flattop boulder of dark gray basalt. Years ago from my vantage point on horseback I saw the top of the boulder had been worked by human hands to form a rainwater cistern. Someone had patiently carved the basin by removing only small amounts of stone at a time. To do this the carver had to use a stone harder than the dark gray basalt—maybe a fist size chunk of the meteorite iron like the one I found in the big arroyo. It appears to have been used as a hammer.

I don't often pick up or carry back very large rocks because most days it is all I can do to carry myself up the big arroyo and home. But one day I saw a rock I couldn't resist: a chunk of gray basalt the shape and size of a book—a perfect altar for my turquoise ledge stones. But by the time I got home with the rock, the muscles of my right shoulder and arm were so sore I had to visit the acupuncturist.

Now I don't try to carry back the tempting rocks I see; instead I check on them each time I walk and I imagine how I might get them home without crippling myself in the process. Gunny sacks, backpacks, a wheelbarrow, even a burro might be what I need.

There is a flat smooth white quartzite, very hard and fine-grained, that is about two feet long and six inches wide. The water carried it to the side of the big arroyo where it snagged against other rocks and now the white stone is almost vertical. I don't know what attracts me to this white rectangular stone; is it because the stone would work well for grinding corn?

If I put my hand on a rock and it does not come loose from the earth the first time I try to pick it up, then I leave the rock where it is. It reminded me again how the old folks used to admonish us children to "Let it be!" To leave things as they are, all things in this world— animals and plants and rocks. Human things had to be respected too and the special places where the ancestor spirits resided.

Turquoise is the ritual color of Tlaloc, the Nahua God of Rain. In the surviving codices of the Nahua people, Tlaloc usually appears dressed head to toe in feathers, clothing and adornments all the color of turquoise.

The Hopi language is closely related to Nahuatl. Many words are identical; the word for "ear" is one. The old Spanish maps that label northern Arizona and northern New Mexico "Aztec territory" are not fakes. All this territory is the realm of speakers of the Nahuatl-related languages, thus those Indians and mestizos who travel or migrate from Mexico need no permits or visas to be here—this land is theirs too.

At the beginning of the eleventh year of the drought, in 2006, a group of Hopi traditionalists decided to make a run from northern Arizona all the way to Mexico City to the carved stone monolith of Tla-loc, to ask for the rain and snow that were desperately needed. Tlaloc is Lord of the Rain as well as one of the Nine Lords of the Night. He is often portrayed wearing goggles formed by two live rattlesnakes.

To bring their prayers to Tlaloc, the Hopi runners followed an ancient ritual trail from Hotevila village in northern Arizona through New Mexico, El Paso and Ciudad Chihuahua to Mexico City. Along the way, they made stops at certain sacred springs and rivers where the runners and those who accompanied them offered prayers and pol-len or corn meal to the water before they collected small amounts of it which they carried in a ritual gourd canteen.

The sacred run ended at the fork of two small rivers not far from the Anthropology Museum in downtown Mexico City. A Hopi elder prayed and poured some of the water from the gourd canteen before the great stone statue of Tlaloc that stands outside the museum; then the elder went a short distance to the fork of two small rivers. The small rivers were as polluted as the sky above the great city but no matter—the elder poured the water into the river fork and just as he did, a big eagle appeared out of the smoggy sky and circled overhead calling loudly before it flew away.

The Mexican people who joined the Hopi group in Ciudad Chi-huahua as interpreters saw the eagle appear in the sky that day. As they described it to me six months later, they were still excited about what they'd seen and what then happened later. They'd been educated, as we all have, to expect no miracles from Tlaloc. But in the Americas, the sacred surrounds us, no matter how damaged or changed a place may appear to be.

Three months after the Hopi group completed the sacred run, on June 16, 2006 the rain clouds began to roll in from the eastern Pacific, to Sinaloa, then the clouds moved up the lovely backbones of the Sierra Madre and the Sierra Madre Oriental all the while pouring the pre-cious rain that brought relief from the drought.

In Tucson where the drought had lasted so long even the desert vegetation was beginning to die, the rain smell was intoxicating—I couldn't work on this manuscript. I stood outdoors on the porch and watched the rain shimmering from ridge to ridge in the wind; sometimes in the mist I thought I saw tall figures of rain beings. I put out buckets and tubs to catch the rainwater for my plants and then I tried to videotape the rain until my hair and clothes were soaked.

For the next six weeks, the rain clouds gathered every day from Mexico City to as far north as the Hopi villages. El Paso and Las Cruces, New Mexico were flooded again and again. Chihuahua got more rain than anyone had seen in eighty years. Over and over the storms followed one path, the reverse of the path the Hopi runners took in March, from Mexico City through Ciudad Chihuahua, El Paso and Las Cruces. I noticed that oddly, Palm Springs, Las Vegas and Salt Lake City got no rain at all during that time.

Winter came and so did the snow; Tlaloc sent snowstorm after snowstorm—more than an inch of snow fell here in the Tucson Mountains. People drove up from the city to show their children the snow and I reached for my video camera.

It snowed in Phoenix for the first time in forty years. There was more snowfall than Albuquerque had seen in more than forty years. Denver got buried too. The airports were shut down and the interstate highways out of Albuquerque and Denver were closed.

CHAPTER 27

Although it is late September, the days are still very warm. The other day my search for evidence of a turquoise ledge took me up the arroyo to the point where it narrows dramatically to down-cut through solid basalt and limestone. Nearby there is a spring that bubbles to the surface for a week or two after the rains come; for years a cottonwood tree lived by the spring although the location is outside the natural range for cottonwoods. The tree lived near the spring for years, but died during the early years of the drought.

Now a mesquite tree grows in its place. The tree is large and robust but it grows horizontally just above the ground across the arroyo from side to side. I had to crawl over the mesquite's trunk to get past it.

I could see that the mesquite tree had grown vertically for many years. But then a heavy rainstorm must have come with runoff water that roared through the narrow rock gorge with such great force that the tree was flattened to the ground but not uprooted. Now it grows horizontally, safe from floods.

I continued up the arroyo. On a bar of sand and gravel I found two rocks with a few streaks of turquoise. The rocks didn't really fit in my pockets and felt uncomfortable there but I carried them anyway.

After the arroyo passed through a ledge of the basalt, it forked. I took the right fork, which was much narrower and was overgrown with catsclaw bushes and mesquite branches with thorns that tore at my clothes. The erosion wasn't as deep and there wasn't nearly as much rock debris and gravel here. It didn't look promising for turquoise so I decided to turn back. Next time I would take the left fork of the arroyo; it was wider and I knew it passed the site of an old mine shaft where water dripped from the ceiling and flowed out the shaft entrance—just the environment needed to make turquoise.

Sometimes early in the morning when I walk the trail the air is cool and faintly scented with rain. Just before the sun rises over the mountains, incandescence floods over the bright greens of the mesquite leaves and the jade greens of the tall saguaros. A breeze stirs and there is a silence as it might have been five hundred or a thousand years ago. No sound anywhere in the distance from a train, jet, car or even a dog. Here the desert is as it always was.

Up ahead a small arroyo intersects the trail. The branches of catsclaw and mesquite that overhang the arroyo make a delicate shade with shadows in diamond patterns. Suddenly I realized there was a giant rattlesnake there in the shade and shadows, stretched out twelve feet long, its body as big around as a bread loaf. I stopped in my tracks; my heart pounded. I looked again to make sure I'd not mistaken a long mesquite root in the sand for the huge snake.

Alert and motionless, the snake watched me. The eyes were pale yellow and its head was bigger than my two fists put together and at least five feet above the ground; the black forked tongue flicked out level with my chin. The rattles on the end of its tail were the diameter of a man's thumb.

I saw the black forked tongue move more slowly, and felt the sun's light on the right side of my face. The shadows in the small arroyo shifted and the shade receded, but I could still see the snake's head slightly turned now as if to look back.

I took a few steps closer up a short incline and I lost sight of the snake for only an instant. But when I looked again at the intersection of the trail with the small arroyo, bright sunlight filled the space. The shade and its shadows were gone and the giant rattlesnake with them.

I didn't notice the great ant palaces in the desert until I began my walks. The first ant palace is under a square of basalt the size of a book in the middle of the trail up the hill. The trail and the slope of the hill divert the runoff after storms from the ant palace entryway. The overhang of the square basalt protects the palace entrance from foot traffic. Why build the ant palace in the middle of the trail? Because the passers-by—human and otherwise—drop bits of crumbs or seeds that enrich the ants' storehouse.

The second ant palace I saw was a short distance past the Gila Monster Mine and the flat grassy place where the deer and javelina dance at night after rain. This ant palace is on the low ridge that parallels the trail; I noticed it because there is a perfect circle of small stones around its entrance. The rocks look as if they landed there like meteorite fragments. I thought of the Star Beings.

Today I left on my walk much inspired by the two little notes I wrote about the ants and their mountain palaces yesterday. But as I walked I realized that I didn't remember exactly where the book-size basalt was, except that it was on a slight ridge of rock higher than the trail. I had the camera with me the day I noticed the ant palaces but something stopped me from taking their photographs as I passed them. The rhythm of my walk determined part of it—I didn't want to slow down. Also it was because photography or video distracts me so I prefer to remember being in the actual presence of the rocks rather than recording them electronically.

Today I discovered a wonderful ant palace in the dark basalt bedrock below the blue gray limestone; it was outlined in small stones in a semicircle. Did the ants remove the stones from their nest? Or did the ants move the rocks there to divert runoff from the palace entrance?

I thought I was more certain of the location of the ant hill with the circle of stones. I must have missed it because I was looking at the large egg-shaped rocks as big as a man's head. One of them was cracked open by prospectors searching for geodes of silver or gold.

Today I noticed many of the ant palaces have plants growing near their entrances and I realized this was not accidental. This is a result of the ants intentionally leaving a seed out to germinate. When the plant goes to seed, the ants will only have to carry the seeds a short distance.

The ants by the gate outside the national park made a new pile of stone granules to repair the mound that washed away in the rain after horses and people trampled it. They excavated fine gravel first then formed it into a steep-sided cone to protect the ant palace entrance from floods.

Not far from the ant hill, on the left side of the path, so the morning light illuminated him, was a small silvery blue rattlesnake, maybe a Mojave and not a Western diamondback. He made no sound or move. He pressed himself flat in his pancake posture to be less visible. He seemed not to mind that I mumbled "Hello!" as I stepped around him.

This morning I walked the same path as the day before. Overnight dark rain clouds had blown in from El Golfo, and the air was damp and sweet with the smell of rain and greasewood and wet stones.

On my walk yesterday I didn't see any turquoise stones but today suddenly almost as soon as I stepped off the trail into the big arroyo I spotted a large turquoise rock right where I'd stepped the day before. The rain brightens the turquoise color but still it seems strange that I saw the stone today but didn't notice it yesterday. I found a tiny hard turquoise on the road to the Gila Monster Mine. Did someone bring it from the arroyo and drop it there?

This morning while I was out back feeding the military macaws, I heard a squirrel chattering incessantly at the water trough in the back above the old pool, and when I went to see what was happening, there sat a big bobcat nonchalantly lapping up water. He knew I was watching him but he didn't care. This bobcat lives in the neighborhood and isn't afraid of humans or dogs. He is the same height as my ninety pound pit bull but the bobcat's head is twice the size of the dog's.

Today's March shower—the first storm since the end of January—was enough to fill the small cisterns carved into the boulders along the arroyo. There was a bright blue turquoise rock in plain view where I walked yesterday. It wasn't there yesterday. Did the rain bring it? On a previous walk without the rain's help I found a round nugget of pale blue turquoise on the trail I'd walked dozens of times before. Later when I held this piece of turquoise against my cheek, the stone felt heavier and cooler than the others.

Does Turquoise Man travel with the rain? Well of course. He calls for the rain so the runoff water comes to the arroyos where deposits of copper, aluminum, iron and the calcites drink in the moisture to become turquoise.

I always assumed Mexico and the land to the south had deposits of turquoise. Macaws and macaw feathers were brought north, but I used to wonder what it was those rich Mexican Indians wanted badly enough to walk a thousand miles with live macaws on their backs. It wasn't until I found a book about the turquoise mosaics at the British Museum that I learned they had jade and jadeite in Mexico, but turquoise was rare and thus the most precious stone, most desired by the deities for their ornaments and ceremonies.

During the classic period of Teotihuacan, the Nahua Empire sent out traders with macaws and feathers north along the turquoise trail to Arizona and New Mexico to bring back the turquoise so highly coveted. The turquoise exchange accounts for the well-traveled trade routes the Spaniards found as they followed their captive Indian guides north.

Turquoise is a favorite color for ka'tsina masks. The paints on the ka'tsina mask are what make the mask alive. When the old paints are scraped off prior to repainting, the paint scrapings from the masks are taken to a ka'tsina shrine for disposal. Otherwise even the paint scrapings have the power to harm someone.

The Long Horn ka'tsina's turquoise-colored mask has one long horn because he brought long life to the people. His right eye is short so that "witches" or "the two hearts" who pretend to be kind but secretly crave violence and misery, don't live long. His left eye is long so the people of one heart will live a long time. Turquoise is worn to ward off witches.

Years ago at a Zuni Shalako ceremony, a housetop collapsed with many spectators on it. Apparently they'd failed to place turquoise under the floor of the new room being blessed by the Shalako dancers.

Xiuhtecuhtli, Lord Turquoise, is also the God of Fire. He wears a mask studded with turquoise cabochons for moles on his face. He is also known as Ixcozauhqui, Old God. His turquoise mosaic mask survived the conquistadors and ended up in the British Museum.

Xiuhatla means turquoise water.

Xiuhatl is the turquoise waters of Paradise.

Xiuhcalli is the house of turquoise that belongs to Quetzalcoatl in Tollan.

Xiuhuitl herb is the color of green turquoise; xiuhtoz means "turquoise parrot" and is a fictional name used to designate a ghost warrior.

Xiuhtzoneh is the name of the mountain at Tepozotla where the Toltecs mined a turquoise lode, the only source of turquoise inside Mexico.

CHAPTER 28

I t's early May now but the morning was still cool. I'd gone a good distance up the wash to the sharp turn at the natural cisterns of blue stone in the area of the lost petroglyph. I was thinking about the turquoise stones I'd picked up over the thirty years I've lived here. The big ones only had splashes of turquoise or tiny thin threads of turquoise on their surface. The smaller rocks are better—all the thin crumbly surface has worn away in the abrasion of the arroyo, and only the turquoise remains—polished by the tumble in the muddy water, and pebbles.

I glanced down the sandy delta where I never found turquoise stones and this time I saw a rock with a tiny bright spot of turquoise in the shape of a cloud.

A short distance away I found another small turquoise rock in the shape of a half moon. The swirling action of the floodwaters in the arroyo churns the deposits of sand and stones over and over. The delta where there's only sand and a few pebbles on the surface probably has turquoise pebbles buried six feet below that get churned back up in a flash flood.

Along the way I picked up two shards of bottle glass. The glass is dense and heavy so I know it is old, from the 1960s or even the 1950s when the glass had some lead or other metals in it. If left for many years in the sun, the clear glass turns bright amethyst.

Most times I find glass fragments of recent manufacture. The glass is very thin because they've mixed in plastic resins to make it lighter-weight, but not stronger. In Tucson the thin glass of bottles of carbonated water often explode in the heat and blast their shrapnel in every direction.

I see fresh wood dust under the small palo verde killed by vandals a few months ago. I felt very badly when I found it lying in the arroyo because the foothill palo verde grow very slowly and this one must have been thirty years old. But now the insects are eating it and I am reminded the desert has its ways to work out death and life.

I was walking down the steep hill near the Thunderbird Mine, and I was almost to the bottom, keeping up a good pace while careful not to stumble, when I looked over to the right, and coming at a good pace too was a Gila monster. The big lizard saw me just at the instant I saw him. He flicked his delicate black forked tongue at me, and in my surprise I blurted out "Hello." Such an ugly sound ruined our introduction. The Gila monster didn't flee but he turned his back to me and hid his head in a small desert sage brush so he wouldn't have to see something so large and frightening.

As I walked along the path, I paid special attention to the ant palaces along the way. I took notice of them when I passed by; each colony did something different—perhaps owing to the unique conditions of their location in the desert. Some went underground at sunrise while others stayed on to work in the heat.

The perfect rings of bright vermillion caught my eye. They encircled the stone entrance to the ant palace. The ants gathered the fallen blossoms of the ocotillo and intended to move them into their nest after the flowers dried. The brilliant orange red of the tiny flowers was incandescent in the early light.

The storm came suddenly, and oddly there was not the thunder and lightning that usually accompany hail and rain. The hail was the size of corn kernels. The storm lasted only an hour or so but when it was over, I could see the big arroyo was flooded from bank to bank. The damp air amplified the sounds; I heard the low whir of the floodwater as it crossed the paved road with its slurry of pebbles and rocks.

The curved beak thrashers sang their rain songs full of trills and arpeggios while the Gila woodpeckers shrieked with joy. The rain makes the desert birds amorous. Even a moderate rain may allow the desert birds and others the sustenance to raise their young successfully.

Next day's storm was short but violent—a great deal of rain and hail fell in a short time. The trail was badly eroded; the path the rain-water carved was filled with sizeable rocks and pebbles so I had to pay attention to my footing. The damp earth felt wonderfully moist with an energy that helped my feet spring along.

As I walked along, a light breeze moved steadily, full of the scents of wet earth and wet bark and leaves. I even smelled wet roots. The tiny gnats the hummingbirds love to eat rose from their damp earth beds under the foliage as a gossamer golden cloud in the morning light.

I was interested to see what had happened to the ocotillo flowers the ants had out to dry by their palace entrances. With such a strong wind and heavy downpour, I assumed the orange red blossoms would blow away.

The ants were out working on their entrance when I got there, rearranging the protective barriers of coarse sand grains and tiny pebbles that kept yesterday's deluge from flooding their palace. Amazingly, the masses of tiny orange and red ocotillo flowers the ants stored outside had not been dislodged by the wind and rain, only slightly shifted.

How do the ants get the dried flowers to stay put during storms? Glue? Weaving? Magnetism? I took a closer look at one of the tiny dried florets and saw that the anthers and pistils had dried into hooked tendrils that the ants had interlocked to form a blanket of blossoms. The ants attached the tendrils to large grains of ant hill sand where they remained, impervious to wind and rain until they were ready to be taken underground.

The small mesquite lizard in the front yard likes to sun himself on the round stones shaped and smoothed long ago by human hands. The lizard has other good rocks in the sun to choose from but for some reason he prefers the smooth man-made surfaces.

CHAPTER 29

t's the beginning of June but the early mornings are still cool enough
for a walk. Today as I was returning from my walk, and still some
distance from my driveway, I noticed two piercing laser-bright red
lights in the mesquite tree in my front yard. How strange they were! At
first I couldn't imagine what I was seeing, but then I realized it was the
early morning angle of the sunlight that caused odd visual effects this
time of the year, and what I actually saw were the hummingbird feeders an eighth of a mile away. The sunlight shone through the red sugar
water which acted as a lens to focus the light.

Under the mesquite tree I saw a dozen or more brown ants bringing down a cicada ten times larger than they were. The cicada struggled feebly from the effects of the ant venom, and I noticed the cicada's
second skin was separating for a molt, and part of the old exoskeleton
seemed stuck to its wings and tail.

One hummingbird came to the feeder while I sat on the porch. She
is the female with the black line on her tail feathers. I said, "Where
were you? I missed you." The hummingbird darted away. I forgot the
human voice out loud sounds ugly to the hummingbirds. I should have
whispered. She didn't go far but I didn't want to disturb her again to
ask her the whereabouts of the other hummingbirds and the bees.

The sudden rain last week gave the greasewoods enough nourishment
for another flowering this spring. I hope the bees and hummingbirds are

not missing, only browsing nearby in all the many waxy white saguaro blossoms and sweet yellow greasewood flowers.

The night-blooming cactus, la reina de la noche in the clay pot, the one I started from a twig, had a single gorgeous perfumed blossom last night and early this morning. Then it was finished.

The reinas are indigenous to the Sonoran Desert. They frequently grow under jojoba bushes for partial shade but this makes them difficult to locate unless they are in blossom. The bulk of the reina is a tuberous root underground; what appears to be a leafless stick pokes up through the ground and the jojoba branches. In early summer the leafless stick forms a bud and just after sundown a large white blossom emerges. Then their heavenly perfume gives them away. The scent is delicate and haunting, never heavy or cloying, and reminds me of the lovely perfume of the white orchid flowers of the *Brassavola nodosa* from Central America where it blooms for the autumnal equinox.

The scent of the brugmansia blossoms were a disappointment—I expected they'd be as fragrant as the purple datura but they were lovely to see. They require a good deal of water and rich soil—both in limited supply here. No wonder they grow best in the Quechua graveyards in the mountains of Peru. In the twilight their pendulous yellow blossoms are ghostly, resembling the dead souls on the branches of the Tree of Life.

On my walk this morning I picked up a rock the size of my two fingers with speckles and threads of turquoise. The rock is light greenish gray basalt and the turquoise is a light green blue that collected in a triangular crease near the lower middle of the rock. On the far right end, midpoint, there is a raisin of iron ore.

This morning, instead of coming in to work on the manuscript, I sat in the shade on the front porch and watched the mesquite lizard catch the tiny gnats that swarmed around the lower limb of the big mesquite tree. The lizard had lovely patterns of ivory and copper over brown and darker shades that mimicked the bark of a mesquite tree. Suddenly the lizard moved, then turned and bounced up and down on its front legs to assert his dominance over his territory, but why?

I looked around and about eight feet away on the trunk of the smaller mesquite tree I saw a larger spiny desert lizard I call a "sky lizard" because of its brilliant blue color. Sky lizards like to sit at the top of the stucco walls of my house in camouflage, their blue silhouettes hidden in the blue of the sky.

The spiny lizard intensified the brightness of his iridescent turquoise blue and he puffed up his spiny neck with its elegant black necklace marking. Fat with all the gnats he ate in the tree, his tail was a luminous pale turquoise blue, the color of the summer sky overhead. His ribs and chest were intense turquoise of the greatest substance and purity, and the blue on his head and his back was the shade of lapis lazuli.

The mesquite lizard appeared unconcerned about the puffed up spiny lizard and instead watched the Gila woodpecker that flitted around the hummingbird feeder until it managed to find a place for its claw so it could tip the feeder and its contents into its beak.

I left the house early as the sun was still behind the Catalina Mountains to the east. The air was cool, and I could smell just a hint of the dampness, the last trace of the sudden rainstorm of a few weeks ago. The scent of the greasewood was pervasive because the bushes are covered with tiny waxy yellow flowers. A few orange carmine blossoms remain stored outside the ant palaces but I saw no ants.

At the ant hill which had been trampled by humans and horses earlier in the month, I found the damage had been repaired by a rainstorm which smoothed away the boot-prints and hoof-prints into a concentric circular pattern. I saw seven or eight ants working on the entrance to arrange the grains of sand the rainstorm brought before it got too hot.

I heard loud noises of rocks clattering in the nearby arroyo where I had seen the giant rattlesnake. I stopped and stood still and a herd of six or seven large mule deer does stared at me, uncertain whether they should run. I went on my way at once to reassure them I was no threat.

All the trees and shrubs are bright green and many are blossoming again. Each rainstorm in the Sonoran Desert brings another springtime of wild flowers and cactus blossoms even if it only lasts two weeks.

In the big arroyo right after the rain I found three pieces of turquoise rock uncovered by the runoff. But since then I've not found any; I noticed the floodwater left a layer of dove gray clay on the pebbles and rocks, so the turquoise isn't as visible. To wash off the clay, a gentle steady rain is needed; then I'll be able to spot the turquoise rocks again.

Each time the trail went downhill and across even the smallest arroyo, the cool moist air rushed past my face in the most delicious manner. I felt my skin drink it in. The cool air held subtle perfumes of the catsclaw and mesquite that blossomed following the rain. In the big arroyo the flow of cool air had much more of a woody green herbal scent.

A short distance past the Gila Monster Mine I caught a flash of turquoise out of the corner of my eye. I picked up a piece of orange quartzite the size of my fist with a streak of turquoise across its face. This was quite a distance from the big arroyo where I imagined the ledge of turquoise to be so it served as a reminder: turquoise may be found anywhere in these hills where there may be more than one turquoise ledge.

In the arroyo I noticed a small rectangular turquoise cabochon of a very nice sky blue and green. I brought it home but I lost it for a while under papers and notes on my writing desk. When I located it again, I took a closer look at it, and I realized one side resembled the turquoise mask of Tlaloc.

I picked up the trash I found too—a faded scrap of a Starbucks wrapper, a piece of brittle weathered gray duct tape, a shard of a green bottle and a large shard from a clear glass bottle. I am intrigued to see the items that somehow find their way and travel down the big arroyo.

A few days later, I set out on my walk on the trail just after six a.m. The previous day's rain wasn't as heavy as three weeks earlier when all the erosion occurred on the walking trail and my driveway, but it was just what the new foliage from the last rainfall needed in order to go on blossoming—the mesquites and the catsclaw bushes all are in bloom a second time in just three months. The breeze was cool and smelled faintly of the flowers and the camphor of the grease-wood. Some newcomers complain that the desert "has no seasons," but the desert has many seasons; each time it rains, we have another springtime.

At the point in the big arroyo where the basalt boulders leave scarcely enough space for a horse and rider to pass, the trail goes up and through the remains of an ancient tumult of stones, pebbles and sand. Stones the size of bread loaves and cantaloupes formed a long narrow ribbon along the sandbars. In the sandbar I found a piece of turquoise rock—the second such since the flood in the big arroyo had moved so much sand and stone.

A light, brief rain from the previous day had washed off the mud left by the floodwater and exposed the turquoise stone which was about the size of the end of my thumb. I saw it so plainly there on the nar-row ribbon of sandbar above the big gray basalt boulders. Its color was so bright and intense in the morning sun and leftover dampness of the night shower; the rain brings out the intense turquoise blue. The writ-ing I saw on the stone was in turquoise threads. As soon as my eyes fell on the markings, my brain registered both "turquoise" and "writing" at the same time.

I recalled reading that the Chinese got their written language from sacred stones from a mountain somewhere. The "writings" or natu-ral marks on the stones gave the Chinese the idea of a system of marks and drawings that would send messages. I imagined them poring over the stones with the markings or "writings," certain these were messages from the supernatural world, interpreting each mark, each figure before they copied the marks and kept the stones themselves as a reference once the message of the stone was deciphered. The turquoise stone I found read thus: a flying bird, a rain cloud over Africa.

CHAPTER 30

keep other rocks I find on my walks, not just the turquoise. On my writing desk today, I have a piece of quartz crystal with smooth faces that reflect sunlight. I like to keep favorite rocks near me when I'm writing although they barely leave me any space to work. They catch dust and spiders' webs.

The small spiders in my studio leave tiny fluffy white web strings and balls all over the faces and chests of the Star Being portraits. I don't like to disturb the spiders by dusting the portraits. It is possible to use a lamb's wool duster to remove the spiders' webs and eggs without harm but the spiders are forced to relocate.

Good news. The wild bees that water at the small tank by the cistern pool have returned in their usual numbers. I was afraid they might have lost their home to the real estate developers as the others had.

I ran outdoors as soon as I heard the mastiffs barking excitedly as they do when they have some poor creature cornered. Slow moving tortoises, Gila monsters and toads are at a disadvantage with the mastiffs. A big Gila monster had bitten Lyon on the mouth, and his lip was swelling and bloody; it had to bite and hang onto the the mastiff's lip to grind in the poison because the lizards don't inject with fangs like rattlers do. The coral pink and shiny black lizard lay motionless and I saw blood so I thought it was dead. How could it survive the jaws of a mastiff? I felt very badly about the beautiful lizard.

I took the mastiffs indoors and immediately came back out to bury the remains of the lizard, but when I got back to the site, the Gila monster was gone. I walked around and searched carefully under bushes in case it had crawled away to die but I found no trace of the creature in the dogs' yard. I felt much better knowing it had escaped. I don't know if it lived or died later but at least it was able to escape on its own.

I found an immature Gila monster in the front yard some years ago; I hope this wasn't the one that got mauled this morning. I feel badly that I didn't get out there faster to help the lizard escape.

Dogs have evolved with loose skin on their heads and necks to help them survive snakebites. The snake fangs catch in the loose skin and inject the venom under the skin but not in the muscle where greater harm is likely to occur. If a dog weighs thirty-five pounds or more and is in good health, a snakebite to the head or neck will usually not kill it.

Gila monster venom affects dogs much differently than rattlesnake venom. It acts as a sedative, and a bitten dog will seem to have little pain. The rattlesnake venom is so painful that the dog will pant and pace restlessly. Gila monster venom is prescribed in small amounts and injected to control diabetes that can't be controlled otherwise.

Lyon is a seven year old purebred English mastiff. Over the years he appears to have developed a partial immunity to rattlesnake venom from frequent warning bites on his head and snout. He's already been bitten twice by rattlers in 2007.

I kept a little blue notebook I titled "Rain 2007." I have a number of notebooks titled "Rain" and a year; but open them and they are blank except for one or two pages with writing. Sometimes this is because it only rained once or twice in six months and I lost interest and lost track of the notebook.

Maybe the weather is about to change. The rattlesnakes sense subtle shifts in barometric pressure so they move and change locations days before a storm arrives in Tucson.

This is why I can't travel anymore: well-meaning house-sitters removed the rattlesnakes that customarily lounged in the coolness of my front porch by the pots of geraniums and datura. One of the twin rattlers was removed and relocated—not far, I hope. A tenth of a mile is still within a snake's range. That was the distance the firemen took the big brown rattler last year when the other house-sitter called them.

After I returned, I noticed the snakes out by the macaw aviaries seemed much more jumpy around me. The rattler with the big head was coiled next to the small blue plastic water tub under the small mesquite tree. But he abruptly changed position and put his back to me. Another rattler by the old macaw cage hurried away when I came with the hose. They didn't like the house-sitters.

I found a small owl feather with an amazing intricate pattern of small white circles mixed into the bands of silver and pale beige. Was it a silvery white barn owl or a great horned owl? Perhaps a greeting from the owls that hunt around my house at night. I put the feather in the shade cloth but when I came back it was gone. The breeze took it or it went with the breeze.

The big heat arrived on the second day of July with the enormous sky canopy of blinding white sunlight. The Sun blazes hotter than ever because its expansion as a red giant has accelerated. I imagine the coronal mass ejections that hurl great hurricanes of solar particles at the Earth; many of the charged particles pass right through us and the Earth and continue on. I think I can feel the particles pass through me, leaving behind coded messages in my bloodstream.

The air is so dry that 106 degrees Fahrenheit feels like 88 as long as one has shade and plenty of water to drink. The heat expands the molecules of air so sound doesn't "travel" as readily, and with the rising heat comes an eerie silence. Birds and small animals lie low to find some relief. A slight breeze stirs and cools my body. A wind chime rings hesitantly at first and then it rings with abandon. The edges of my eyelids feel burned or parched so I think I will move indoors.

Today the air smells like scorched paper or wood about to catch fire; it is so dry the fine mist from the hose evaporates before it touches the macaws on the high perch.

This morning I found a lizard, dead standing up, his eyes open, so at first I thought he was alive but sick and paralyzed. It was a "sky lizard" with a brown collar, blue belly and blue tail. He was facing north. What could have killed him but not eaten him? Did he die suddenly of natural causes? Did a stray particle from a gamma ray or supercharged cosmic ray strike it dead in its tracks? Heat didn't kill him; lizards love the heat. He had no old injuries—there were no marks or signs of damage on him.

In the desert one seldom dies without quickly becoming a meal for another; thus we aren't dead for long before we become part of the living creatures and plants.

CHAPTER 31

At five a.m. the sky over the Catalina Mountains is an ethereal mist of lavender pink. The humidity in the air above the peaks reflects the light of the sunrise blocked by the mountains. I hadn't walked in weeks and all the lovely colors of the morning called me out. I took off my sunglasses and hooked them over my shirt in case I needed them later.

The ant palace on the first hill was all closed up as if the ants expected rain or more hot weather. At another ant palace the entrance was open and a few ants were standing nearby as if they were about to call it a day as the sun rose higher.

I see fewer shoe prints on the trail since the big heat descended. I found two turquoise rocks soon after I turned into the big arroyo. The startling bright turquoise was right where I'd walked many times before. Was it there before but flipped over to hide its turquoise side? The flood last month rolled it over so the turquoise was visible. The rock is a gray limestone the size of the tips of my fingers and thumb held together. The turquoise has orange brown iron spots scattered over it like dust.

The second turquoise rock was about the same size but was a reddish brown iron-bearing stone with turquoise that resembled lichens of bright green. I put the turquoise stones in my jeans pocket carefully so I don't lose them; I keep any broken glass or other trash I pick up in a separate pocket to protect the turquoise rocks.

Under the mesquite trees in the bottom of the arroyo the javelina herd dug out wallows in the sand to find any dampness, any coolness in the terrible heat. When I got home from the walk I realized I had dropped my sunglasses somewhere along the way. Early in the day sunglasses aren't as important, but later on they prevent heat radiation from entering the eyes and heating the brain.

Rain clouds broke the heat wave in Tucson on July 5, but in the Pacific Northwest and Idaho and Montana the atmospheric high pressure intensified the heat so temperatures were higher to the north than here in the desert. Medford was 109 degrees and Boise was 108 while it was only 103 in Tucson.

As I walked the last stretch of the arroyo I found two fine pieces of turquoise rock. The first was a flat orange brown rock the size and shape of a Sonoran red spotted toad or a silver dollar. On its flat side, there were seven distinct spots of turquoise as if painted with a brush to look like a spotted toad. It made a fine spotted toad fetish to bring rain.

The second was a small nugget of turquoise I spied in the fine sand and loam deposited by the receding water. This was a nugget the size of a jellybean of solid chrysocolla-impregnated chalcedony with all the extraneous basalt and limestone worn away by the rocks and water of the arroyo. The nugget had a flat side that resembled the face and head of a coyote.

In the breeze I made out the scent of sweet wood incense from a distant pine forest fire. Later I looked toward the city and the entire valley and sky over Tucson were filled with white smoke, and I wondered if the smoke came from the same source as the sweet wood incense I smelled earlier.

During the heat wave the day is consumed by watering and feeding the five macaws and two cockatoos outdoors, so they are prepared to endure the heat. The mastiffs have to be fed to get them ready to spend the day indoors.

The windows indoors are covered with shiny silver Mylar emergency blankets or "space" blankets originally developed by NASA to protect the astronauts. Tucson at the end of June and in early July is nearly as hot as the surface of Venus, so the space blankets work great, and they are inexpensive. The only problem is to find the right tape. It was so hot the duct tape I used to fix the emergency blankets over the windows wouldn't stick, and the blankets fell down and I had to use thumb tacks to hold them instead.

When I first came to Tucson thirty years ago I heard about eccentrics (usually older women who lived alone) who covered all their windows with aluminum foil followed by a layer of newspaper. Now I've become one of those eccentrics. Light is heat. The dim interior of my house in the summer saves me hundreds of dollars in electricity for cooling the air.

Outdoors on the aviaries I have layers of shade cloth and rolls of willow fencing over the cage wire to give the big parrots the maximum shade and protection from the heat.

I found my blue lens sunglasses on the steep hill just below the Thunderbird Mine. The glasses landed on the ear-pieces, no damage to the lenses. I saw the strange saguaro "boot" again; it looks like a mask. The saguaro forms a hard gray shell-like tissue around damage to its skin, sometimes in the shape of a boot or shoe. I spotted a second saguaro skin that looks like a mask in the debris at the side of the arroyo. I debated bringing home the two "boots" to make them into masks to hang on the wall. I decided to let them be as they are. Near the home stretch of the big arroyo I found a small nugget of turquoise in the deep sand.

The following day on my walk, I was stunned as I approached the big arroyo near the end of the road. The graceful sandbars with the delicate patterns of pebbles and small stones were gone—gouged out and removed by the same machine that smashed the gray basalt boulder and took it away in pieces.

The day I discovered the destruction I didn't tell anyone. The loss and outrage I felt choked me. I knew the local authorities didn't bother to enforce the laws intended to protect the land from damage, and that angered me even more.

I didn't want to write about it; I didn't want it to be in the *Turquoise Ledge* manuscript. I had decided before I started the memoir that I wanted as much as possible to avoid unpleasantness and strife and politics as much as possible. But the beautiful gray basalt and pale orange quartzite boulders had been torn loose from the sides of the arroyo and dragged out of the wash and skidded up the old road to "landscape" the yard of the preposterous house with its prison tower and prison wall.

Small stones and rocks were gouged out of the center of the arroyo to make a level yard for the ridiculously huge house. Boulders and rocks, the fine sand and the pebbles that formed the sandbars along the edge and middle of the arroyo to slow the erosion were gone. The gaping hole left the young mesquite tree and its roots vulnerable to flash floods.

The owner of the grotesque house could have easily afforded to buy rock and sand excavated legally from a quarry. Instead he acted out what he saw as his manifest destiny: to destroy whatever he wanted to destroy willy-nilly no matter the impact on others or himself—that's the credo of southern Arizona, and much of the West.

I was shocked at the damage because I thought the arroyo's proximity to the national park safeguarded it from such damage; I thought the flow of the water in the arroyo was protected by Federal water law. I am always surprised at how easily the wealthy in Pima County can flout laws intended to protect the desert terrain and groundwater. They break the law and then pay a dinky fine to the County which allows them to leave the offending damage or structure in place for a matter of a few hundred dollars. This is the reason much of Tucson looks slightly askew and a bit trashy.

When I approached the damage in the arroyo the next day, I tried to remain calm. I recalled my old neighbor, may he rest in peace, the author Edward Abbey who made famous a certain course of action in his novel *The Monkey Wrench Gang*.

The Earth-avenging protagonist and his pals drop monkey wrenches into bulldozer gear boxes at destruction sites and unbolt power transmission towers from their pedestals. In law school they called such action "self-help" which is frowned upon by the police and the courts because it makes them irrelevant.

But instead I resort to another kind of remedy: I begin to visualize the man with the rock-moving machine as he pulls the wrong lever one morning and drops a boulder on himself. He lives alone in the huge house so he lies squashed under the rock for a good while before anyone finds him.

With that image of the man's moisture squashed into the humble desert earth he violated, I think of rain—great long rainstorms from Lord Huracan far to the south who, once every thirty years, sends Tucson great deluges of rain that last for days and wash away trees and highway bridges and parts of mountains.

The violence of the flash flood powers the redemptive process. Over the years I've seen floods completely change the appearance of the big arroyo.

Just past the machine's destruction I glanced down and found a flat stone with a deposit of sky blue turquoise in the shape of the United States and Mexico. The Earth doesn't cease her blessings just because humans foul Her.

The first storm clouds since June 17 appeared out of the southwest. Just in time to water us thirsty things. It broke the back of the monster heat.

Another gathering of rain clouds.

Our beloved ancestors return to us as rain.

The black mountain peak above the house is veiled in fog and misty clouds in swirls of wind out of the south.

CHAPTER 32

I broke my foot on July 11, 2007, the sixth anniversary of my mother's death. At about six a.m. I went to let the two mastiffs in the living room out. The three steps down into the living room were built incorrectly, too narrowly, and too close together to be safe. It was early, I was too lazy to turn on the light and I thought I was on the bottom step when actually I was on the middle step. My left foot took all the force and weight of my body as I fell from the middle step to the living room floor. As I went down I heard a loud sickening crack.

Early on a Friday in the summer, I knew all the doctors would be gone far away from this blast furnace, off to the cool golf courses of Mission Beach and La Jolla. At the time, the average wait time in a Tucson emergency room was four hours fifty-eight minutes.

I thought: why inflict four hours and fifty-eight minutes of the emergency room on myself while I'm suffering with a broken foot? I took two ibuprofen tablets and hobbled around to feed the dogs and parrots before the worst of the swelling and pain set in. I sat with a big cold pack on my foot and watched *Sesame Street* with the gray parrot.

I knew the doctors didn't put rigid casts on broken bones in the foot; I figured that was all they'd do for me at the emergency room after four hours and fifty-eight minutes and a charge of five hundred dollars or more. So I decided I would take care of my foot myself. I called Caz and asked him to buy me a cane and one of those ugly postsurgical sandals. My health insurance doesn't cover anything but major catastrophes anyway. I decided next week I'd let the acupuncturist work on the foot, which was completely black now; if I went this week it would frighten her.

My younger son, Caz, came and fed the dogs and parrots the next day so I could stay off my foot. I never thought about it until now but with one foot gone, the stress on the remaining foot and leg was shocking. I forgot; it had been years since I'd lost mobility; one cannot order the remaining limbs to take up the burden of the failed limb without much protest by the sore strained muscles unaccustomed to the sudden shift in weight. The cane left my hand and arm sore. I had to face the facts: if I ever lost my mobility permanently, I'd have to find someone to help me or I'd be forced to part with my beloved dogs and parrots because I could not feed or care for them properly.

The broken foot forced me to sit on the front porch and observe the sky and the gathering of clouds.

> More rain
> good rain
> all love and gratitude to the clouds who come
> from white shell houses afar.
> In the swirling mist
> cloud breath beings sweep
> along the slopes of the dark peak.

For eleven days straight, the rain came into Sinaloa and Sonora along the Sierra Madre and the Sierra Madre Oriental fed by the twin tropical storms named Cosmo and Dalia.

Thirteen nights after I broke the bone in my left foot, it was healing nicely thanks to the benevolent energy of the Nine Lords of the Night who wished to see me back on my feet so I could continue painting their portraits, and thanks to the little needles my acupuncturist used twice a week, beginning the tenth day after my fall.

On the fourteenth day after I broke my foot, I was up watering plants in the front yard when I caught a glimpse of a piece of turquoise rock I had picked up long ago on a walk probably in the big arroyo. It was in the dirt in an old flower bed. I had to smile. This was the second time since my injury the turquoise rocks came to me. I have them to write about even if I can't walk far, and of course I have the big rains to write about.

A few days later on a rainy Saturday, I used my special waterproof notebook paper with special waterproof pencil to sit outside on the front porch and write during the rain because a breeze would blow the raindrops onto the porch from time to time.

The following day I hobbled out to water the fig tree in its pot of dirt and lo and behold I saw a turquoise rock the size of a pea. How did the little rock get there? Was it in the soil from this hilltop or was it one of the rocks I picked up years ago and tossed into the pot? This nugget was on the ground in the back yard where the erosion is loosening the pebbles and gravel in the layers of white caliche dust. I realized then how old all this rock is, how the turquoise ledge may have been very large—as big as a mountain ridge—when it was blasted to smithereens by the big volcanic eruption millions of years ago and its turquoise was scattered all over the area.

The turquoise pieces I've found since I broke my foot came to me so I could keep writing about the stones even while I couldn't walk in the big arroyo.

CHAPTER 33

After the rainy August dawn comes a blue sunrise—sunlight through blue violet storm clouds from horizon to horizon. Clouds that are as thick as dog fleece or goose down. They are heavy with mists, fogs and gentle rains.

I'm on the front porch with my waterproof notebook paper and waterproof pencil to watch the gentle mist, rain and fog enclose the high mountain peaks to the west.

I've got all the buckets out and even a deep ceramic bowl under the front porch eaves where the gutter failed along with nearly everything else that inept handyman once did here. The raindrops ring against the metal buckets and thud on the plastic.

I try to imagine the prayers the runners said along the way in March 2006 as they ran from Hotevila to the carved stone image of Tlaloc in Mexico City.

The rain in the empty metal bucket makes a strange sound, like that of a small human voice vocalizing Ahhahah Ah! Not in pain or distress but maybe in delight and celebration.

I keep watch on the twelve pails, buckets and two big plastic garbage cans I fill with rainwater. My potted plants and trees need the rainwater to wash away the salts and minerals left by the well water. As a child I watched Grandma A'mooh, Aunt Alice and so many others at Laguna who caught and stored rainwater in fifty-five-gallon barrels to drink and to wash their hair with.

The ancient ones are nearby. Sometimes late at night in the wind you can hear them sing or on a long hot summer afternoon you can hear them laughing and talking in the shade. Maybe the old ones that used the concave metates under the big palo verde trees on the hills a thousand years ago, maybe they brought the turquoise up from the big arroyo just as I have.

Six weeks away from the big arroyo and the search for turquoise stones. My eye is on the lookout. This afternoon towering mountains of cumulus clouds, remnants of a Caribbean hurricane, appeared on the horizon.

The little spiders in my studio increased as I spent more time at my desk after I broke my foot. I moved some webs but used a clean dry rag and then left it outside where the spiders might escape overnight. I transferred the spider egg sacs to the rain lily leaves where they may hatch. They seldom bite me and if they do it is because I've accidentally squeezed one with my elbow against my writing table.

It's almost eight weeks to the day since I last walked before I broke my foot. The hurricane rains were lovely last night. This morning the desert is wet—so many shades of green. In the bright sunlight everything that is wet reflects a mirror light. The reds and yellows of the limestone are fluorescent. The bones in my foot feel healed and I can't resist a walk.

The trail is a beloved friend I realize now. I didn't know how much I missed it until I started to walk today. I intended to go left and take just a short walk in the arroyo, but my feet wouldn't leave the trail. The fresh rain breeze in my lungs felt exhilarating. My left foot felt good to be on the trail again. Both feet in contact with the welcoming trail made me feel so alive. Oddly, it was my right ankle that I sprained when I was twelve that protested after the lay-off.

I took my time and kept walking to see what had been going on along the trail while I was laid-up. One ant was out early to see what he could find knocked down or blown in by the wind and rain last night. All around I could hear the calls for celebration and the singing by the cactus wrens and thrashers.

Water was gurgling in the big arroyo where it surfaced then disappeared again below the sand. In other places, water dripped from the rocks and filled sandy basins no larger than my hand.

I saw traces of soapy froth from yucca roots flooded by the heavy rainfall. I was the first human over the trail this morning, but the javelinas had already been down the big arroyo ahead of me. From the darting patterns of their v-shaped tracks and the damp sand and pebbles kicked loose, the javelinas had been dancing there the hour before to celebrate the gorgeous rain.

What an unexpected gift this rain! It means the arroyo may begin to transform the damages the man and his machine caused. I felt an effortless connection with every part of the trail. Even the steep eroded hill by the Thunderbird Mine seemed less rough and difficult than it had been the last time I walked here eight weeks ago.

Since the damage to the big arroyo, I no longer assumed I would find the trail as it was the last time I saw it.

I had to walk more slowly over the unfamiliar terrain left by the heavy rain and runoff. I also very much anticipated what I would see when I reached the place torn up by the man and his machine. After all these years in Tucson, I'm still not accustomed to the way untouched rocks and hills and the living creatures here can be crushed alive by these men and their machines without a second thought.

At the site of the damage the deep ruts left by the machine were partially filled with freshly washed sand and pebbles from the rain. Many of the smaller rocks damaged by the machine had been carried downstream or buried. But the holes left behind by the big boulders that were gouged out by the machine would need far more time to fill in.

I walked a short distance past the damage and found a turquoise rock on the new sandbar left by the flood. The rock fit in my hand like a triangular egg with a turquoise frog shape on it. The rainstorm water had brought this turquoise rock here. I went only a few feet farther and spied another turquoise rock; this rock also fit in my palm, but was flatter and had a layer of turquoise over one end in the shape of a bobcat's head.

A third piece of turquoise rock I found was the size of a grape with coppery brown rock surrounding the turquoise layer which is shaped like a star.

On this walk I missed seeing the red grinding stone in the middle of the wash but thought perhaps I'd been distracted and overlooked it. I saw deer and coyote tracks at the edges.

The wide ledge of bluestone was more exposed now than ever before. Small pools and basins in the bluestone hold the rainwater. The sand that once covered the bluestone got moved by the water, and accumulated around the boulder and covered up the petroglyph. Somewhere I have a photograph of the petroglyph from twenty years ago before it got buried in sand.

The flood carried away the remains of the poor palo verde tree that had been previously uprooted by vandals, but later a home to wood bees and wood ants. The scent of the catsclaw in blossom and the damp woody stalks and barks drying in the sun give the breeze a wonderful perfume. What blessings this rain and this Earth!

I picked up bits of trash washed down the arroyo by the rain: a plastic dental floss container, a fragment of brown bottle glass, a white paper dust mask. The turquoise "mystery cabochon" I passed up on the trail by the rodent hole then turned back for was actually a wad of blue chewing gum discarded by some park visitor.

The next morning the arroyo was bank to bank with javelina tracks. The air was scented with barks and roots and sweet desert woods and was deliciously cool this second day after the sudden big rain.

Still no red grinding stone. In the runoff flood after the rain it didn't stand a chance. It must have tumbled end over end with the other rocks and tree roots and debris. Foolishly I had thought the water would go around it and leave it be.

The big arroyo has no attachment to the way things are. The arroyo is the space the water and the boulders and other debris pass through in floods, the space that desert animals and I move through. The space that is the arroyo changes with every flood.

A distance past the old culvert, as I approached the straight stretch of arroyo, I found a turquoise rock the size of a Brazil nut and the shape of a baby sea turtle; a layer of turquoise marked the turtle's shell.

During the time my broken foot had prevented me from walking the trail, I found so many turquoise rocks around the house and yard I began to wonder if the turquoise stones really were everywhere—not just in the arroyo. Now that my foot is better I can walk the hilltop around the house to take a further look.

The other afternoon I wandered up the hillside past the big power pole. At its base there was a pile of dirt left over from the drilling that had been done to set the pole. In the dirt I found a round turquoise rock the size of a grape—more evidence that there is turquoise under the hill where my house is.

CHAPTER 34

Every summer my great grandma A'mooh grew cosmos, four o'clocks, morning glories and hollyhocks. I plant pots of cosmos in the autumn now and think often of A'mooh. In her yard there were the lilacs and the old-fashioned rugosa rose bushes, and next to the swing on the long porch there were two shrubs with cascading branches of tiny white flowers that she called "bridal bouquet." A huge datura plant had grown in the sandy floodplain soil in her back yard; she called it a "moon flower" because the blossoms opened at night.

My garden is fifteen or twenty mismatched clay and plastic flowerpots on the porch of my studio under the big mesquite in the front yard. I drag this potted garden back and forth from the sun to the shade in the summer.

In November I sow seeds before the cold weather comes. The seedlings like the milder temperatures and they grow quickly after the equinox. By the end of January my front porch is perfumed by pots of datura, alyssum, cosmos and snapdragons. On the nights the temperature falls below freezing, I make tents out of old towels and sheets to protect the cosmos and datura. I drag the pots back into the sun all winter, then back under cover at night, over and over. This is the fate of any gardener of alien plants from outside the desert.

There is no point in preparing a flower bed. The desert trees and shrubs can send out roots overnight to suck the water from a flower bed or tree well; the mesquite tree in my front yard will even steal the water from my clay and plastic pots if I don't block the drainage holes in the bottoms of the pots with pieces of slate. The pots are discolored with streaks of gypsum from the well water and some of them are cracked.

The garden shade, the green leaves, the seeds and the water buckets attract birds and rodents which attract the rattlesnakes. The cool of the dampness and the deep shade of the pots give great comfort to the rattlesnakes that live around and under my house. Snakes will perish in direct sun and the summer midday heat in a matter of minutes much as we humans can die of heat stroke. Besides their heat detection sensors, rattlesnakes also have organs to detect the coolest spot in an area.

One morning I walked back and forth on the porch with the hose watering the flowerpots, past the geranium that overhangs its pot and sweeps the porch bricks. After an hour or so I took a break and sat down where I could see the small brown rattler coiled up under the overhanging geranium branches on the porch floor. My feet had only been inches from him all that time but the snake recognizes me—he must do this often but I never noticed him until today. He seems unconcerned about me; I'm not enough of a threat to make the snake want to leave the sweet cool shade of the clay pots where ground squirrels and sparrows stray from time to time.

Over the years I had planted a good many cacti from outside the Sonoran Desert only to watch the birds and rodents feast on them. Sonoran varieties secrete bitter or toxic juices that protect them if their spines and stickers don't stop predators. I can't resist night-blooming cacti. I grow the indigenous reina de la noche but also three others that are not native and must be protected from pack rats and from freezing. I grow the night-blooming cactus for the subtle glorious fragrance of the blossoms that last only one night.

I grow pots of datura because datura withstands the heat and ultraviolet radiation of the summer. By day, the alyssum, snapdragons and datura survive in the shade; at night the big white datura blossoms are heavenly fragrant.

The daturas are interesting to grow because they are a vital part of the life cycle of the beautiful hawk moths that may grow as large as hummingbirds. The hawk moths visit the datura flowers on moonlit nights guided by the perfume and the luminous white flowers the size of saucers. The moths lay their eggs in the dirt around the base of the datura plant and the larvae grow into huge beautiful bright leaf green caterpillars with white markings. The voracious caterpillars then strip the datura plants of their leaves and buds before they spin their cocoons.

At the end of September, the heat began to recede, and a rainstorm revived my garden. The pink and the white rain lilies bloomed and I kept watering them after the rain left—for the bees and the butterflies and for me.

One morning as I watered, I saw two large grasshoppers, amazing in their beauty and their size. Their outer wings were emerald green in the center with peacock green along the edges; the inner wings were hues of magenta red and magenta pink with lacy leaf patterns in bright yellow. Their faces and necks were outlined in bright yellow on jade green, and their antennae were bright orange with bold black stripes. They sat in the cluster of pink rain lily blossoms they'd been eating. They regarded me fearlessly, with great majesty. Their bright black eyes looked intently into mine.

As soon as I saw them, I wanted to sketch the grasshoppers in colored pencil, but I was busy and went off to do other chores. I worked on the manuscript. I forgot about the grasshoppers.

The next day I found one of the big grasshoppers under the potted fig tree. He walked unsteadily as if drunk or sick. His antennae moved feebly, but he didn't seem afraid of me. I picked him up carefully and moved him so he wouldn't drown when I watered the fig tree. I wondered what had happened. Poison? Then I remembered: his life was the length of a summer; he was dying of old age. Still he was arresting in his beauty and his steady gaze connected with mine. The vivid colors and intricate markings were unlike any I'd ever seen. I left him in the rain lilies to die in peace.

The next morning I found the grasshopper in the rain lily leaves, "dead" some might say because he didn't move, but he was still brightly colored, so there was life in him yet. I gently picked him up and brought him into my studio. I needed to hold him in place somehow; all I had was a shot glass where I stood him up so I could see his thorax plainly.

As I sketched him, I realized he wanted a portrait in the manner of the Star Being portraits I'd painted. Later, after I finished the grass-hopper's sketch, I brought out a big canvas like the ones I used for the Star Being portraits, and I prepared the canvas with stucco and left it to dry.

I was thinking about how to paint the grasshopper face-on in the manner of the Star Beings; it presented difficulty because of the shape of the grasshopper's head, so I didn't work on the portrait. A few days later while I was outside to watch the rain clouds gather from a hurri-cane in Mexico, I noticed another of the big colorful grasshoppers under the mesquite tree by the front porch. It looked me in the eyes, and I knew at once this grasshopper was a messenger from Lord Chapulin.

Get back to work.

I thought a profile was a tempting variation from the portraits I'd done, so I got out my sketchbook and colored pencils to attempt a sketch in profile but I just couldn't get it right. Chapulin didn't want a portrait in profile; he wanted his portrait face-on, like the portraits of the Star Beings.

I had to work awhile to get the face-on pose to look right. At first I drew the eyes on the sides of the grasshopper's head, but this was incorrect; the eyes were more to the front of the face. As I sketched, I understood Chapulin wanted to be seen and remembered as he was on the big fiesta day in August when there were so many good things to eat, and he celebrated by wearing powdered turquoise all over his head and face out of regard for Tlaloc, Lord of the Rain, whose color is turquoise.

I relied on my colored pencil sketch to draw the outline of Chapu-lin's portrait on the canvas. In the sketch his buckskin leggings and moccasins could be seen, but on the canvas, only his head, chest and waist fit. I was pleased with the work I'd done, so I left the portrait for the rest of the week while I worked on the manuscript.

Another week or two passed. One day I noticed one of the big "painted" grasshoppers on a datura plant outside my studio window; the grasshopper gazed in at Lord Chapulin's portrait on the easel. I felt uneasy because I'd done no work on the portrait for a long time.

Then one morning outside my studio under the mesquite tree, Lord Chapulin himself approached me. He came straight toward me and climbed up from the ground to a sandstone bench to get closer to me. He regarded me gravely and remained motionless on the sandstone while I looked at the hues of green, the magenta pinks and reds, and the black and orange markings so I'd get them right when I painted him. Then he lost interest in me, and turned his attention to the rain lilies that stirred in the breeze.

A day or two later as I watered, I splashed a pot of purple alyssum and suddenly there was Lord Chapulin, indignant and glaring at me. Forget about your writing—complete my portrait.

That night when I went to plug in the lights under my car to ward off pack rats, in the beam of the flashlight I saw a team of brown ants struggling to carry a dead grasshopper that resembled the others, but this one was much smaller, with lighter yellow green hues on the outer wings, and light pink on the inner wings. The grasshoppers wouldn't last much longer.

The next morning I hurried back to the portrait before I forgot the pink hue, and I repainted the dark magenta on the portrait's inner wings with a light magenta pink—the effect was a rosy magenta. Perfect. Exactly what Chapulin desired. I knew what Chapulin desired because he communicated with certain thoughts that would cross my mind, thoughts about what he wanted for his portrait, thoughts he sent directly to me.

At one point I whited out a lot of a dark green color I didn't like, and Chapulin's portrait looked ghostly and I called it Ghost Grasshopper but I couldn't leave it that way. Chapulin wanted to be portrayed as he was in life, not death. Still, the grasshopper figure all in white on the red background looked really cool.

Lord Chapulin is secretive and mysterious. Those of his kind may appear only once in eighty-four years while others return in cycles of seven or twenty-one years. When the portrait was finally completed in the last week of October, I opened the front door one morning and there was Chapulin warming himself in the sunlight on the top branches of the greasewood bush that faced the studio window where his portrait sat. I watched him for a while to figure out whether he liked the portrait, but I couldn't be sure. So I turned back to paint the white flowers on his belt; as I touched up the green on the wings I felt such happiness and pleasure. Later when I looked out, he was gone.

I watched for Chapulin and the others whenever I watered. I even looked for dead grasshoppers, but they all were gone without a trace; carried off by the ants, scattered by the wind.

CHAPTER 35

On my walk this early October morning, two horsemen startled me. I didn't realize I walked in such a deep meditative state as I was down the trail to the big arroyo. I really had trouble coming back down to Earth. "Oh you startled me!" I said. Horses are so large I should have heard them or seen them sooner than I did. The riders seemed a little intoxicated by the power the horses gave them. I was reminded of a phrase in my new novella: the Spaniards in the New World had "the advantages of gunpowder, horses and dogs." I was glad I carried my ultralight five shot .38 revolver that day.

Encounters with wild beings aren't nearly as jarring probably because I am watching for the wild creatures but not expecting humans, like the two horsemen.

Later I met up with them in the hikers' parking lot; I'd managed to walk the same distance in the same amount of time as the horses.

I often think of Geronimo and his ragged band of women and children in their final years of resisting the U.S. troops. Five thousand of them had pursued forty or fifty Apaches, mostly women and children. The troops rode horses, while the Apaches traveled on foot. In the steep rocky terrain the horses were ineffective; they went lame and slowed the troops; if the Apaches got a horse they promptly butchered it and dried the meat. Travel on foot was the fastest way over the steep rocky trails of Sonora and Chihuahua.

Another turquoise rock washed out of the dirt in the back yard. The off-white limestone is about two inches by one half inch with odd deposits of turquoise in the moon-shaped indentations. "The end is broken off creating"—my notes are incomplete; I wonder if I can find this rock and complete the sentence. I turn to my collection of turquoise rocks. No labels, no plastic containers. Just handfuls of turquoise pebbles and rock fragments mixed with dust and paper clips on my desktop. Nothing.

Then to the other tables that I've covered with turquoise rocks; and from the description I wrote, I only had to pick up one other piece of rock before I spied the correct one. It is almost arrowhead-shaped with the point broken off. The off-white limestone appears pockmarked and in the tear-drop indentations in the limestone small spots of turquoise in calcite and metal salts are attached.

So I would end the unfinished sentence like this: "a resemblance to a broken arrow tip." The white limestone also has turquoise on the other side in a sort of cheesy-crust texture but with no eye-catchers like the pockmarks or moon craters with turquoise spots.

The turquoise is quite hard to scratch with a fingernail and is not chalky. My note continues: "The limestone is some of the whitest I've found to contain turquoise." Again comes the question—did it occur in the layers of whitish caliche on this hilltop or was it found elsewhere and brought up here by humans? Like the old trade beads I used to find in the back yard, like the other pieces of turquoise I had found in planters and clay pots and around the house while my broken foot healed.

On my walk this morning in the big arroyo I was thinking how delicious the cool air was, slightly moist; how when the time comes, I wanted my ashes scattered there and just at that instant I glanced down and there was a small turquoise stone.

On the past three walks, I've found no turquoise—pebbles or rocks. This points out how infrequent and how wonderful the discoveries of turquoise stones really are.

On the days I find no turquoise I appreciate how rare the stones are. Could they finally run out, be as exhausted and finite as other minerals have become? The next time I find a turquoise stone it will be in the big arroyo, probably in a place I've passed many times.

A speck of turquoise the size of a rice grain caught my eye; it was the only turquoise on a rock the size of a cantaloupe. I picked up the rock for a closer look at the speck of blue stone then I returned the rock to its resting place in its imprint in the sand.

I stopped to scrutinize the provocative shadows on the high mountain slopes of dark basalt in the shifting light; they might be caves or shafts of lost mines. In the shifting light of the desert, the wonder is that somehow it was visible at that moment but not at another.

The trail changes. Somehow the angles and the earth soften despite the dryness. Horses ridden in the big arroyo churn and crush the stones in the sand and free the turquoise nuggets. Otherwise the weight of the horses breaks the crust of the deep arroyo sand and requires far more effort for me to walk there.

My son Caz and I were digging a grave for our old black dog Dolly this late November day when I spied a piece of dark green malachite. It was the only pebble in four or five shovelfuls of dirt. The stone was the size and shape of a dove's heart. Dolly's farewell to me. The ghost dogs came to her for three nights while she was dying, and on the fourth night they took her home. We dug the grave just outside her beloved yard. She's not here anymore, but she's not far away.

The malachite stone is so smooth and polished; it seems out of place in the caliche. I couldn't miss the connection with Dolly because the stone is so far from the arroyo. The green is a sable green, dark but touched with red iron oxide just under the surface as Dolly herself was pure black but with a sable undertone. That was to make it clear the heart came from her, a gift to let me know she is safe and free now with the other ghost dogs, and every night she sleeps in her yard.

Spirits inhabit the same spaces, only they fit into dust motes so we can't see them and we think they aren't there, but of course they are, just in a different sort of space, not gone or destroyed.

For the past weeks that I did not work on the mural of Turquoise Man, I didn't find any turquoise rocks on my walks. Then the morning after I worked on the mural of Turquoise Man with special attention to many small turquoise cabochons on his bracelets and necklace, I found a fine oval nugget of turquoise chalcedony with a bit of iron, nestled in the sand between the arroyo rocks by the path in plain view—again was the turquoise nugget lying there all these weeks and I didn't see it or did it arrive overnight?

It all depends on how the light shines off the sand and the rocks in the arroyo, I decided. During the time of no turquoise I did see turquoise—a big rock which I left in the arroyo with five tiny turquoise bits the size of grains of sand—proof my eyes did detect even small bits of turquoise during that time.

I found a hand tool of gray basalt that fits in my palm with a groove pecked out—what for? A cradle where pebbles could be rolled and shaped into beads? A stone to shape arrow shafts? Maybe a stone to crush and mix paint—all traces of the mineral paint long ago washed away.

Yesterday I left on my walk later than usual, in the early afternoon. For the past two days clouds had filled the sky; they moved too high and too fast for rain, but kept the Sun covered and increased the humidity. I thought it was the afternoon light that made all the gray blue rocks appear more intensely blue but this morning I noticed that the turquoise rocks on my writing table absorbed the moisture from the clouds and their blue color intensified.

The turquoise only forms because water interacts with the calcite and the copper and aluminum. Raw turquoise and chrysocolla never stop absorbing moisture. The heavier, harder chrysocolla-impregnated chalcedony does not absorb moisture so dramatically.

I found a nice cabochon of turquoise today just after I realized that Turquoise Man and the mosaic turquoise mask at the British Museum are one and the same. I found another cabochon—malachite green, red iron and yellow with the small blue stone dotting the top of the malachite. I found a rough stony turquoise rock with a lovely mountain scene in all shades of blue green—lichen green mountain slopes, and a sunset sky of pale orange limestone.

As I age, I appreciate how the old women in my family felt about their run-down houses: let it stay with its leaks and holes until I'm gone and then they may tear it down. Years ago my friend Mei-Mei told me about an old man who owned thirty-five acres in the middle of downtown Scottsdale, most of it planted in grapefruit trees. In the winter he sold the grapefruit in front of his driveway. The roof in his big old hacienda style house leaked terribly, so he bought rolls of clear plastic sheeting at the lumber store and nailed drapes of plastic across the ceiling over his bed.

"8:30 Coyote" shows up twice a day, usually twelve hours apart, to tease the big dogs. The mastiffs bark madly but the coyote saunters to the water pan; Coyote has a lovely tail, wide and full, glossy and thick, though it is only of average size or even a bit smaller. A yearling female perhaps, but such a nice coat—usually yearlings struggle their first year.

In the big arroyo near a natural stone step that makes a sort of cradle for the finest sand I found a tiny nugget of turquoise that stood out in the grayish white wash sand. In its journey down the big arroyo, the mother rock that bore the turquoise nugget got worn away or crushed down into pieces and finally the last piece of mother stone broke away and the tiny but solid nugget of turquoise continued the journey alone, polished by the fine sand in the rushing water.

The turquoise diggings near Cerillos, New Mexico are called Mount Chalchihuitl. "Chalchihuitl" is the Nahua word for jade. Chalchihuitl supplied most of the turquoise used in the famous Mixtec and Nahua turquoise mosaics.

This turquoise may explain the huge pueblo located just west of the diggings, on the flat grassy plateau not far from Santa Fe. With eighty kivas and eighty plazas, this pueblo's size is comparable to Aztec and Maya cities. Turquoise financed the great pueblo that lies undisturbed under the sand.

The mine at Chalchihuitl did not require earth-moving machines or destruction to obtain the turquoise. The ancient people used to pour water into the rock that held the turquoise and overnight the water would freeze and shatter the rock holding the turquoise. People picked it up from the ground. The ledge at Chalchihuitl still yields turquoise after nearly a thousand years.

Such a large pre-Columbian city near Santa Fe helps solidify the Nahua claim to the four corner states of Arizona, New Mexico, Utah and Colorado. A barrio in Santa Fe is named Tlalacan—supposedly for the Tlalacans who came with the Spaniards. But suppose there were Tlalacans already in the Santa Fe area long before the Spaniards because of the turquoise trade?

Here where the turquoise exposes itself, and can be found on the surface, the small bits don't matter because the mosaic makers must break the turquoise into small pieces anyway.

When I was a child, people at Laguna and people in the Spanish-speaking villages nearby used to paint the doors and window frames of their houses bright turquoise blue to keep away witches. The Spanish-speaking people used to save the bright blue stamps that sealed the Bull Durham tobacco bags, and whenever they had headaches they wore the bright blue stamps on their foreheads to stop the pain.

PART FOUR

Turquoise

CHAPTER 36

The steep slope of the basalt ridge below the old Thunderbird Mine shaft showed me an amazing bobcat years ago as I rode my horse, but also the Gila monster, and only recently the maroon red horned lizard. Why might I notice more wonderful beings here than other spots?

Maybe the steep slope slowed the horses I rode and I had time to observe my surroundings more closely; now when I walk, the slope slows me down so it is possible to see more of what is alive in the world.

On the hillside, some distance from the big arroyo, near the ant palace, I found a piece of turquoise rock. Does this mean there is a turquoise ledge up here somewhere too?

It's mid-November and the bees are back. The wild Sonoran honeybees migrate with the hummingbirds. The bees' return coincided with the return of my long-time friend, the male white-eared hummingbird. During the hot weather months, the bees and hummingbirds migrate to the mountains. At least a dozen varieties of hummingbirds may be seen at Ramsey Canyon in the mountains near Sierra Vista in the summer months. Now that the weather here has cooled off, they are back.

The wild bees also flock to my garden of flowerpots under the big mesquite tree next to my front porch. The bees are hungry and thirsty; they frantically swarm over the hummingbird feeders. Wherever there is shade and water a great many desert creatures come to find comfort so

I'm careful to keep the ceramic water pots away from the paths because they attract rattlesnakes.

The bees and I have known one another for a long time. We first met when I used to have water hyacinths in the rainwater pool. I never harm them intentionally and they never sting me intentionally though of course accidents occur from time to time, but we harbor no hard feelings.

I wasn't thinking of the wild bees when I filled the pots with water. I was thinking of the rattlesnakes that look for water; I hoped the rattlers would water out in the yard, and not at the dogs' water bucket next to the front door. The bees came and began to swarm around the water bowls. The bees were unfamiliar with the water bowls and a great many fell into the water and buzzed like speed boats on the surface until they reached the side or drowned. I rescued them with twigs and leaves.

The black plastic lotus tub I keep for my old pit bull to cool herself in exerts a magnetic attraction and many bees drown. I look at the other bees for their reactions to the plights of their fellow workers. They seem unconcerned about the bees in trouble in the water. The drowning bees pile on top of one another to create a staircase out of the bodies of their comrades. I saved bees only to watch them fly and land in the water again, but others seem to learn caution and to be tentative at water's edge. The commotion warns the other bees to be careful.

Later I hung out the hummingbird feeders so now the wild bees know me best as the one who brings sugar water. The wild bees vie with the woodpeckers and hummingbirds for a turn at the sugar water.

The wild bees sometimes fly in front of my face, intently but without hostility; recently I read that animal intelligence researchers had determined that domesticated bees learn to recognize the faces of those who bring them sugar water. Now I feel no apprehension when the bees fly near my face because I know they are only trying to identify me.

In Chiapas, Mexico the wild honeybees are docile and at ease around people. In the market in San Cristobol de las Casas the bees landed and crawled over the trays of creamy sugar candies and the candy sellers made no move to shoo them until a customer bought a piece of candy.

Around the world recently the keepers of domestic bees report empty hives. No dead bees are found, yet they are gone. After these reports, I worried the wild bees here might also disappear, so I began to pay more attention to them.

First came the sound. A faint hum that rapidly became louder. I knew what to look for: a great swarm of bees because once before I'd heard the sound and saw a great swarm of bumblebees flying very fast. I estimated their speed at forty or fifty miles per hour. This morning the swarm was honey bees, only half the size of the bumblebees but they flew even faster. Both swarms of bees I saw flew from north to south.

Around the time of the first rains in April, the wild bees stopped visiting the hummingbird feeders; I hoped they were merely harvesting the mesquite and catsclaw in bloom then.

After rain the hummingbirds and even the Gila woodpeckers quit drinking the sugar water I offer because the desert pollens and tiny insects hatched by the rain are far more tasty and nutritious than sugar water.

This morning the sunlight caught a piece of glass near the place the javelina have their celebrations after the rain, not far from the Gila Monster Mine. I picked up the glass and it was a five inch clear piece sharp as a dagger. I carried it in my pocket for a while but later lost it in the big arroyo. I found a wonderful nearly round malachite blue stone the size of a quail's egg.

According to Nahua tradition, there are four Tlaloc or Lords of the Rain who control the precipitation. The Tlaloc reside on mountaintops and in caves. They brew rain or hail and snow in great vats on the mountaintops at night. The Tlaloc also reside in Tlalocan, the Watery Flowery Heaven where only a few are on the list to join them there: warriors, women who died in childbirth, people with stunted growth, the handicapped, those with leprosy or dropsy or gout and those who drowned or were struck by lightning went to Tlalocan. It was said that those who hoarded turquoise died by lightning or drowning. I wonder if I'm hoarding turquoise by keeping the stones and pebbles I find on my walks? I prefer to think that writing about the stones is a way to share the turquoise.

On my walk early this morning the air was so invigorating and the desert plants so lush, and the green blue light so beautiful with the sun behind the mountain that I made up a song as I walked down the long steep hill below the Thunderbird Mine:

> beauty beauty
> beauty beauty
> beauty beauty
> as I go oooooooh.
> Heyah! Heyah Heyah Heyah ah ah!

I can spot the grains of turquoise on a rock the size of a bread loaf even when there's only one or two grains the size of a particle of sand. I picked up the rock to look then I replaced it so it would continue to make grains of turquoise.

I'd been cleaning the parrot patio and had left the front gate unlocked because I intended to do some more sweeping and removal of debris. I knew the gate was unlocked when I let the two blue and gold macaws loose in the patio enclosure with the caged cockatoos, but the macaws had not opened it for months because I kept it chained and locked. I thought they'd given up testing the gate. I looped the chain through the gate loosely.

When Bill and I returned from town with groceries around three-thirty p.m. the macaws had worked loose the chain and the patio gate was open. Brittney was clinging to the gate but her long-time companion, Rudy Scruffy, was gone.

I ran around the house and checked all the trees in the yards for the macaw, but no luck. The sun had already dropped behind the foothills west of the house.

First I walked north and east to the vacant property suddenly abandoned this last spring. I walked toward the tallest trees in the area because macaw keepers will tell you the macaws fly to the highest point when they escape.

The lost macaw is turquoise blue and bright yellow. I walked around the empty house and called the macaw's name. A heavy silence pervaded the place. The house belonged to ghosts. It is too old and too small. The new buyers will demolish it. I checked the tall mesquites and palo verdes near the house but saw no macaw. I began to walk rapidly back up the hill to the house.

I checked on Brittney, the remaining blue and gold macaw. She wasn't eating because she was upset her companion was gone. I saw a dead dove in the macaw cage and surmised that after the macaws opened the outer gate to the aviary, wild doves went inside to eat the scattered seed and the old pit bull trapped a dove in the macaw cage and killed it. The ruckus of the dog after the dove would have caused the macaws to screech so loudly the dog would have had to retreat, in the process dropping the dove.

I almost didn't dispose of the dead dove because the sun was down and it would be dark before long. I regretted so much my carelessness with the chain and lock on the gate. I felt sorry for the lone bird; I didn't want to leave the dead dove in the cage overnight.

I removed it and thought about tossing it down the hillside just outside the yard where scavengers would find it. But I didn't want to attract scavengers near the house at night because that would cause the dogs to bark and howl in the middle of the night. So I took the dead dove down the hill to the area a little north of the corrals and I left it for the hungry scavengers.

I don't know why I had the impulse to continue walking past the corrals into the palo verde. A better use of my time would have been to go back into the house and begin to make LOST PARROT posters to hang in the neighborhood. The sun was behind the mountains now and everything was in heavy shadow. I didn't think she'd gone down below the house but I searched there anyway. I found nothing near the water trough or on the roofs of the outbuildings. I walked farther behind the west side of the old corral into the palo verde trees toward the fence and hikers' parking lot although I didn't think she'd be there.

Then straight ahead of me on a lower branch of a big palo verde tree I saw her. It was as if the macaw brought me directly to her. All these months of training my peripheral, unfocused vision to note turquoise in all its shades had helped me spot the lost turquoise and yellow macaw despite the approaching darkness. She had chosen a palo verde tree and a low branch so the hawks and owls could not see her, but I might. She had remained close to the parking lot for the hikers where the cars and human activity would keep the predators away until night fell. She was very anxious to climb onto my arm and held on firmly. She did not try to fly away even when Bill drove up the driveway behind us.

CHAPTER 37

t crossed my mind that I might live on top of a turquoise ledge but I dismissed the thought and now here was evidence again. Recently there was the marble of turquoise where the hole for the power pole had been bored down, and then the sliver of calcite with a splash of turquoise from the ground in front of the gate to the front yard.

I was with Robert looking for possible locations for a house so I went into the old circular corral. At one time it was made the old-fashioned Sonoran way with long mesquite poles stacked and woven together as the ends. I noticed an outcrop of rock.

The rock outcrop must have been covered with dirt those years I kept horses in the round corral. I know I would have noticed the outcrop with the thin streak of turquoise across it. It took seventy or eighty years of horse and cattle hooves pounding the corral ground, which wore away the bluish gray basalt that surrounds the white layers of calcites, to expose the bright spot of turquoise. Here is another turquoise ledge.

By the end of the year I realized there were turquoise ledges right here on this hilltop—out back where I found the malachite or green chalcedony when we buried Dolly. All this time I was thinking about a great ledge of solid turquoise somewhere up the big arroyo in the mountains, while a ledge was here, right under my nose, right under my house.

On the eve of the winter solstice a magical thing: I found a small turquoise stone on the closet floor of my bedroom.

Not long afterward, I was walking down the west side slope below the house to check my trashmidden. I was looking down for trash when I spotted a caliche outcrop that was secreting turquoise of a bright deep blue—no green tones at all. The color was more pure bright blue than any of the turquoise rocks from the big arroyo. This is how the year of walks ends.

On New Year's Day 2008 I went for a walk to the big arroyo and found more boulders and sand removed with a great deal more damage done to the big arroyo by the man and his machine. Only now, eleven days later, do I feel like writing about it.

I regretted I had not reported the original incident in July—broken foot or no broken foot. The gray basalt and quartzite boulders might have been saved from destruction and the small creatures in underground nests—the lizards, snakes, tortoises and tiny owls—might not have been crushed under the wheels of the machine.

I kept thinking if only I had said something in July; instead I gave in to my misgivings about the indifference and ineptitude of the local county government. A special buffer zone which extended out a mile from the Saguaro National Park might have protected the boulders if I'd acted.

On January 3, I made the first call to report the new damage. The Pima County Environmental Protection Agency office is part of Pima County Development Services. This alone should have prepared me for what followed.

The Pima County EPA informed me they didn't have jurisdiction over the strip mining of desert arroyos for aggregates no matter how close to the buffer zone of Saguaro National Park. They directed me to the Floodplain Management Division.

Ah yes! I thought. Of course this damage affects the floodplain. The removal of the boulders, rocks and sand accelerated erosion—that lovely mesquite tree whose roots had helped stabilize the sides of the arroyo was about to topple in the next rainstorm because the man and machine had gouged out the rocks and sand at its base. Without the boulders, the runoff flowed faster and there was nothing to slow it—no sandbars to hold the precious rainwater so it could soak in.

A Floodplain Division hydrologist paid the arroyo a visit and reported the damage she found was "not significant." Now I was beginning to understand why much of the landscape in Pima County looks the way it does—trashed and ruined.

As I was writing this and going about my routine on the morning of January 11, 2008, I had no idea that just outside three of my military macaws had been attacked by owls before dawn.

I had bought Sandino twenty years ago as a mate for my first military macaw, a hen named Paco. My other military macaws were birds I had rescued in one way or other. They are big wonderful birds but they are predominantly green and not as lucrative for sellers as the scarlet or blue and gold macaws. A few years ago breeders in the Tucson area had begun to get rid of them. I felt badly to see the birds go unwanted so in 2003, I bought a pair for $500, from a veteran with Gulf War illness who could no longer keep them. Prophecy Bird came with a mate but she later died.

My nickname for Prophecy Bird was the "Hello Bird" because he was able to say "hello" a dozen different ways in higher or lower tones, faster or slower. Sometimes he allowed me to touch his head or wings—he'd been a pet at one time—he could be quick with his beak but he never behaved aggressively when I went inside his cage. I called him Prophecy Bird because often I heard him talk a great deal; sometimes he conducted both sides of a conversation but I was seldom able to hear clearly what he said.

I bought the other macaws—Bolee and her three chicks—in the spring of 2004 from a local parrot breeder. Bolee's mate had died the previous year. I really only wanted the hen, Bolee, as a companion for my military macaw Sandino, but the breeder would only sell them as a "package." Sandino had been without a mate much longer than Prophecy Bird had. I planned to get him a new mate next.

I put Bolee in the six foot by twelve foot aviary with Sandino; and the three youngest birds, Tony, Binny and Sugar, I put in the biggest aviary, the fourteen foot octagon, to be nearby their mother, Bolee. The diameter and height of the aviary saved the lives of the three young macaws the night the owls came.

During the cool weather months I sometimes delayed feeding and watering the birds until the afternoon so I might have the morning hours to write. I went from writing and working on this manuscript to binding a copy of my new novella, *Ocean Story*, for my sister Wendy on her upcoming birthday January 18.

Finally at around four-thirty that afternoon of January 11, I went out to the aviaries. I noticed something was wrong right away because Prophecy Bird wasn't there to greet me. I walked over to his aviary and the first thing I saw was a severed foot in the middle of the floor of the cage and a pool of blood. I knew at once it was an owl attack. I was heartsick.

I expected to find him dead in the nest box, but he was still alive. I tried to get him out of the box but he turned away to a corner to let me know he just wanted to be left as he was. The sun was behind the mountains. I had to think what to do. I left Prophecy Bird in his nest box and went to feed and water the other macaws in their aviaries.

I saw Bolee, the military macaw hen, at the back of the cage on the floor. That was unusual for her to be standing on the floor, but when I looked more closely I was horrified to see that Bolee was dead but not lying down. She had spread wide her lovely wings a last time for balance because both her legs were gone; she held the cage wire in her beak to steady herself as she died. It took me awhile to loosen her beak from the wire so I could bury her.

I think Bolee fought to her death to keep the owls away from her three offspring in the octagon aviary next to hers. All my attention was on her so I didn't notice Sandino had lost a leg.

I was in shock. I had to take care of Prophecy Bird, but I already had a sad feeling that he was dying. I went and got a ladder and a towel to wrap around him to catch him. I saw he was in the corner of the barrel, his back to me, and when I made an attempt to put the towel around him to pick him up he turned back twice as if to beg me please to let him be, to let him go in peace.

Sandino seemed o.k. Healthy parrots perch on one leg—in the twilight I couldn't see his injury. I set up a light near the octagon aviary to discourage owls that night. I had a feeling Prophecy Bird would die that night.

The next morning I found poor Prophecy Bird dead in his oak box and buried him. I loved him dearly and even now I miss him. As I walked back from the grave, I took a look at Sandino in the aviary and it was then I finally saw the jagged ends of the leg bone, and realized he had lost a leg in the owl attack.

Sandino had pretended to be o.k. and had fooled me as he hoped to fool predators. I don't know why Sandino didn't die of shock as Bolee and Prophecy Bird had. I felt so badly I had overlooked the terrible injury; but maybe it was good that Sandino had the night to stabilize before he faced the vet office and the surgery.

The orthopedic vet who amputated the remains of the leg was experienced with large birds. He'd seen similar injuries in the Harris hawks and red-tail hawks the State Fish and Game officers brought for treatment. Great horned owls tore the wings off red-tail hawks and falcons, and sometimes their feet.

Twenty-four hours later I brought Sandino home to a different life. I put a macaw cage in my bedroom because it was the warmest room in the house; I wanted Sandino nearby so he knew how much I loved him—I was determined that he survive.

I called my son Caz, who helped me fortify the octagon aviary with hardware cloth and layers of shade cloth to further protect the three young macaws in case the owls returned. I hooked up a light and left on a radio tuned to a talk show station to discourage the owls at night.

For eighteen years I had kept macaws in aviaries outside without any trouble. The great horned owls often came around my house at night, and I loved to hear their HOOO! HOOO! Sometimes I found an owl feather at the water dish near the aviaries, but they never bothered the macaws. Not long before the attack, I'd seen a large handsome horned owl on the top of the utility pole near the big arroyo. There were so many rodents at night for the owls to eat, I didn't worry, I never dreamed the owls would choose the macaws instead. But in those eighteen years a great deal had changed as the city sprawled across the desert.

That the owls attacked not one but two aviaries in the same night seemed excessive until I thought about it. I recalled the strange uncomfortable energy in the atmosphere here in the hills in the days after I had found the new damage in the arroyo and made the phone calls to the local authorities.

The big arroyo itself is an ecosystem. The animals and humans use the arroyo as a way to traverse the steep rough terrain of the cerros and basalt ridges. Large arroyos may cross private property but the wildlife and pedestrians and equestrians have a right of way to pass through the arroyo; no fences or dams or other obstructions are permitted. Because runoff water concentrates in the arroyo, the wildlife of the desert gravitate there to feed or hunt. The excavating machine not only tore up the boulders, it disrupted the entire area, and left many creatures homeless as well as hungry and thirsty.

The suffering and distress of so many living beings from the same location of the desert created an anxious angry energy of conflict that permeated the area. I felt it strongly; the disturbance was real and pervasive, even on a psychic level. The fury of the owls was powerful, but the man with the machine was full of fury as well.

January is the month the birds and animals give birth and raise their young ahead of the brutal summer heat. The pair of owls killed my macaws to feed their owlets. If the owls had been able to find game elsewhere they would have done so, but the big construction boom with cheap mortgage money had brought the bulldozers to the desert hills to crush and scrape the earth for grotesque mansions where the owls once hunted.

The machines dug up the earth and destroyed the nests of rodents and birds in the owls' habitat, and disrupted hunting and water sources. The bulldozers sent the hungry owls to find food for their nestlings in my aviaries. I love the great horned owls; I don't blame the owls for the attack on my macaws, I blame the men in the bulldozers who crush the desert. I blame the imbeciles in Pima County government who fail at everything except collecting taxes and bribes.

The strange angry energy loose in the Tucson Mountains in early January was also fed by the machine man's anger at the visits from the county authorities. He tolerated no interference from any government; he was a law unto himself.

Six or seven days after the owl attack, Bill and I were awakened one night by a loud sound that shook the bedroom. It felt and sounded as if some large object had hit the wall outside the east-facing window. Whatever it was struck the wall about seven feet above the ground.

Bill went back to sleep, and it was then I realized something strange was going on—not of this world because the four mastiffs outside the bedroom door had slept through the loud thud of the object that hit the side of the house. The dogs' self-preservation instincts kept them safely asleep as the wild violent force raged outside the house.

I got up and in the bathroom I was able to hear a sound from outside the east-facing wall but as if no interior walls or exterior wall existed. It seemed like the low guttural canine sound of a growl just before it turned into a howl. The word "werewolf" at once came to mind.

The odd energy came in a straight line from the site of destruction in the big arroyo east of my house.

The four dogs remained asleep. I went back to bed. I wasn't afraid because all nine of the Star Being portraits were facing the east that night, and protected the house from the "werewolf energy" sent my way by the machine man.

After the owl attack I was too sick over the loss of Prophecy Bird and Bolee, and too anxious about Sandino's survival, to think about writing. I had to give Sandino antibiotics twice a day so I stopped my walk so I'd be there at the right times. I wasn't able to write or paint or do anything but check on the remaining macaws and watch television, which served as a kind of narcotic.

The owls attacked the macaws on January 11 but I wasn't able to bring myself to write about it for months. When my beloved grandpa Hank died, it took more than ten years before I was able to write about the morning he passed away, in the poem titled "Deer Dance/For Your Return."

I was fourteen years old the morning Grandpa had the heart attack. We were all together that morning: my younger sisters, my parents, and Grandma Lillie. I was the only one of them who knew mouth to mouth resuscitation; in the early 1960s, Laguna Pueblo had no ambulance or emergency room. The U.S. Indian Health Service doctor lived a half hour away. I did my best, but Grandpa's jaws were clenched shut and I could not open them; I think he was already gone.

After the doctor got there, he pounded on Grandpa's chest so hard I heard ribs break. Grandpa was only sixty-nine, and had never been sick or had any symptoms or bad habits other than he smoked two packs of Camels a day. He'd never been inside a hospital in his life, so it was just as well he left the way he did that morning. His death ended the happiness of my childhood; the family slowly unraveled after that.

CHAPTER 38

The portraits of the Star Beings gave way to what I call star maps, but maybe these are just group portraits of the Star Beings. There are billions of galaxies so I figure somewhere in the Universe there is a galaxy that matches the star map I've just painted.

The portrait of Lord Chapulin turned out very well. Could he be an associate of the Star Beings?

The first two pieces of turquoise stone I found on my next walk were scarcely streaked with turquoise but that meant my eye for turquoise hadn't lost its accuracy during my lay-off. The third piece I found is the size of a sparrow egg, though not so egg shaped as seed shaped.

Before the last storm I worried the buds on the jojoba might freeze but it was a warm rain with no frost. Now I see purple ajo flowers on tall slender stems across the hillsides; on the ground tiny red and white flowers form lacy mats that are fringed with tiny green leaves.

In the big arroyo I found a small piece of light gray feldspar the size of a quarter with a turquoise spot in the shape of a soaring condor.

The breeze is cool despite the sunshine of this lovely day in February. Purple blue lily-shaped flowers of the ajo, the wild garlic, are the first to push up through the soil. The hungry creatures depend on tasty little bulbs. The yellow gold desert poppy flowers are the size of hen's eggs this year but they aren't as numerous as in 1978, my first year in Tucson.

Once in a hundred years you might see the hills solid blue with desert lupines, solid gold yellow with desert poppies as they were in 1978. I had moved to Tucson only a few months before, so I had no prior experience with which to compare the lush abundance of blossoms of all kinds. Over the years I realized how singular the wild-flower bloom in 1978 was.

On the long steep hill below the Thunderbird Mine something darted off the trail to my left. A lizard. But when I reached him I saw it was a special lizard, a horned lizard the size of a half dollar, no larger, but it was the most amazing color I've ever seen for a horned lizard—an intense iridescent red orange and magenta red orange—the same red orange as the streak of iron in the limestone and clay on the hillside where the trail passes. When I moved closer to get a better look it became frightened and hurried under a gray leaf burr sage. I immediately regretted the move; next time I'll remain motionless.

I spent two days assembling the new cage for Sandino, the one-legged macaw. I covered the wooden perches with soft old towels to protect his remaining foot before I moved him into the cage. He's got a red spot on his heel. The vet warned me about sores on the remaining foot and toes. I hope it's just the new cage and new perches and not something I failed to notice sooner.

Later I walked and in the big arroyo I found a rock streaked with turquoise where I've walked many times before; only today the light made the turquoise rock visible. It's a slender outcrop of reddish brown limestone about four inches long and the strands of green blue and blue are a half inch wide. I stacked up three flat rocks on the side of the arroyo to mark the place. Was this part of a turquoise ledge?

On my walk in the big arroyo the next day I found three turquoise stones—a green blue stone, triangular and the size of a parrot egg, and two others more blue turquoise, one on a rust orange stone the size of a sunflower seed that is speckled with turquoise, and the other a tiny sliver of pure blue turquoise no larger than a grain of rice.

Here are the turquoise ledges I've located so far:

Right at the front gate to my house there is a gray basalt rock with a trace of lime or calcium carbonate with four tiny scattered deposits of turquoise. My earlier suspicions of a ledge here when I found stones in the back yard in July and August were confirmed. A week or two ago, below the house, on the steep west slope I found small pieces of bright blue calcium carbonate cabochons on a wafer thin ledge of calcite.

In the old round corral last December I found a ledge with a bit of turquoise made visible after years of rain eroded the ground broken by horses in steel shoes. So I've learned that I'm surrounded by turquoise ledges. The water in the big arroyo means the ledges there may be larger.

The really huge fat red diamondback appeared this morning, the last day of February. "Dove Eater" I call it. The snake was on the move, and later, from the Weather Channel I learned a late winter storm was moving in from the north.

The desert is green and brushy from all the rain this year. The curved beak thrashers and the cactus wrens are whistling deliriously with joy; so many seeds will follow these blossoms that bud overnight in the gentle warm rain.

It rained before dawn so this morning the telephone doesn't work because the wire to the house is old and gets wet. The satellite Internet is out because of the thick clouds between the relay tower on the mountain ridge and the satellite. When it rains one should hang out wool rugs and wool clothing for a wash. I brought out both of my Guatemalan woven palm leaf sombreros which require rainwater twice a summer at least or the crowns of the hats will crumble.

I was thinking about my birthday that comes in three days, on March 5. I looked at a star map to see what stars and constellations were overhead when I was born: the planet Venus was spectacularly high in the west horizon. Also present: Sirius, the Dog Star forty times brighter than the Sun, Hydra the Snake constellation with Alphard the solitary star halfway up the snake's neck; blue Regulus brighter and hotter than the Sun; and Pollux and Castor, bright eyes of a great serpent.

Sirius is one of the Star Beings who peeps in the west windows on long winter nights after big Venus is finished spying.

The wild flowers are more numerous than they've been in years. The gold yellow desert poppies are pools of color in the emerald and jade green of the desert. The white six-pointed Mojave desert stars blossom first on the purple blue outcropping of rocks and form great constellations on the dark stone. Desert chicory send up big white ruffled flowers amid the jojoba leaves that shade them. Yellow fiddle necks, taller larger purple frills, and the twin blue violet lily-like flowers of the ajo are also in bloom.

Lupines lupines lupines purple red blue—even taller than the orange poppies. Tiny yellow flowers of the goldenrod fill the air with the scent of honey. White desert zinnias bloom early and so does the rattlesnake weed with its small blankets of tiny calico red and white flowers.

Everywhere I see the tall stalks of white penstemons that cover the rocky hillsides—the pink and purple penstemons only bloom in sandy moist arroyos.

I found a small piece of white glass, polished smooth by years of tumbling down the arroyo over the sharp edges of rocks and sand until it almost looks like quartz crystal. I found a piece of reddish gray basalt with white calcite crystals in its center like an eye. I spied a bright bit of turquoise in the center of a bean-size reddish pebble.

Today, March 5, 2008 I am sixty years old. My mother and I shared this birthday and used to celebrate our birthdays together whenever we could. So I think about her today.

On my walk this morning I found no turquoise in the big arroyo but did find a piece of turquoise rock at the foot of my driveway, near the small outcrop of turquoise in the round corral.

On my walk this morning I kept thinking about the digital camera and taking pictures of the backlit wild flowers and saguaros as I walked. That spoils the walk. And thinking about what things on my walk I will write about later spoils the walk. No camera, no notebook on the walk. What I can't remember without a notebook, and what I can't describe without a photo, may come back to me sometime when I'm writing or dreaming.

After I'd been finding the turquoise stones for a while it occurred to me that I should have kept a record of where I found them, bagging each stone and labeling it with the location and date, so if there were a clustering of finds I could focus my search there.

Instead I bring them home and put them on my writing desk, until I write about the walk where I picked them up. I don't keep them in boxes because I like to see the turquoise rocks together, in the air and light. I can identify many of the pieces when I handle them because I wrote about them.

The walks are my cardiovascular workout so I don't break the pace of them to slow or linger over an area to try to find special stones. They have to catch my eye despite the pace; I try not to break stride when I pick up the pieces of turquoise. I find that I go into a different state of consciousness when I walk—almost like a trance in which I'm not fully aware of where exactly in the big arroyo I found them.

I read about the trance-walking the Buddhist monks in Tibet used to perform; a tall dark haired white man used to run the Tucson Mountain trails in a trance. I saw him pass by for a couple of years; the local weekly paper did an article about him and then he was gone. Maybe he was training for running in Nepal and needed to live at a higher altitude, say Santa Fe or Albuquerque.

You watch strangers for years and you begin to expect to see them but then they disappear and you wonder what happened. In communities like Laguna-Acoma and the land grant villages, the news always got around and you heard what happened to people you'd seen come and go but didn't really know. Out here in the wilds of the wider world, people disappear and you never hear of them again.

Old René was a Tohono O'Odom wood seller who came every year, sometimes more often, to sell me loads of mesquite firewood. He was from the village of Santa Ana west of Sonoita, Sonora but it was my impression that he hauled the mesquite from somewhere south of Sasabe. He and I both were happy when he became my exclusive wood seller. He always brought big loads of wood with good-sized pieces, not just small branches and twigs, the way some wood sellers did. Sometimes in the summer he'd appear without warning in my driveway with firewood because he needed cash for some family emergency. Then like now, the people didn't have a lot of cash; the gambling business of the tribe hasn't really changed that.

One time he arrived at the bottom of the hill unexpectedly while I was here alone. Right as he honked his truck horn, I was trying to glue a small cherry wood bench I managed to put together from a kit. I had no way to prop up the glued wood and I couldn't let go until the glue set a bit or it would be ruined. By the time I put down the glued wood and went down the hill, René had already left.

The next time he telephoned, and I bought a two cord load of mesquite. As he unloaded the wood, I noticed a change—he was still a big man but this time he was short of breath and had to stop each time after he threw a few pieces of wood out of the back of the pick-up. I could see his health wasn't good. He offered to stack the wood for me but I told him I wanted to stack it for the exercise. I always paid him what he asked and that day I didn't have the right change and neither did he so I told him to keep the $10. I never saw him again.

CHAPTER 39

S andino seemed to recover from the surgery. I watched him and could not decide if he was energetic or strong enough to play with the toys I had hung inside his cage with him. Sandino had always lived with a mate in a large outdoor aviary, so I had no way of knowing what was normal behavior for him indoors. But he ate well, and I kept my thoughts positive.

I watched his remaining foot closely; if anything happened to the foot a serious parrot disease called bumblefoot might set in as a result. I worried about a small red mark on his foot I noticed in February. I decided I wanted the new vet to take a look.

I called a parrot veterinarian, Dr. Samuels, that my friend Nate recommended. By great good fortune he had a cancellation for the following Monday at eleven a.m. Before he examined Sandino, I explained the owl attacks to Dr. Samuels. When he saw how traumatized and sad the attacks had left me, he was kind enough to respond with this story:

When he first moved to Arizona, he lived near Prescott and raised Amazon parrots in outdoor aviaries. Parrots began to disappear while he was away at work. He lost a number of birds and thought it must be the neighborhood children who were opening the cage doors. One afternoon he returned home early and he caught two red-tail hawks attacking a parrot, trying to pull it out of the cage. It had been the hawks, not neighborhood children, that took his parrots.

The red mark on the macaw's remaining foot was a callus and meant nothing. But Dr. Samuels weighed Sandino and found the macaw was terribly wasted despite his good appetite and high spirits. He found signs of an infection inside the site of the leg amputation. The vet said the infection inside the leg wound was "devouring" all the nourishment from any food Sandino ate.

I was sick with regret. I delayed the return vet visit so I could focus on the manuscript. Now it sounded and felt to me that my beloved Sandino, dear friend for eighteen years, might die because of my inattention.

Dr. Samuels said he felt cautiously optimistic he could save Sandino. Sandino was in high spirits; I could tell he wanted to live. I told the vet I had a good feeling about the bird's survival, to go ahead with the surgery.

The vet called me at home when the surgery was completed. Sandino got through the operation just fine although it was in the nick of time because the infection had nearly spread to the bone. He prescribed a different antibiotic than the first vet, and I became an expert at administering the medicine to make certain the macaw took all of it.

Yesterday I walked the trail for the first time in weeks since the loss of the macaws and my periodontal surgery. I was thinking about how many pieces of turquoise I had gathered, so many that they cover even the surfaces of my writing tablet and work areas, but when my eyes caught a glimpse of turquoise I had to pick up the rock. It is intensely turquoise blue green and the size of my thumb, in the shape of a scrotum.

Now with the rain and cooler nights, the seeds of more wild flowers are bound to swell with moisture and sprout. Spring out. The wild flowers are dancers honoring the Sun and the Earth. The white chicory wore a large white hat that honored the white light of the Sun; others were slender green dancers with purple feathery hats. The frilly full dresses of the arroyo lupines required no hats or headdresses. The desert sennas wore flowery masks of white and yellow petals.

Today one of the turquoise rocks leapt from the top of the fireproof file cabinet to the floor. When I picked it up I saw it was the most lifelike of any. When viewed from left to right it looked like the head and neck of a great rattlesnake; when viewed from right to left, it was the head and neck of a great ancient dragon of goodness and great good fortune revered by the old Chinese. I found this piece of turquoise rock at the foot of the driveway, near the turquoise outcropping of the old corral.

Oh here comes the light gray foggy rain shimmering across the hilltops in the breeze.

Today I went down the steep slope west of the house. I wanted to check out the turquoise formation I found at the base of the west slope and while I was looking for it, two bright blue soft stone turquoise pieces caught my eye. About twelve feet farther down the slope I relocated the ledge of calcite that is making chrysocolla right now.

The two cabochons I thought were turquoise because they are green blue and so hard turn out to be "chrysocolla-impregnated chalcedony" according to the Smithsonian book *Rock and Gem*. Chalcedony is quartz that was compressed while it was cooling so it's harder than turquoise. Also there are iron pyrites in the two cabochons so they give the appearance of coming from the same source.

It's late March now. Last week I found no turquoise in the big arroyo. All the lovely wild flowers with their incandescent greens caught my eyes, and they're all I could see. I got home and right at my front gate, where the path I walk every day is eroded, I glanced down and there was a bit of turquoise rock in a very hard white calcite chip about an inch long and a quarter of an inch wide.

Where the trail crosses the small arroyo with the black rock, I found a large piece of old glass that nearly filled the palm of my hand. Its edges were completely sandblasted and smoothed. In the beginning, the piece of glass must have been the size and thickness of the bottom of a mason jar. The jar came from one of the old ranch dumps from the early 1900s. The shard of glass traveled with the rainwater down the hillside from the ranch house. Once in the small arroyo the piece of glass was tumbled smooth in the arroyo sand and heated by the sun for eighty years and was transformed from transparent glass to a pale aquamarine opalescent glass that had the appearance of a natural mineral, no longer "man-made."

On the trail before the Thunderbird Mine, I stopped to blow my nose and up jumped an astonished mule deer doe that stared at me wide-eyed before she vanished into the flowering palo verde forest dense with yellow blossoms.

I didn't find any turquoise rocks because the early light was diffuse. I picked up shards of broken bottle glass. Then in the big arroyo I heard rocks crashing and I stopped and turned and there she was again, the same doe, staring at me, and I at her. We both had made half a circle and met up again.

I turned and continued on to show her I meant no harm.

Backlit by the rising sun, even the dry grass stalks and empty seedpods glitter; the spines of the saguaro and cholla are incandescent in the early light. The cool air is perfumed with the blossoms of palo verde and catsclaw along the arroyo. The thick new growth and the blossoms on the palo verde obscure my view of that oval orange rock on the hillside.

Awhile later in the big arroyo, out of the corner of my eye I caught a glimpse of turquoise; in an imprint left by a horse hoof I found a tiny bit of turquoise on a square gray limestone. Then up ahead there was a bright spot shining on the ground; I picked up a fragment of crystal quartz that blazed with the light of the sun.

CHAPTER 40

Now Sandino lives indoors in my painting studio in a big cage where he screams and deafens me further. I try to wear headphones most of the time I write anyway. He is supposed to be my muse, but I don't know if he will help or hinder me.

I painted a memorial painting in tempera to commemorate Bolee and Sandino; I gave her two legs because she is in the spirit world now and is whole again; Sandino is portrayed as he is in life, with one leg.

About three hours ago Sandino started splashing in his water cup, dousing himself with his beak full of water, flapping his wings and crying out with joy. Now on the southwest horizon I see the ocean's clouds dark blue with rain, hastening to the northeast.

The parrots and macaws sense the approach of rainstorms long before humans unless the humans have Doppler radar or satellite images. The ancestors here in the Southwest called the macaws and parrots "rain birds," and painted their images on pottery water jars because the water-splashing of the parrots as they bathed attracted the rain clouds.

The desert birds, the thrashers and cactus wrens, sing their rain songs as soon as they smell the sweet rain in the air. The raindrops are an aphrodisiac for the parrots and the desert birds. Tarantulas and desert toads also smell the rain; ditto for the rattlesnakes and the horned lizards.

No thunder, no macho winds, this is a gentle female ocean rain. Later, a big rain cloud over the mountain peak is so luminous it has to be the Sun's eye.

The macaws and parrots are able to talk to the clouds, to the ancestors; which is why a macaw oracle was consulted to learn what the dead wanted and what the dead were angry about. (The dead become rain clouds—so if they are angry, they won't appear and the living will die of thirst.) The macaw oracle's words were interpreted by the oracle bird's "human servant" who also collected the fees for consultations.

The rain clouds block the sun. The rain evaporates as it falls into the desert heat and reaches the ground as a cool cool breeze that smells of rain. When the masses of nimbus and cumulus clouds began to arrive and covered the sun, a small brown rattler went toward the gate to the patio where the cockatoos sounded an alarm. The snake stopped and looked longingly at the gate all blocked up with wire mesh and rocks so it couldn't get inside. The patio was a good hunting area after a rain. The snake seemed to consider whether he wanted to bother to exert himself to push under the rocks blocking his way, but then gave up and went into a thicket of aloe veras.

Early May. On blue paper white and gray pastel clouds and the words in turquoise ink:

Welcome to the first rain clouds of the summer. I hope they linger while I draw them.

On beige paper in white pastel nimbus and cumulus clouds and the words in black ink:

Some believe the smallest clouds are babies and small children who died.

Then one cloud's constant transformations all alone in the bright blue sky got my attention. In white pastel on the beige paper I drew a sequence of this cloud as it changed shape and shifted over ten minutes.

The sequence begins at the top of the page. I stopped a moment to smear the white pastel into wispy tendrils of the cloud in the six forms it took. When I looked up again at the sky the cloud was gone.

Clouds in white pastel on beige paper and these words in black ink: *More clouds.*

In purple ink these words:

It was as if the clouds were communicating with me by changing shapes in the high winds above.

The clouds changed shapes so rapidly the thought occurred to me this might be extraterrestrials contacting me.

Two nimbus clouds in white pastel on beige paper. In purple ink these words:

The clouds were teaching me how to communicate with them.

It requires long periods of watching the sky in stillness. I seem to have the most interesting encounters with single clouds. Large masses of clouds pay no attention to me.

———◆———

As I walked into the room I share with the one-legged macaw, I was surprised by a fresh light scent. Sandino had shredded a big red apple that smelled of spring flowers, not apple.

Spring comes to the desert again and again with each rainstorm. The rain I smell in the wind leaves me exultant to be alive in that moment. What I like to do after a rain is go outside early in the morning as the sun rises above the mountains to see the night-blooming cactus flowers; their double and triple blossoms are the shapes of comets and supernovas incandescent with celestial light. Their perfume is hypnotic. In the backlight of the rising sun, the dried seedpods appear as exploding stars—dazzling with their reflections.

Later that morning I noticed a bushy tailed squirrel intent on teasing or attempting to frighten something by flicking his tail and fluffing it—fully extended, the hairs made a halo of the shining sun. He didn't mind me watching him, he was so focused on his adversary. At first I looked around the ceramic water bowl and saw nothing, and almost gave up. Then I looked more closely and saw a small rattler curled around the water bowl next to a fence post. The rattler ignored the squirrel that kept looking to see if the rattler was still there. Did the squirrel have a batch of babies nearby? The doves are like me, they don't see the small snake curled up against the fence rail when they land on the water bowl.

The bushy tailed squirrel came back a third time to wave and shake his fluffed up tail in the small rattler's hunting area—that is probably the plan—to ruin the hunting for the snake with his squirrelly dance that alerts all in the area of the hunter.

This late May morning Sandino sensed the approach of the rain and bathed himself with much enthusiasm. Four hours later a petite rain paid us a visit. The palo verde, mesquite and ironwood are all in bloom. The true garden is the desert outside my yard.

Two days later in the big arroyo, I found two pieces of turquoise rock both the size of a small button. An orange butterfly with arabesques in black on its wings greeted me with kindness and ceremony on the trail.

I have a dozen or more sketchbooks and notebooks only partially filled, then abandoned for years only to have me find them and start using them again for drawing and painting and writing as well. The linear time line is thus tangled and confused as it deserves to be.

The pack rat is trying to move into the barbeque grill Charlie abandoned when he left a few years ago. Is this the same rat that was inside the engine compartment of my car despite the light bulb that burned there all night?

A few years ago I might have tried to kill it with a rock or stick, but right then I didn't feel like killing anything, not even a pack rat. Now that I'm older, I can't bring myself to kill anything except assassin beetles—I even help scorpions reach safety. But I kill assassin beetles, my karma be damned, because their bites almost kill me.

So I showed the old pit bull dog the burrow where the pack rat ran. The dog sniffed the barbeque grill where the rat fled and now the dog is vigorously chewing the steel frame that holds the bottled gas under the grill.

The raven couple called back and forth to one another along the big arroyo. I listened for the voice of their raven child but I wasn't sure I heard it or one of them. I hope their chick survived the attention of the owls and red-tail hawks. The old pit bull is still chewing the grill's door, trying to reach the pack rat that's long gone.

The big black collared lizard king I nicknamed "Godzilla" is out and about this late May morning hunting the golden cockroaches I disturbed by moving flowerpots around. This dark mesquite lizard rules all the shady area under the tree and front porch including but not limited to the damp flowerpot bottoms and all the golden cockroaches hidden there.

I saw a light brown lizard without a collar and hope it is the same lizard that was inside the oak barrel debris. I couldn't see the lizard when I started to move the debris in the macaw cage, and the lizard got knocked unconscious. I thought it was dead. I almost threw it out into the desert. But when I went to pick the lizard up, I saw that it was alive, barely, so I took it to a safe shady spot under the mesquite tree. A short time later when I looked, the lizard had regained consciousness and was gone. I kept a lookout in case it just crawled off to die, but never saw any sign of it until I saw the light brown lizard today.

CHAPTER 41

I read that the way to distinguish real turquoise from chrysocolla is to lick the stones and your tongue will stick to the chrysocolla but not to the turquoise. I licked all the turquoise stones I had on my writing desk. My tongue stuck to nearly every one of the turquoise rocks except for the two big nuggets. With further reading I learned the two cabochons are probably "chrysocolla-impregnated chalcedony" with the hardness of seven—chalcedony is harder than turquoise, and heavier and denser than turquoise.

I found another turquoise ledge off the west side where we throw biodegradable items. A turquoise ledge of very blue, sky blue chrysocolla but soft as calcium carbonate from fossil seashells. So the house I live in sits on top of a chalky turquoise ledge of brightest blue.

I try to leave the house before the sun rises over the Catalina Mountains across the valley to the east. When the sun breaks over the Catalinas, the Tucson Mountain peaks catch the first light and glow an incandescent yellow gold that makes them look purple then orange. The early morning air of the desert is incomparable—it is delicious— the air is cool with the least hint of moisture that holds the scents of clay and stone and even the perfume of the late-blooming catsclaw bush. Later the heat parches the air and the scent will be of wood about to combust. Early in the morning is the time all creatures in the desert move about; the pack rats are light-sensitive and must be in their nests by dawn. The night hunters, the bobcats, pumas and the snakes, begin to head for their day shelters from the sun. The cactus wrens and thrashers call; the doves begin to fly to water.

Sometimes it is completely silent. No human sounds (unless you count my breathing), no engines, no trains, no barking dogs, no airplanes, just the sound of the wind moving through the palo verde and saguaro and for a moment even the desert creatures are quiet. I might be standing here a thousand years ago, or ten thousand years ago.

The ancient people stood here and looked at the Catalinas with the sun rising over them; they watched for any clouds that might come. Clouds from any direction were always welcomed.

During the 2007 snake season, the mastiffs finally managed to kill the big rattlesnake that lived under the dog shed. One evening when I brought them in at bedtime, I saw that Snapper and Lyon had been bitten though they weren't swollen much; Lyon was bitten on the foot and Snapper on the lower lip, but they both had developed immunities to the venom, so were barely affected by the bites. The next morning when I fed the dogs I wasn't paying much attention and when I walked past the dog beds I got a big shock. There was the dead rattler, its huge head smashed flat, and its four foot long body torn into three pieces.

Now the squirrels are excavating a huge cavern under the dog shed which now teeters on the edge. That's what we get for the killing of the big snake.

I blamed the manuscript of my memoir for the anxiety, the ringing in the ears and the poor concentration I had; I'd never had such a strong visceral reaction to writing before. But now I've realized the true source of my symptoms—it wasn't just the childhood recollections that started to get to me as I wrote this book.

Over the past months, I'd managed to poison myself with a strong electromagnetic field in my house electrical wiring. I had plugged in a gizmo to drive away rodents about eight months ago. I didn't leave the device plugged in all the time because I had a pet mouse I called Mystery Mouse. I worried the device might irritate her so I called the 800 number on the device and spoke with a polite man who could tell me nothing about the device or how it worked except that it was safe for humans and pets.

I was familiar with the research done on the dangerous effects of alternating current's electromagnetic field on the cellular development of zygotes. But the desire to find an easy fix to the rodent infestation in my attic led me to delude myself with the false assurances the device was safe for children and pets. I threw caution aside when I plugged in the device. It caused all the wiring of my house to give off an electromagnetic field that slowly destroyed any creatures unable to escape its force field.

Mystery Mouse died in late April. Once she was dead I left the device plugged in all the time because I didn't have her comfort to consider anymore. I thought large creatures like myself were not affected by the field.

Within five days of leaving the device plugged in, I was ready to go to the emergency room. My ears were ringing loudly, my heart was pounding and my blood pressure was uncharacteristically high. I felt anxious and unable to sit down at my laptop to work on the memoir. I blamed writing the memoir because my symptoms got worse when I worked on the computer due to all the electricity required to run it and the peripherals.

About that time the roofers came to fix the front roof of the house. The roofing foreman noticed the lights we use in the engine compartments of our cars at night to keep away the pack rats. I told him about the plug-in device, and he said his roofing company used the same plug-in device. It worked great, he said, no rodents, not even birds would fly inside their warehouse anymore.

That was when I let go of my self-delusion and realized what was wrong—it wasn't the writing of the memoir that set off my pulse and blood pressure. The anti-rodent gizmo's electromagnetic field utilized all the electrical wiring in my house to create a strong wave signal twenty-four hours a day. No wonder the spiders indoors had virtually disappeared; even the assassin beetles were gone. The rattlesnakes didn't leave because they lived under the floor below the grid-work of electrical wiring in the walls.

CHAPTER 42

The Quicholi festival for Mixcoatl, the Maize Mother, is a celebration that uses a great many arrows which are made and offered to Huitzilopochtli, Lord Hummingbird the Warrior, and to all warriors who died in battle to commemorate the descent of the stars into the interior of the Earth.

On the turquoise mosaic, the outer band represented warriors who are war-like star deities such as Tlahuizcalpantecuhtli and Huitzilopochtli; so the Star Beings are linked to turquoise, which shows their status as the highest. Now astronomers say that great ice comets collided with the Earth and brought all the water there is. So the comets were the Star Beings that brought life to Earth; without water there can be no life as we know it, and no turquoise.

I thought the rattlers wouldn't climb up the tall clay pots but my neighbor found a big rattlesnake in one of her large clay pots on her wooden deck. About that time I watched a really big rattler crawl over—not around—a stack of bricks by a flowerpot which means the snake could easily climb into my tall flowerpots if it wished. Fortunately the snakes seem to prefer the dirt that dampens between the flowerpots under the mesquite tree to the flowerpots themselves. My neighbor's wooden deck gets too warm and is probably the reason the snakes crawled up into her flowerpots. The snakes here haven't done that yet. Not yet. But I now look before I reach in the flowerpots to test the dampness of the soil.

The big rattler was lying in the shade in wait for a mourning dove. He was on the other side of a big pot with gourd sprouts in it. I couldn't see him. I was wearing my sound cancelling headphones when I stepped outside to the porch; I think the cockatoos had been screeching so I left the headphones on.

Although I barely heard it I felt the vibration of the rattling. I took off the headphones and located the snake before I stepped around the big pot and found myself face to face with the big snake. I don't like to be surprised by snakes; it means I'm not paying enough attention to my surroundings.

The light! The light! This first morning of June on the stretch of the big arroyo just above the old iron culvert that resembles a coffin, bright in the sunlight I found a small cabochon of turquoise in the shape of a heart on a gravel bar I've walked past a number of times recently but never saw. Was it there those other times? When did it appear? Was it visible only in the 6:20 a.m. light? Maybe the light at 8:30 a.m. is brighter but the wrong angle, and so bright the turquoise stones appear to be enameled.

Now the misty breeze smells just like the ripe prickly pears boiled for syrup. The rain smells of wet cactus. The wind came from the east and there was little thunder or lightning. It was a gentle rain that soaked into the ground. The air had been so hot but now suddenly the breeze off the rainstorm feels almost icy. The palo verde covered with dainty yellow flowers sway in the wind; at their feet the drifts of fallen blossoms swirl.

The cooler air lingers in the low-lying places, the arroyos. It feels delicious on my face and is lightly perfumed with the late-blooming catsclaw bushes in the arroyos. The wild flowers that bloomed in February, March and April are dry stalks, their seedpods the shapes of spiders, bees and stars. They are luminous—backlit by the rising sun—as lovely in this light as they were in flower.

At 5:15 a.m. the sun is up but not quite over the Catalina Mountains. To walk or not to walk? I tell myself the more walks I take the more material I will have for the manuscript. Yes, no. I decided yes, a slow walk. I didn't have any coffee. I left the dogs indoors but I uncovered the one-legged macaw's cage.

I started out and felt a bit odd on the first hill from not eating. But I can think of no better place to die than out on the trail in these hills with the saguaros and all the other beings I love. But after the first hill I get warmed up and feel better the longer I walk.

The low angle of the rising sun through clouds filters the light through a yellow shimmering haze that makes the early morning golden. The dry stalks and leaves and the seedpods were backlit by the sun and transformed to flora of light in another dimension.

I saw a set of large boot-prints on the trail. A big man. Size 13 DDDDD. I see little tracks of night insects and night rodents in the fine dust inside the boot-print; he was here yesterday.

After the Gila Monster Mine the boot-prints stopped, and I saw only rabbit and javelina tracks and those of insects on the trail which filled my heart with relief and happiness. At the javelina dance place I found no dancing tracks. They dance here because the soft sand feels good and there are no pebbles or stones to stub their cloven hooves. They take their dirt baths in select spots where the runoff moves the rocks and pebbles and leaves only the finest soft sand and clay which they carefully prepare by pawing it with their hooves and rooting it up with their snouts and curved incisors.

The morning after the first rain I will be sure to walk to see what sorts of gatherings went on here last night. From the fresh tracks in the damp sand, I can tell the deer reared up on their hind legs and danced in mock combat with one another. They frolic because the rain fills them with joy and erotic excitement.

For years I rode my horse along the trail I now walk. The horse watched the footing and did all the work while I enjoyed the view from the top of the horse. Now I walk and I keep my eyes on the trail while scanning up and around from time to time. I stop now and then to listen as my father taught me for deer hunting.

I am losing my hearing from all those years of my childhood when I happily watched my parents fire high-powered rifles and large hand guns without ear protection so I probably miss a great deal but still I can hear the happiness of the curved beak thrashers and speckled cactus wrens over the recent rain and the wild flowers.

CHAPTER 43

I like to think about the interesting things I saw on my walk. The round orange rock on the hillside north of the Gila Monster Mine pit is one of those "arresting" things. It is a bright orange granite that is not abundant but still present here. The shape is nearly round and I imagine I'm not the first to notice it. Someday I want to detour from the trail and hike over to the orange hillside to look at the bright orange round rock close up.

The rain made the desert trees and brush so lush and thick I have difficulty locating the round orange rock on the hillside these days.

Two days ago on June 15 the first clouds—small and round, fluffy and fast-moving—passed through headed northeast. Some of them resembled birds flying backwards, or flying antelopes in threes and twos, and a bear crossing the sky, followed by a frog and a squirrel. They fill the horizon, fleecy on the edges from the winds above that push them. A swimming snake, a swimming fat man who just lost his flipper. A reclining nude woman with two heads. Out of the west, long thick strands of clouds parallel one another, like herds of elk and herds of buffalo. Clouds are constantly changing, especially these fast-moving clouds, that remind me of wild horses with wind whipped manes and tails. It is possible to communicate with the clouds—I don't know why—I just speak to them.

One hundred eight degrees Fahrenheit. The air itself is hot and heats my silver bracelets and earrings. I learn to cover my brown skin with loose white cotton or linen; I never go out without dark glasses or a wide brim hat.

Occasionally I take a different route. Not long ago I walked north of the Gila Monster Mine, past an old digging, and toward the hill with the arresting orange rock. Distances and the rough terrain of the desert can be deceiving; I wanted to have some idea of how long it might take me and how difficult it would be to reach the orange rock.

The desert brush was heavy and the terrain was rocky at the foot of the hill. I decided to put off the orange rock for another day. I found the easiest path was to walk down the center of the small arroyo to avoid the catsclaw and mesquite along the edge. I saw deer tracks and javelina tracks there. The mountain lion and bobcat probably hunt around here.

I feel I must share the well water with the wild creatures. When my last horse, the sweet Prince Charming, suddenly got sick and died, the horse water trough in the corral was no longer required. I'd have more water for us humans if I stopped filling the trough in the empty corral. But too many wild creatures had come to depend on the water in the corral in the thirty plus years that people kept horses and water there, from javelina, deer, bobcats, coyotes and all number of birds—including owls and hawks. I call it the "memorial water trough" in memory of my two beloved Arabian horses Hudson Bay and Prince Charming.

I try to keep the troughs and dishes completely full of water so small creatures can climb out if they fall in. Alas this morning I found a half dozen hatchling Gambel's quail drowned in one of the round flat water tubs down at the old corral. I felt so badly because I didn't anticipate such an accident with the tiny quail. I set out the dead chicks where hungry creatures might find them; this is the only consolation the desert offers for death. Long ago the Tibetan Buddhist priests were given "sky burials" under the stars, on remote mountains where hungry creatures could find and consume them.

I've lived here thirty years and I still have so much to learn about the desert and its living things. The round water dishes needed large gravel, and small stones on the bottom to create secure footing, and shallows so that rocks would protrude above the water's surface allowing the tiny quail hatchlings to climb out if they fell in, as in natural water holes.

Even after I filled the water dishes with stones and made a ramp into the water trough, I found a single tiny quail drowned the following morning. I added more rocks and so far it's not happened again.

In the intense heat there is silence. The molecules of air expand so far apart that vibrations can't bridge the gap between them, and the sound stops. There is no wind; nothing moves.

We are waiting for the rain. Along the high plateaus, veils of blue mist trail out of the clouds' blue bellies; even when the big-bellied dark blue clouds amass around the mountains' peaks, the air is so hot and dry the raindrops evaporate before they hit the ground.

In fewer than three hours the sun will reach the "North Corner of Time" as the old-time people at Laguna Pueblo called it, or the summer solstice. In the old days down here, the Tohono O'Odom women harvested the carmine red fruits of the giant saguaro cactus with their long poles made of saguaro ribs. They brewed a sacred wine from the ripe fruit and drank it in order to visit with the ancestors and beloved family members who had died.

Last week a Tucson newspaper printed a list of the city's most memorable summer storms. The first date was my favorite: on July 11, 1878

five inches of rain fell on Tucson in seventy minutes and caused a sea of water to wash away most of the downtown area.

The first day of summer is 110 degrees Fahrenheit by 2:00 p.m. I was up early and sat outside to watch the fat fluffy clouds along the southwest horizon. I tried to sketch them but they seemed to evaporate into the heated sky.

Late in the afternoon thunderclouds began to roll in from the west. The spine of the Tucson Mountains and the highest peak are in full sun but here on the northeast slope my house is temporarily in the shade of a huge cumulus cloud as the other clouds gather around the black mountain peak. Across the valley to the east over the high blue mountains, tall waves of bright white and dark blue clouds rise in the forms of great cliffs and giant mountains fifty thousand feet high.

Two days later I opened the door early in the morning and the air smelled heavenly—rain! The scent from yesterday's clouds took all night to reach us down here. I walked outside and it was so cool. All the living beings from the palo verde trees with their green bark to the ring-neck lizards are drinking up the precious moist air through their skins. I can feel my hair drink the moisture in waves and the skin on my face feels refreshed and cool.

It was such a lovely morning I didn't want to go back indoors, even to put on my clothes. I don't care who sees me in my nightgown which is nothing more than a very long t-shirt. I walked down the hill to the corrals to check on my new arrangements of the water dishes and the new ramp into the water trough.

As I walked I looked at the dark basalt hills, and at the cactus and shrubs and trees; all of them were in harmony with one another, and I felt within that beauty. In an instant I saw that even man-made things—the roll of old fence wire, the old rail ties withered by sixty years of the heat and the sun—were in the light of that beauty. In that beauty we all will sink slowly back into the lap of the Earth.

CHAPTER 44

Yesterday the temperature reached 111 degrees Fahrenheit. No wonder the clouds suddenly vanished while I was trying to sketch them. The heat evaporated the clouds. When I went outside to spray the macaws, there was a breeze and the hose spray wet down my clothes and the breeze cooled me so 111 didn't seem quite so bad.

But now the humidity is coming, and it will make the air feel hotter.

I brought the garden hose to the pots of water. The bees didn't like the disturbance but the water was so low it would have been gone before morning. I dumped the water buckets and rinsed them clean before I refilled them; not one of the bees gave even the slightest hint of anger. They are accustomed to my commotion with the hose and buckets.

Ah the wind off the thunderstorm on the other side of the mountains is cool and sweet with the smell of rain!

The first rain of summer. The air smells magical, the rain on the trees and shrubs releases leaf resins and rare balsams—invigorating scents of bark splashed with rain, all these subtle perfumes loosed and carried by the wind.

The raindrops were so few and far between they left the dirt speckled and dotted, "pinto" with darker damp spots.

The one-legged macaw, Sandino, is very fond of Tigger, the old pit bull dog who cleans up the parrot food he scatters with such glee. Seeds and parrot formula are nothing for Tigger. The dog once ate fresh rattlesnake dung as I looked on in revulsion and disbelief.

This is Sandino's first summer indoors in the room where I work. He gets around on one leg very nicely in the big cage. He uses his beak and flaps his wings for extra lift if he wants to move quickly. Sometimes he shrieks in alarm if shadows of large flying birds cross the sky outside his windows. Luckily music soothes him. He enjoys all the Carlos Santana albums I listen to while I write.

Sandino plays tug of war with his rubber ball with the bell inside, and he rings the copper sheep bell I hung in his cage. I never really got to know him before the owls killed his mate, Bolee. She was fiercely possessive of him and flew at me to drive me away from their outdoor cage.

Now the one-legged macaw is possessive of me and sometimes he reminds me of a bad boyfriend. Parrots are notorious for their jealousy. He demands a great deal of attention from me; otherwise he hangs by his beak upside down from the top of his cage and flaps his wings and screams. I wear headphones while I write so his screams don't deafen me more than I already am.

Yesterday raindrops and thunder. Again today there are rain clouds and thunder. On a green paper in white chalk I drew the horizon line which is the spine bone of the black mountains and towering high above, mountainous white and gray clouds.

Later, as the huge white rain fell minute after minute, it occurred to me that I might have inadvertently written down the Nahuatl words to a rain cloud spell.

Ca! Caca! Aye! Frog!
Cacalachitli! Clay rattle!

Cacalotl! Raven!
Cacapaca! Clapping!

My poor garden in clay and plastic pots is a disaster. The summer was cooler and wetter than usual so my plants in pots should have thrived. Instead, they died of overwatering for two reasons. First, I was not counting on there being so much rain in the afternoons. I always watered in the morning when the sky was clear, but later in the day, the rain came and the result was too much water.

Second, all my anxieties (about the manuscript, finances etc.) seemed to surface while I watered. On hot days it is healthy and natural for plants to wilt temporarily, not from lack of water but to protect themselves from the heat.

After the air cools, the wilt disappears and the plants are fine. I knew this, but whenever I saw a wilted plant, against all common sense and reason I had to give it water; this was a compulsion, although I knew overwatering during the heat kills the plants at once.

The alyssum is drought-resistant but I overwatered all the pots of alyssum and killed them; ditto for the datura, even my rare blue single hybrid that I killed when it was at its prettiest. For three years I coddled three large brugmansia plants, a pink, a double yellow and a double white. I put their pots on rollers and moved them indoors in the cold months and out to the shade on the hottest days. The yellow and the pink brugmansias bloomed in the winter months, but the white never did. This summer I managed to overwater all three and that was the end of them. Only the rain lilies were able to survive my anxious overwatering during the heat.

I tried to grow gourds but the squirrel or Ratty the pack rat ate them almost as soon as the seeds sprouted. One or two gourd sprouts grew a few inches and got my hopes up for them before they were eaten that night.

The cacti managed to escape overwatering. But I perched one of them in a clay pot atop another overturned clay pot that sat on a steel table. The steel table becomes a solar grill by day. By the time I noticed, the cactus had baked.

Once again the rolls of robust blue cumulus clouds hug the black mountain peak as they did yesterday about this time in the afternoon. Now a cool wind, the sky a deep solid blue behind the peak, and then a high bank of blue blue storm clouds. At first they were tall and resembled canyons, mesas and mountains; then they transformed themselves into great blue temples of stone at Cholula and the massive stone towers of Teotihuacan and Tikal. But later when I looked for the clouds they had vanished without a trace I thought until this morning at dawn when I inhaled them as the rain scent in the cool air.

This lovely late June day the air is calm down here but overhead the wind must be racing, because the nimbus and cumulus clouds are stampeding across the blue sky, the fast winds driving them to the mountain peaks of Utah and New Mexico. Some of the clouds are shaped like sea mammals—dolphins and small whales; one has the shape of a pelican. But cloud-shapes are human whimsy. The clouds have a language but it's not one of shapes.

One rain cloud broke into two rain clouds.

I was only gone inside long enough to wash some dog dishes. I heard thunder in the distance while I was putting the dishes away. I came back outside on the porch and all the big silver blue fluffy clouds had transformed into pale purple violet tendrils of rain that reached down to the black mountain peak but evaporated before they reached the ground.

A sudden shift in the wind blocked the sun with thick masses of clouds that cooled the air even faster. In the old days they used to say that San Juan Day, June 28, was the beginning of the rainy season in the Southwest. The villages had big fiestas for San Juan probably because John the Baptist sprinkled water on people. Long before San Juan, traditional

Pueblo and Nahua people used to attract the rain by sprinkling precious water on everyone who turned out for the summer gathering.

Although the blue violet clouds and their raindrops don't reach us, still we Earth creatures find cool comfort in the damp breeze that blows steadily off the peak. The wild bees are still out so that means they think we won't get wet.

The white wing and the mourning doves drink water from the pots in my front yard. I had to adjust the safety grill on the blue plastic water dish out back because another baby quail drowned. I no sooner filled the two water pots full to overflowing than a redheaded house finch and his plain gray mate came for a drink.

The following day the clouds that fly past are large and in the shapes of flying birds. A great cloud is Lord Macaw with long tail feathers streaming behind him, rain that reaches the earth. I can make out eagles and woodpeckers, all flying in the opposite direction of the wind.

Now the clouds amass thickly; a giant frog face snake of silvery blue cumulus. Raging rivers, great ocean waves crested in silver foam—the layers of cumulus swell out of the sky in large masses that resemble nude humans at an orgy.

Later on the evening news the weatherman reported the clouds brought dry storms full of lightning that sparked wildfires in the Rincon Mountains southeast of Tucson.

I have two Nahuatl-English dictionaries. One is compact, palm-sized but thick, and is modern and practical. The other is Bierhorst's old dictionary that grew out of the translations of *Cantares Mexicanos*, the epic poem of the Nahua people written in glyphs and paintings on folios of folded amate paper the color of white clay.

Some days I don't feel like working on the manuscript so I read my two Nahuatl dictionaries for coded messages that may inspire me to write. It is possible to do a great deal with a language we don't speak or understand, as long as we freely employ our imaginations and have access to good dictionaries. Today as I browsed through the a's and the c's (Nahuatl has no b), my eyes were attracted to the Nahuatl words that appear to me to be onomatopoeic; but I also look for rhyme or the repetition of sounds in a single word. I used the "ca" sound of Nahuatl to write my rain cloud spell awhile back, so I started with "ca" again.

"Ca" means because of you.

"Cacahtli" means water dweller with a loud croak.

"Cacacuicatl" means toad song.

"Quiahuitl" means rain.

"Oquiah" means it rained.

"Ehecaquiahuit" and "yehyecaquiahuitl" both mean rainstorm.

Are the "Eh" and "Yehye" sounds before the word for rain intended to be exclamatory or prayerful?

"Quiahuatl" means rainwater.

Just after I wrote down the list of words in Nahuatl and English suddenly a white rainstorm arrived out of the southeast with only a little thunder and lightning. White and gray nimbostratus clouds roll over the hills. Now we are in the clouds!

As the huge white rain fell minute after minute, it seemed there might be something about Nahuatl words written in ink on paper that works as a rain cloud spell. I will have to continue to experiment with this.

As I browse in the Nahuatl-English dictionary I also watch for words that are combinations of other words; the Nahuatl word for cloud is "mixtli"; the Nahuatl for snake is "coatl"; the Nahuatl for tornado is "mixcoatl" but "mixcoatl" is also a cloud companion, a ghost warrior or ancestor. "Cuahtilli-n-totolye mochiuh ocelomixcoatl" means: he's become an eagle, a jaguar, a cloud companion!

The Bierhorst dictionary shows a number of meanings for each word. Often a double meaning refers to the ghost warriors. For example the Nahuatl word "celiya" means to take root, to sprout or to grow green again, but it also means returned ghost warrior. The word "cempohualxochitl" means marigold but also means revenant warrior. It is apparent that many Nahuatl words have a double meaning which links them to ghost warriors so the revenants hold a central position in the Nahua cosmology. Could it be that the revenants are responsible for bringing rain?

"Calli" means house.

"Mixcocacalli" is the House of the Cloud Companions, the dance hall or music room where the ghost singers perform the ghost songs, often in the form of lullabies.

"Ahua conetel!" means Hail little baby and is used by the ghost singers to address the revenants. "Ahuitzotl," little longed for child, is another term of endearment used to call the revenants.

"Olini" means to stir, to come to life as the ghost warriors do when they arrive on Earth.

"Matlahuah calli" is a pack basket used for carrying the revenants from Paradise to this world.

"Malina" means to be spun or whirled, and refers to the ghost warriors as they emerge from the matlahuah calli.

CHAPTER 45

Another gardening error—fatal for my double white daturas. I misidentified some voracious speckled red bugs as ladybugs. These flying red bugs are the same size and shape as ladybugs and mimic the ladybugs' red color. They lack the precise black spots of the ladybugs and have instead asymmetrical black splotches. I thought they were a variation of the ladybug.

I didn't want to kill a species of ladybug so I took awhile to observe their numbers and behavior. After they attacked the double white daturas I realized they were not ladybugs. They denuded the young white daturas and devastated the purple datura so I made a concoction of dish detergent, garlic olive oil and red pepper from Viet Nam to spray on the ladybug imposters.

While I was observing the initial effects of my spray repellant from my chair on the porch, I heard a rustle in the dry leaves and stalks around the clay pots. I turned and caught a glimpse of the head of the garnet and ruby red racer snake who's lived in my front yard more than fifteen years. She stopped but didn't seem to mind me looking because she knows I won't harm her.

I turned away from her to reassure her so she could proceed by me, and as she passed I looked down at her (she's four and a half feet long so it takes a moment for her to go by me). I was shocked to see a slash wound in her side that was draining infection, and then came her tail—the very tip of her tail was gone and had traces of dried blood on it.

My long-time racer snake neighbor had been in mortal battle last night or early today. But with whom? Roadrunner? Owl or hawk? Any one of them might slash and eat a red racer snake.

I knocked the ladybug imposters from the tattered remnants of the datura leaves; the red bugs lay on the ground as if dead. I thought probably the dish detergent and red chili sauce suffocated them. But about twenty minutes later the red bugs regained consciousness and flew away.

I was about to go indoors to escape the flies when I heard the rapid beak clatter of a roadrunner. One suddenly flew up from the bird water dish to the fence and was gone as fast as a thief. Right then I knew who the likely attacker of the red racer snake was. Would a roadrunner eat a hummingbird? I suspect it would; Lord Roadrunner eats anything alive, and is very quick.

I went to fill the water trough down at the old corrals. The small water pans were dry and the level of the trough was low. As I waited for the trough to fill, I saw a small covey of half-grown Gambel's quail coming to water. When they saw me they skittered across the old corral and retreated to the bushes—survivors of the heat and rain and my carelessness that drowned six chicks earlier in the spring.

All the desert is bright new green and the cactus wrens and thrashers excitedly chirp and sing for all these lovely afternoon and evening rainstorms.

Today the clouds form heavy layers on all the mountaintops. I feel I can't communicate with so many clouds. Across the west and northwest sky the clouds unreel themselves. Suddenly bird songs and birdcalls create a cacophony of joy; for the desert is bright green and the rains come.

Masses of tall silver blue rain clouds stream down from the Sierra Madre Mountains into Arizona and New Mexico. I make sketches of the clouds with light gray and white chalk on a page of light blue paper. I found the cloud photographs Stieglitz called "Equivalents" among some post cards years ago. Whenever I look at them, I want to make cloud prints from contact negatives on blueprint paper.

The second time I wrote the same Nahuatl words in my notebook the blue rain clouds gathered and the rainwater overflowed the barrels. Apparently, certain Nahuatl words written in ink on paper can bring rain clouds at certain times.

Then I remembered where I had gotten the notion that words in ink on paper could bring rain. My friend Linda Niemann found the rain book in Mexico City in 1993 and had given it to me. The book was made of traditional amate, paper from the bark of the fig tree, by Sr. Alfonso Garcia Tellez in 1978 in the town of San Pablito, Pahuatlan, Puebla.

In times of drought the people of San Pablito made a pilgrimage to a cave in the mountains three days' distance from their town, bringing a small handmade foldout book of amate paper to ask for rain. Sr. Garcia Tellez wrote the words in the rain book by hand, in Spanish; facing each page of text were paper cutout figures also made of ochre and brown amate paper. The figures represent "dioses" or spirit beings, mostly cultivated plants, who also plead for rain.

The rain book is an offering the people bring to the cave but it also tells the people how the pilgrimage should be conducted. At one time of course the text was written in Nahuatl or some related dialect, not Spanish. The amate paper itself was held in great esteem, so the paper cutouts themselves are powerful. My theory is the paper cutout figures compensate for the use of Spanish. The Nahuatl words are much more powerful for rainmaking than the Spanish; it is enough to write the Nahuatl words on paper, no amate paper cutouts are needed.

After I added two more words to my original Nahuatl rain prayer in ink on paper, rain clouds came and stayed for three days:

> Ca! Caca! Hey Frog!
> cacalachitli   clay rattle
> Cacalotl cacapaca Raven clapping
> atlatlacamahmanilizti thunderstorm
> ayahuitl fog mist of ghost warriors

"Atlatlacamahmanilizti" is made of the sounds of a thunderstorm: "atla atla camahma" is rolling thunder and "nilizti" is the crackle of lightning.

———◇———

My niece Halley told me this: Two of her friends moved to Tampico, on the Bay of Campeche in Mexico, to teach school. The mayor of the city was showing the new teachers around the town when one of them asked if hurricanes ever struck. The mayor quickly assured the teachers Tampico would never be threatened by hurricanes— "it was a certainty," he said. "But how could this be so?" the new teacher asked. The Bay of Campeche was a "calving ground" for tropical storms so it was odd that Tampico would be spared. The mayor took a deep breath. "I might as well tell you," he said. "We people here in Tampico believe the UFOs protect us and keep the hurricanes away."

The mayor told them at one time a rumor had raced through Tampico that the UFOs were going to leave. All the townspeople hurried down to the beach to watch them depart. Of course the townspeople were very concerned about what might happen to their town without the UFOs to protect them from hurricanes.

The townspeople waited for two or three hours but they didn't see any UFOs departing, so they went home, and Tampico remains protected from hurricanes by the UFOs.

In the middle of the night a gentle steady rain fell—no lightning, and only a little distant thunder. My son Robert said last night when he got home the giant toad was guarding our front door.

I wonder if it's the same giant toad I rescued a few years ago? That one had lived under the bricks of the front porch but rodents had removed the soil beneath the bricks. The big toad may have burrowed beneath the bricks of the porch floor too, when the bricks suddenly shifted and caused a cave-in that partially pinned him.

He was there a good while before I found him and looked the worse for it from dehydration. I got a bucket of water and poured a little water on the toad and on the bricks around him. I was alone the afternoon I found the trapped toad, but I had a short steel bar called a "wrecking bar" and I was able to pry up the bricks and free him.

I moistened the toad again in the sand of the tree well by the porch. I poured more water on the ground and the toad dug into the moist sandy soil. After a time I checked the damp sand of the tree well and the toad had vanished.

The five hundred year drought cycle is well under way here; as a result the desert toads in the Tucson Mountains have scarcely spawned pollywogs since 1983, when a hurricane came into the Gulf of California and headed straight to Tucson with flooding rain.

The pollywogs need clean water that is still or slow-moving, with enough volume to last until they become little toads. If the rainwater pools are too shallow or scarce, the big toads won't lay eggs; they sense that offspring will not survive. Instead they conserve fat reserves, feed on insects all night and bury themselves in sand during the heat of the day while they ride out the drought, and wait for the hurricane rain to return.

The rain clouds assemble in their colorful dance costumes of white and pink mother of pearl, coral, lapis and turquoise, lined up in rows across the sky as the ka'tsina dancers do.

The light this afternoon is a soft green from the hills where the rain clouds are gathering. The leaves, grass and green bark of the palo verdes give off an incandescent glow that turns the bellies of the clouds pale green.

CHAPTER 46

I got up early to walk the next day because it had rained during the night and I wanted to feel the coolness and freshness of the breeze before the heat of the day descended. The ground felt softer and fuller from the rain. All the shades of green from the grass and leaves gave off a soft glow in the early morning sun.

In the big arroyo I saw fresh V-shaped tracks of three or four javelinas that passed through ahead of me, but no sign of humans. The rain had been heavy enough to send the runoff down the arroyo; its appearance had been transformed overnight. Stretches of rocks that jutted out fully exposed before the rain now were partially buried in the sand and pebbles. Small rocks I'd not seen before were brought to the surface and others buried; small branches and other debris washed up on the sandbars on either side of the arroyo.

After great downpours and floods, the bed of the big arroyo changes greatly and only a few features in the bottom of the wash remain identifiable. The banks and ridges along the big arroyo were not affected, although an epic flood or earthquake could reshape them. Even this small flow of runoff had moved a great deal of fine sand; it was exciting to see the arroyo's new contours.

The sunlight was only beginning to illuminate the arroyo directly so I didn't expect to spot any turquoise stones. As I approached the small boulders surrounded in fine white sand I saw the most amazing object lying on top of the freshly washed sand. Amethyst light shone through it as if it were a gemstone. The runoff down the arroyo from the rain had uncovered a large shard of purple glass.

When I was a child there was a collector of purple glass who made me aware of its value. Of course collectors only want whole objects, not shards, but I still picked up the piece of purple glass at once as I had when I was a child. It was part of the thick bottom of a mug—the glass shard was almost solid and molded in a fluted form.

Before 1960, clear glass for molded beer mugs and vases was manufactured with an ingredient which caused the glass to gradually turn purple after years of exposure to sunlight. There was only one possible source for this piece of glass—the old ranch trash dumps from eighty years ago. The nearest of the old ranch dumps was two miles away.

The shard of purple glass had traveled a great distance downhill from the old ranch trash dumps, where it lay in the sun for at least twenty years before it began to turn purple.

I felt lucky to find it. If another human had passed by before I did or if a pack rat or a large raven had noticed the amethyst shine, the purple glass might have been gone before I walked by.

In thirty years here I've learned to marvel at the survival of anything alien or man-made in the desert heat and terrain. At some point after the glass shard began to purple, it had been hit by rocks as it tumbled in floodwater, and a hairline fracture occurred. The fracture line is a pale pale violet; it seems to have slowed and clouded the process of purpling in the glass fragment.

When I first came to live here in 1978 I rode horseback in the area frequently where I discovered a number of house sites that were only rock chimneys. No other traces of the houses remained; the palo verdes and burr sage had obliterated any evidence of a foundation.

After Arizona got statehood in 1912, eager gringos flocked to seek their fortunes here. They moved their small herds of cattle and built their houses up here in these hills before the summer heat arrived. They probably lasted only a few years or until the cattle drank the well dry. Then they moved on and left the houses to the pack rats and vandals from town.

Whenever I am near the ocean at El Golfo on the shore of Sonora, I follow this practice after high tide: I get into my clothes slowly as a sleepwalker might. Out the door, I shiver in the damp air and cold that settle over the desert coast ahead of dawn. The ocean leaves wonderful gifts to find—pink fluted seashells, a seal's skull with a bullet hole, a sunbleached whale vertebra the size of a steering wheel and a topaz egg of sea glass polished like a jewel.

The hurricane remnants fly overhead bright silver and wind-fluffed. This summer was the coolest, rainiest summer since I moved to Tucson. The afternoon thunderstorms every day reminded me of the five or six year period from 1957 to 1962 or 1963 when I was a child, and the Laguna-Acoma area was blessed with rain showers every afternoon around 5:30. In those years the old-time people used to pray at dawn for the Sun's children, the rain clouds, to come.

The Tohono O'Odom people west of Tucson get rainstorms every afternoon during June and July. Few other places are so blessed because the O'Odom people know how to ask the ocean to send rain.

Usually the foggy mists of the rain beings move slowly and dance slowly and gracefully. Today the first rain beings came swirling rapidly in a heavy white rain off the mountain peak that was invisible in the clouds. The fogs and mists took on forms of wraiths in the white rain; they crowded themselves together pushing one another much as men will to show affection to their comrades. I watched them hurry along in their formations, long lines of beings extending down from clouds of the white rain, and suddenly the word "legions" came to mind: legions of revenant warriors, ghost warriors, marched out of the clouds and across the slopes of the black mountain peak.

After the legions passed, little showers followed their path from time to time all day long.

The rain yesterday evening filled the rain barrel almost to the brim. Earlier I transferred the rainwater to the smaller metal can to make room for more rain as the storm clouds approached late in the day.

I made sure the lids were off the rain barrels before I went to bed. When I went out this morning and looked into the barrel, I saw a beautiful hawk moth, one of the biggest I'd ever seen. It was floating motionless on the surface of the rainwater. Oh no! If I'd kept the lid on the barrel the hawk moth wouldn't have drowned. Gently I scooped up the big moth and it moved feebly. I held it in the palm of my hand close to my chest to warm it and it crawled onto the front of my shirt. Heartened by its motion, I took it to the potted jessamine bush and carefully set it down under the leaves out of the direct sun where it might recover or finish dying in peace.

The hawk moths depend on the datura blossoms and pollen for food, and they lay their eggs in the soil under the datura plant. The larvae become beautiful caterpillars of bright green with an elegant pattern of white and black stripes which the big moths retain after they emerge from the cocoons of their caterpillar phase.

About fifteen years ago on the front page of the local Tucson newspaper, an article announced the Air Force and U.S. Defense Department had a project at the base here in Tucson to experiment with hawk moths to see if there were military uses for them. The Air Force researchers glued tiny radio transmitters on the poor creatures.

Later I checked on the hawk moth under the jessamine and it was still there; but next morning it was gone. I hope it recovered and flew off after dark.

Today in the big arroyo I found a petroglyph I'd never noticed on a gray basalt boulder I'd passed dozens of times before. The basalt boulder sits in deep sand near the east bank of the big arroyo. The petroglyph was carved on the side of the boulder that faces west and is in shadow early in the morning.

The petroglyph is ancient and badly weathered so the light must be just right, from the west as it was today. Traces of the overnight rain were still visible on the boulder's face, and the dampness darkened the basalt but highlighted the incised outline of the petroglyph.

The incised image exposed an under layer of basalt which is lighter in color; the droplets of rainwater on the surface of the pecked stone caught the early morning light. The image of the petroglyph seemed almost to glitter when I saw it. It appeared to be an oval within a larger oval outline.

Nearly twenty-nine years ago I found another petroglyph on a boulder as I rode horseback down the arroyo. That petroglyph is no longer visible because over the years, the floods had buried it in rocks, pebbles and sand. The petroglyph I found today is only about seventy-five feet from the location of the buried petroglyph.

I'd been thinking about the manuscript and whether I should walk more to get the book written. I'm ambivalent because nothing gets written while I walk. Now this is my laziness shining through; the hotter the weather, the earlier I have to wake up to walk. But after the rain overnight I woke early in anticipation of my walk in the rain-cool morning air. The discovery of the petroglyph made the prospect of a walk even better.

Surprise! I didn't find a new petroglyph the other day; I merely rediscovered a "lost petroglyph." I remembered that somewhere I had a black and white photograph from many years ago, of a petroglyph in the big arroyo. I rummaged through file folders of black and white photographs and copier prints and I found it.

I took the photograph of the petroglyph in early spring, 1980; since then considerable weathering had worn away and muted the incised outline; back then it appeared as a vertical ovoid circle within a slightly larger circle that in effect outlined it. The image appears to be that of the Sun or a head, in a close-fitting helmet or headdress.

During those years I did not regularly walk or ride horseback in the big arroyo I had lost track of the petroglyph. My memory of the location placed the boulder with the petroglyph incorrectly at the abrupt turn which the arroyo takes right below the flat outcrop of blue schist. I'd also remembered the petroglyph itself incorrectly, as a triangle on its point or as a "V."

Now that I've relocated the petroglyph I see that both the boulder with the petroglyph and the boulder at the abrupt turn in the arroyo have similar triangular stones wedged on point against them. That must be the reason I confused the two boulders and the location of the petroglyph.

CHAPTER 47

I left on my walk this mid-August morning just before the Sun rose over the Catalina Mountains. All the rain and cool summer brought out the yellow five-petal flowers which the plant guide calls "desert senna." Everywhere I look I see the bright yellow five-petal blossoms. The senna family has unusual stamens, each with a terminal pore that requires bumblebees to hang upside down in the flowers and buzz to shake loose the pollen, which sticks to their bodies.

As I approached the Thunderbird Mine I saw an odd sight: a grasshopper of ebony black with lines of white along his head and legs. He was perched on top of a pile of coyote dung almost as dark as he. He appeared to be eating the dung. Later I read that the black grasshoppers are poisonous so birds don't eat them; the article said the source of the poison was unknown, but I'd say coyote dung might be one of the sources.

The rain left the prickly pear cacti plump with moisture, thick with buds and luminous waxy flowers of yellow and yellow orange. Once the blossoms dropped, the green bud pods began to fatten; the ripe fruits are the brightest luminous carmine red and as lovely as any blossom, and this year they are the size of chicken eggs and in their abundance they lie scattered everywhere. Birds and rodents feast on the cactus fruit but so do the coyotes and even the bobcats and the mountain lions.

In the sandy bottom of the arroyo bunches of red three-awn grass send out feathery purple red tufts on the end of each stem after the rain. Fountain grass with its silvery tufts grows next to the red three-awn grass, and they appear to be related, but the fountain grass is an invader species from South Africa that was introduced about fifty years ago.

The feathery tufts of the grass glitter with tiny droplets from last night's rain. With the dark gray basalt and light-colored boulders of tuff and limestone, the glittering stalks of grass are magical.

A short distance past the bunches of grass I stopped because I heard a strange sound that might be air rushing out of a cave, or the low hum of a great hive of bees—the sound of the Earth breathing. I listened carefully. The sound seemed to come from behind the basalt boulders surrounded by thickets of catsclaw and mesquite.

I glanced up at the sky above the cove formed by the thickets and the basalt boulders; strands of low clouds swirled away from the cove. I checked the rest of the sky and none of the other clouds were moving like that. I thought about walking back to the cove to take a look, but something about the sound made me think of a sacred place I should stay away from out of respect. A Lakota story about the coming of the bison to human beings involves a cave with wind rushing out of it.

I continued my walk in the arroyo to the flat top boulder with the old petroglyph; like the other flat top boulder only a short distance away, the stone on top of the boulder had been chiseled out to form a rainwater cistern.

At Old Laguna village the natural cisterns in the expanse of light yellow sandstone are still carefully protected as a blessed place. In long droughts, the river and even the springs dried up, but the hard, fine-grained sandstone cisterns caught the least rain or snow that might fall from the meager clouds.

I found something really amazing and beautiful today. I decided to walk down to the arroyo to photograph the old petroglyph on the boulder instead of working on the manuscript. Too many disruptions early in the day put me in the wrong mood for writing.

Now that I had rediscovered the petroglyph I wanted a new photograph to compare to the photograph I made more than twenty years ago. Anyway, the morning was too beautiful to remain indoors at my keyboard. Last night a cool rain came and filled the big rain barrel half full and left the air smelling wonderfully of rain. So I got the camera ready, grabbed my hat, my belt with a water bottle, an emergency whistle, the ultralight .38, and off I went.

On my walks I'd noticed interesting rocks that washed down javelina paths from the top of the bank into the arroyo. The rocks I'd noticed were hard fine-grained quartzites of yellow or light orange or off-white, very unlike the other rocks that were mostly dark basalt. Moreover these stones were smoothed and rounded and fit my hand perfectly for crushing and grinding seeds. I thought the stones were a sign of human occupation but I never detoured to find out. But now that I'd rediscovered the petroglyph on the boulder only a short distance away, I knew what I'd suspected was true: thousands of years ago people lived here in the Tucson Mountains.

On my way to photograph the petroglyph I had to pass the rainwater cistern carved in the top of a boulder. The rain the night before had filled the rock cistern, and when I climbed up to its edge I found a small feather, an owl feather. I left it where it was, where Owl the Warrior Scalp-taker, the Sacrificer, had left it.

I'd photographed the cistern long ago for my fictional photo narrative about sacrificial altars. During the ten years I wrote *Almanac of the Dead* I did a great deal of thinking about the Maya and the Nahua ancestors. The photo narrative was concerned with the way words modify how we may see a photograph. Photographs need only resemble slightly what the words with them described for the viewer to "see" whatever the words describe. For the purposes of my photo narrative, the boulder top made a perfect altar; the carved-out rock cistern looked like it would catch sacrificial blood.

I decided not to go straight down the wash to the boulder to photograph the petroglyph but instead to walk along the bank above the arroyo where I felt the ancestors had lived.

I had to pass the rubble that marks the place where a "real estate developer" used a bulldozer to subdivide the land—not to be confused with the man who gouged boulders from the big arroyo with his machine. Nearby the rubble I saw signs of the ancestors' home—dark basalt and pale quartzite grinding stones that had been overturned and everywhere tiny pieces of colorful chalcedony, chert, jasper and flint. I picked up a small piece of bright red jasper and saw it had been hand-chipped; I looked at the others, and then I looked all around and saw colorful unique stones and pebbles the ancestors gathered. Unfortunately the blade of the bulldozer had cut a crude road through the site and most of the hand-chipped stones and other artifacts had been buried under a heap of torn plant debris and dirt.

Only once, years before, I had found a perfectly chipped arrow point of fine-grained basalt near my gate down the hill. Back then I didn't realize the ancestors lived here—I knew they used to hunt here, but that's all. I thought all of the ancient people lived down along the Santa Cruz or Rillito River, not up here in the hills. I had a neighbor two miles away who had found arrowheads near Broken Springs Road, but this was the first indication that the ancestors had lived near my house. No wonder some nights I saw figures in the darkness or heard women's voices singing grinding songs.

I walked a short distance between the skinny greasewoods and I looked down and there on the ground, surrounded by many small stones and chips off rocks that were dark hues, I spotted a white quartz the size and shape of an elm leaf: it was a knife. I was thrilled by its perfection; it was so thin, so finely chipped I knew it belonged to the ancient ones.

I felt a great blessing from the ancestors who lived here and made stones into tools thousands of years ago. The white quartz knife was so prominent among the other small chips and rocks it seemed to me it had been intentionally left there—perhaps on the last night the people ever carved there or danced in the circular area above the boulder-top cistern?

The ancient people here managed to survive the great heat and the droughts, and made their living by the rocks and stones they chipped into knives and awls which they traded for food, just as my Paguate ancestors traded the sandstone griddles for corn in lean years.

I walked around the area and found awl stones used to make holes to sew hides together, and I found sharp-edged stone axes. I found many colorful cherts and blood red jaspers and pale chalcedony, clear rock crystals and even glittering pyrites, but I did not find any turquoise rocks. The ancestors must have found them in the big arroyo as I still do, but I imagine that the turquoise rocks may have been too valuable for the people here to keep and were traded away to the south for macaw feathers or food.

To reduce weight from their packs on the long journey south to Mexico, the indigenous traders scraped the chrysocolla from the copper-bearing rock and powdered it. This "soft turquoise" powder was packed in small dry gourds the traders wore around their waists. The cabochons of chalcedony-impregnated chrysocolla must have brought the traders a good price because it is rare, denser and harder than turquoise.

From Mexico City all the way to Guatemala, the powdered soft turquoise was made into sacred blue green paint to adorn those chosen to be made into "jewels" for Tlaloc, Lord of the Rain.

CHAPTER 48

Regal Chapulin, ebony Chapulin, blackest obsidian, black diamond, black jade. Lord Grasshopper your life span is the length of the ripening of the prickly pear fruits, and the mesquite beans that nourish the coyotes who supply you with the smelly potion which protects you.

I never had seen an ebony black grasshopper before. I thought the shiny black creature with elegant thin white stripes on its legs might be a rare species of grasshopper. But when I searched the Internet, I found many wonderful photographs of black grasshoppers (though none as intensely black or marked as beautifully as the grasshopper I saw on the coyote dung). The web search found three million ninety thousand web sites which have the words "black" and "grasshopper" but which have no relation to the jumping insect. There are shoes called "Grasshopper" which appear to be much desired by web-users.

A number of human beings wear elaborate grasshopper costumes of spandex and latex with large Plexiglas helmets or masks that have antennae and saucer eyes. All of them appeared to be men in grasshopper costumes.

If I'd had more endurance I might have searched long enough to find a woman in a grasshopper suit and insect helmet mask, but I only made it to page twenty-three in my web search of the three million ninety thousand pages of sites with the words "black grasshopper" on them.

The costumed grasshopper people look archetypal in an action comic sort of way. Spider-Man meets Galactic Traveler. I wonder if the grasshopper people attend conferences or throw parties in public gardens.

I was reminded of my series of Chapulin's portraits, and I smiled to think other humans are similarly "arrested" by the regal grasshoppers.

The photographs of the black grasshoppers on the web sites were the efforts of people who appreciated the beauty and size of the creatures. The killers of black grasshoppers posted no photos with their accounts of frenzied assaults on the clouds of insects destroying their gardens.

I had no idea of the significance of black grasshoppers until I read two or three of the web sites maintained by state agricultural departments to help farmers in their states combat the insects. I learned the black lubbers lay waste to all living plants and crops in their path.

One of the web sites concerned a short story by Ernest Hemingway in which the protagonist saw a black grasshopper after a forest fire and believed a green grasshopper was turned black by the fire. Hemingway was mistaken about the fire and the black grasshopper, but he made the black grasshopper a symbol of transformation anyway. He was right about transformation—infestations of the insects quickly turn plants and trees to skeletons.

Lord Chapulin who visited me last year was green, but some black grasshoppers are green; so it may be that Chapulin is only a rare visitor to the desert which explains his stopover to eat rain lilies at my place. He got blown off course on his way to the farms in Yuma and ended up here in the Tucson Mountains. Apparently the black lubbers are around farming areas all the time, although catastrophic infestations occur at seven year intervals.

The most beautiful grasshopper in the world is the color of the rainbow and lives in Madagascar.

It's August 21. This morning I turned the kitchen faucet and there was no water. My heart sank. I always fear the well will go dry. But it's been a wet cool summer and our consumption of water was moderate.

I know all wells will run dry eventually, but I have a feeling the well is not dry; instead some equipment failure has occurred that's bound to cost me a thousand.

The electricity reaches the pump but it isn't pushing any water, the well and pump specialist tells me. This is good news because I thought lightning might have struck the pump, but it still runs. A new pump would be a huge expense. He thinks it is a hole in the pipe. The new pipe and the two workmen and the rig truck won't be cheap. I may run out of money before the well runs out of water.

I called the water truck man and ordered two loads of about four thousand gallons of water to take care of us until the well pump gets fixed. What a pity I didn't have my rainwater storage system in place this summer when we got so much rain. My hope is to eventually use rainwater for all my needs except drinking water. I prefer hard water from the well for drinking.

Today was quite a day. First no water; later Old Green, our 1971 Chevy truck, rolled into the ravine. Just after Caz parked it, the transmission slipped out of PARK and it rolled backwards down the driveway then turned and went down the steep slope in front of the house. Old Green came to rest in the old rusty tin cans and broken glass of an old ranch dump at the bottom of the ravine. The old ranch had a number of dumps, but this one is the biggest.

The run-away pick-up crushed a small saguaro and a number of jojoba bushes and two ocotillos; it hit a big palo verde tree at the bottom where it came to rest. It is a miracle the truck didn't smash down any of the large two hundred year old saguaro cacti in its plunge.

I had my headphones on and was working on this manuscript when it happened so I didn't hear anything. I saw by the expression on Caz's face that something awful had happened. I assumed it had occured in the city and Caz had come to tell me. I never dreamed it had just happened on my driveway. Caz tried to stop the truck from rolling and was skinned up from being dragged by the truck. He might have been killed so we were very lucky after all.

The ocotillos can be replanted, but the rest of the damage, especially to the rocks and dirt, will leave a scar that will last for years, because the desert soil is so thin and fragile here. I don't want to see any more damage done to the desert, so I am inclined to leave the truck in the ravine with the other ranch refuse. To hire a tow truck to remove it will only do more damage to the desert.

Old Green has a good color to blend in with the surrounding desert bushes and plants. I'd like to paint prickly pear cacti covered in red fruit, and palo verde and catsclaw in bloom on it to camouflage Old Green even more. I'd paint desert shrubs on the windshield and windows so the sun wouldn't glare off the glass. It would make a perfect reliquary for my ashes when the time comes, but Robert and Caz aren't amused.

PART FIVE

Lord Chapulin

CHAPTER 49

The blue silver clouds pushed in from the south and covered the sky and the eye of the Sun. A hurricane at the edge of the Baja sent us these rain clouds overnight, and now a cool breeze moves out of the southeast from the direction the hurricane took.

As I sat watching the clouds, the white-eared hummingbird came to the feeder on the mesquite tree, but after one taste he flew away— the sugar water was too stale and full of gnats. Ashamed, I immediately took the feeder indoors to wash it and refill it with fresh sugar water.

One morning when I first started my walks, I left before I refilled the hummingbird feeders, and the male white-eared hummingbird followed me on my walk, chirping and scolding me for a mile before he turned back.

The hummingbirds around my house have been here for years yet I know very little about them. All female hummingbirds are similarly colored an iridescent pale emerald green so I haven't learned to distinguish them. I keep a guidebook handy but so far I can only recognize the male white-eared hummingbird, the male Lucifer hummingbird, and the male Costas hummingbird. The Costas has black and white feathers in his tail.

Once years ago on a cool November morning I found an emerald green hummingbird, dead, I thought, outside the front porch window. I leave my windows unwashed so that birds don't break their necks or skulls against the glass, but dirty glass didn't work this time. I felt such regret.

I picked up the little green-feathered creature to give it a burial of some sort and when I held it in the palm of my hand I felt the rapid beating of its tiny heart. I held it in both hands to warm it, and the heartbeat seemed to get stronger. After a couple of minutes I felt the hummingbird move and when I looked into my hands I saw he was awake, so I offered him my finger and he perched on it. I watched him recover more and more while he sat on my finger, and when I thought he seemed ready, I took him to a flowering brittlebush and he stepped off my finger onto the bush. I stayed nearby and watched until he recovered enough to fly away.

Hummingbirds are very territorial and the ones that live around my house spend a good deal of time chasing one another from the three or four feeders I hang in the trees of my front yard. Among the old-time Pueblo people Hummingbird was considered a great warrior and hunter, in the same category as Eagle and Owl. Hummingbird can't survive in the desert on flower nectar and pollen alone, and must hunt gnats and other tiny flying insects in order to survive the months the desert has no flowers.

This year the abundance of the prickly pear fruit extends beyond the cornucopia spilling around the cactus plants. Coyote dung is black with prickly pear seeds; the ants retrieve the seeds, and outside the entrances to their palaces, thousands of tiny black seeds are kept temporarily until the ants make storage space down below.

As the trail nears the Thunderbird Mine I pass the small barrel cactus I replanted a few years ago. Would-be cactus rustlers dug it up and left it lying root up by the trail to remove later, but never returned. I couldn't find the spot the rustlers dug it from, so I found a place where rainwater flows past and a small jojoba grew to give the cactus some shade. I replanted it there and now this morning the small barrel cactus had five or six blossoms on it, a sign the cactus is happy with its location.

I'm always on watch for snakes as I head down the hill toward the Gila Monster Mine because there is a stretch of fine white sand that the snakes like because they can scoot themselves down into the sand and be less visible. This morning I spotted a small snake curled up there—it was only one or two shades away from being an albino, and blended perfectly with the soft sand. The snake didn't seem to be hunting—it seemed to have spread its coil flat as if to absorb moisture from the sand through his skin.

As I came down the path where the old road drops into the big arroyo I looked down and saw a small outcrop of rock salted with grains of chrysocolla. I walked through the dickhead's private sand and gravel pit. Poor boulders! Slashed and shattered by the steel claw. One of you boulders should roll over the machine and crush that man, I thought as I passed by.

In the big arroyo, I found a fist-size stone mortar of light orange quartzite, and a little farther up the wash in the fine loose sand as I reached down to pick up a shard of brown glass, I spotted a turquoise cabochon the size of a bean.

The hurricane clouds look different than the usual rain clouds. They are fluffy from the strong winds that bring them, and very dense for such silvery white clouds. Usually the thunderclouds out of the southwest have to be very dark to be so dense.

Later an undulating white rain came in graceful waves down the dark basalt foothills of Black Mountain but without thunder or lightning. Now the rain mist breeze is fragrant with the yellow star flowers of the sennas and the cascades of tiny yellow blossoms on the greasewoods, the chaparral.

In a few minutes the clouds darkened and thunder rumbled; a strong wind out of the southwest drove the rain under the porch roof so I fled indoors. I'm wary of lightning; some fearsome natural forces become less threatening the more you learn about them, but lightning isn't one of them.

Lightning is able to travel twenty miles or more horizontally, to strike out of the clear blue sky. A lightning strike affects the body's ability to regulate blood pressure and body temperature, and the rate of the heartbeat. Basically lightning shorts out the body's own electrical system. Half of all who survive a lightning strike are dead within the first year from heart failure.

After the lightning and thunder had passed I went out on the porch again. The rain barrel by the porch was three quarters full. The cactus spines on the saguaro, cholla and prickly pear glittered with the light the raindrops reflected; the greasewoods and palo verdes seemed to grow bright green leaves before my eyes. Their speed in flowering and going to seed lets them take full advantage of the rainy spells.

It is possible to collect enough rainwater to run a household year round if you have a way to store the rainwater. When I first came to this old ranch in 1978, only the drinking water came from the well pumped by the windmill; all washing, bathing and toilet flushing water came from the twenty-two thousand gallon cistern in the ground out back.

It seems a pity to flush toilets with rainwater. Now there is a system which stores gray water from showers and recycles it into the toilet tank. The people who remain here after the groundwater is used up will have to depend on gray water and rain.

CHAPTER 50

My old friends the white-eared hummingbirds are back from the mountains early this year. They have wintered around the house for the thirty years I've lived here. They often come to the feeders when we are on the porch talking, and then after they feed, they perch nearby and patiently listen and watch us.

All the wonderful rain down here lured them back. The feeders were full of sugar water but I had no takers all summer because there were so many blossoms and sugar gnats for the hummingbirds to eat. The Gila woodpeckers that usually drain the feeders were elsewhere too, eating fat larvae and bugs that thrived from the rain.

Hurricane rains' white silver mist curls down the mountainside. The moist air shimmers green, each droplet a tiny mirror of the desert leaves, the cactus skin and palo verde's green bark. The hurricane clouds keep coming—unfurled by the winds, they are heavier and thicker than ordinary August rain clouds.

Ordinary clouds move slowly with nicely rounded bellies on top, even and layered in silver gray and blue. The hurricane clouds rise and crowd close, heap up and tumble over one another with great thunder, and make their way to the Catalina Mountain peaks high above the valley. In the mountain updrafts the clouds take the shapes of blue herons and bison.

The clouds in the distance are as deep blue as the sea with frothy silver white breakers blowing over them from the south. Purple clouds rise behind the black mountains, but in the center of the western horizon through a slit in the clouds the eye of the Sun looks through for only an instant.

Later the sky cools as the Sun moves below the horizon. The purple blue bellies of the clouds spread and flatten—ocean, lake or big river—then a dark rain begins over the Black Mountain ridge. The clouds come in dark blue banks overlaid with wind-frothed silver. In the distance to the west I can see thick wide purple blue clouds as the temperature continues to drop. The wind is out of the southwest where the clouds come from.

This summer of 2008 was the coolest summer ever since I came here in 1978.

Part of the cool summer was the publication of another wonderful book of poems from Ofelia Zepeda, titled *Where Clouds Are Formed*. The poet knows the old names for the mountains in this desert:

> Cemamagi, Tumamoc
> Babad Do' ag, Santa Catalina Mountains
> Cew Do' ag, Rincon Mountains
> Cuk Do' ag, Black Mountains, Tucson Mountains

"There are places where the clouds are formed"—I recalled Ofelia's poem of that title last summer when I felt the rush of the cool air from deep in the Earth and heard the hum; overhead I saw tendrils of newborn clouds rise into the sky.

In 1983 a hurricane came out of the east Pacific and went into the Gulf of California, headed straight for Tucson. The summer had been wet, and the earth was already saturated, and the arroyos and creeks had water. By the time the hurricane came by Tucson only a brisk breeze remained of the wind, but the churning masses of gray silver clouds poured rain from the sky for two nights and two days. The Tanque Verde, Rillito and the Santa Cruz rivers rose out of their banks and washed away condominiums and sections of interstate highway as well as three high voltage power transmission towers and two steel bridges that crossed the Santa Cruz River.

The mountains call the rain clouds; the mountains gather the rain clouds; later the rain clouds emerge in the rushing wind from caves and crevices hidden deep in the mountain peaks.

Now the sky is packed with blue clouds as in a great flood or high tide. Sometimes the storms circle around the Tucson Mountains. I hear thunder to the west in the Altar Valley where the rain clouds travel from the Gulf straight to the farms and villages of the Tohono O'Odom.

Now the clouds look like bundles of long silver tail feathers from a great silver blue macaw that gracefully curl down to meet Earth, dissolving into mists of silver over dark blue violet.

A cool afternoon in the high eighties lured me out for a walk. I decided to go look for unusual rocks along the bank of the big arroyo. The quartz, flint, jasper and chert rocks scattered about differed a great deal from the underlying basalt and light soil; the ancestors were on the lookout for unusual rocks and brought them back to their home. Sometimes I find a small stone with only one or two chips taken from it; maybe the ancestors experimented to see if the rock would permit them to flake a blade or point without crumbling or shattering.

I noticed it at once. This crystal quartz was translucent; it caught the sunlight like magic. It would catch the light of the moon as well. Crystal quartz is infrequent in the Tucson Mountains because the seismic activity and powerful volcanic explosions shattered the quartz crystals.

The quartz crystal I picked up had been carefully chipped to enhance its natural resemblance to a great horned owl. When I hold it under my desk lamp I can see the crystal was worked in the middle of the transparent end to make the slight triangular groove on the owl head between the ears. The eyes and beak can also be seen on the incised surface, and another incision on the right side forms the beak, neck and left wing. The quartz that forms the feet is not quite transparent and was also carved in front to separate the feet from the breast. On the owl's lower left an incision also helps form the feet.

I found another smaller clear quartz crystal not long afterward. One end is transparent, the other end translucent just like the carved owl crystal. Both crystals caught the sunlight so brightly, I wanted to see if they will catch starlight.

Today the wind was blowing from the northeast but felt good because the afternoon sun was strong and the air humid. The wind was blowing hard enough that some sounds were muffled, while others were louder: the wind through the needles of the saguaros made a loud rushing sound; the twigs and branches of bushes and tree branches clattered. I walked around the ancestors' place looking at their scattered chips of stone, and I thought about them. Did they know the last time they were here that they would not be returning? What happened? Where did they go?

Right then in the wind I heard a haunting sound that I remembered from childhood, the distinctive jingles of the ka'tsina dancers' ankle bells, the tinkle as the dancers approached. I looked northeast in the direction of the sound which seemed to come from the big arroyo near the boulder with the petroglyph. The ancestors didn't go anywhere; they are still here, right now.

A long time ago I picked up a small flat piece of white quartz with a sharp edge and the moon shape of a scraper. When I found the piece of quartz I looked for any marks left by chipping, but noticed none at the time. Today I reexamined this white quartz piece, and lo, a belated discovery. Closer examination with a magnifying glass revealed the quartz had been carefully worked with great precision. The ancestor had removed delicate tiny flakes that were almost invisible, with a very small tool that must have required much concentration and patience to prevent the quartz from shattering.

On my walk home with the wonderful crystals in my pocket, I came upon the circular imprint in the sand left by a small snake, and in the center of the circle I found a tiny turquoise stone.

I can't forget the jingle of the ka'tsina's ankle bells I heard yesterday in the wind at the ancestors' place. I will not visit there again for a while.

CHAPTER 51

Late in the morning my son Robert called me outside. He'd just seen the biggest grasshopper ever in the front yard.

Chapulin. Was it Lord Chapulin himself?

What did he want?

I hadn't made many copies of his book, *Portrait of Chapulin,* because I was trying to complete the manuscript. He might be concerned with the delay, so he sent an emissary this morning.

But by the time I got to the front yard, the big grasshopper was gone. In the days and weeks since, I've gone back to that late morning when I missed my call from Lord Chapulin's messenger. I believe he came to tell me his people were coming to stay in my yard awhile to rest and to eat.

This morning I found a big grasshopper in the front yard eating the leftover vegetables I put out for the wild birds. He seemed unconcerned about me but later when I looked for him, he was gone. I found two big grasshoppers together near a pot of rain lilies, but they walked away from me rapidly. They didn't seem as friendly as Lord Chapulin and the others who visited last year. I seldom see them jump; is this because predators might spot them if they jumped?

This afternoon another white hurricane deluge here—a cloud burst as if a giant water tank ruptured in the sky. The fat gray cloud unrolled itself then fell in a shimmering white veil against the dark basalt hill-tops. A warm moist wind out of the southeast drove the clouds rapidly away so the heavy rain did not last.

Before sundown Robert went to see how much rainwater had col-lected in the cistern and found a desert tortoise on the path by the old windmill well. Summer rainstorms bring out the rare desert tortoises, and one must drive carefully and help them across the road if need be.

The tortoise was the size of a dinner plate, large enough to be sixty years old, as old as I am. I kept my distance out of respect; humans are an ugly sight and a shock to shy wild creatures. I used a soft voice because I didn't want to frighten the tortoise. I said, "Oh you are so beautiful." Then I slowly withdrew to get out of the creature's path. In more than thirty years living here, we'd not been visited like this before by such an old tortoise. Truly we were blessed.

The tortoise came to the bottom of the wire fence by the path and stopped. At first I thought the tortoise wanted inside the front yard so I took the old pit bull dog indoors. I took the wire cutters and opened a hole in the wire to allow the tortoise to pass through; he got closer to the fence and to the edge of the aloe plants but he came no farther through the wire.

I came back before long to make sure the tortoise did not venture around to the back yard with the four mastiffs. But the tortoise had dug himself down into the damp soft sand until he was partially bur-ied, and partially concealed by the aloes. Sunset gave way to twilight and the tortoise remained there. How odd that it came there to spend the night. There were other places on the hilltop with soft sand the tor-toise might have used. Why did the tortoise stop so close to us humans with dogs?

The following morning the tortoise was still partially covered with damp sand by the aloes. I checked on him from time to time. I wanted to see which direction he took when he left. At first he came down the path toward the front gate which I left open in case he wanted to come into the yard.

I watched the tortoise from a distance. When he reached the threshold of the gate he turned away and went downhill a short distance then he got on the diagonal path down the side of the hill that faces west. I checked a short while later and he was gone. I followed the path I'd last seen him take, but a thorough search under the greasewoods nearby revealed no sign of him. Tortoises like to make their burrows in the banks of the arroyos just high enough to stay out of the floodwaters. I walked down the steep slope into the west ravine to see if I might find the tortoise on his way to a burrow, but he'd disappeared.

The hummingbirds are contesting with one another for access to the feeder. They whizz around chasing one another; it seems mostly in jest, although last year I distinctly heard the sound of two tiny beaks clicking in combat. With the rain come the tiny sugar gnats that hover in the mesquite leaves; these gnats don't bother humans. The hummingbirds zip and dart through the air and catch the gnats. That's how the hummingbirds survive when flowers are scarce.

Again for the fourth day in a row great dark roiling clouds, armies of ghost warriors many legions wide, rise high over the southwest horizon of the black basalt mountains. While I was out walking I saw Chapulin on a greasewood watch me as I looked for rocks, and then in the yard, another grasshopper. All this rain brings them. Chapulin might be one of the Chacs, one of the Lords of the Rain.

The Anthropology Museum in Mexico City has a large exquisite figure of Lord Chapulin carved out of red chalcedony. The famed "Chapultepec" Gardens are the Grasshopper Gardens, where the Lord Chapulin and his Queen resided with unnumbered relatives and clanspeople in the luxury of fresh running springs and a great abundance of fragrant flowers.

In the *Cantares Mexicanos*, the great epic of Nahuatl literature, "grasshopper" is another name for the ghost warrior. I didn't understand the significance of this until later in the summer when the grasshoppers changed their attitude toward me and other humans.

———◇———

Last night as we sat outside on the porch in the dark, Ratty, our arch-enemy who lives under the aloe patch in the front yard, came out and showed herself to us, almost as if she was greeting us or maybe taunting us—she chews up the wires in the engines of our cars and pulls the stuffing out of the old cushions on the white plastic chairs in the front yard.

Despite the curses we hurled at her when we saw her, Ratty seemed fond of us, and wanted in her way to join us. She sat outside her nest and watched us. The sound of human voices didn't seem to upset her. I started laughing. I told Bill and Robert, "Look. Ratty is sitting with us; she thinks she's our friend. She has no idea she's our enemy." I felt a fondness for her after that. She already figured out a long time ago that I wasn't going to poison or trap her, only curse at her.

People ask me why not get rid of the big rat nest in my front yard. The piled debris crowns the entire four by six foot aloe patch. If it were simply a rat nest, I might have considered its removal. But Ratty and her clan aren't the only ones that live there. A number of rattle-snakes call the rat tunnels under the aloes home and so do the great desert toads.

I know the ancient people here held the pack rats in high regard; in times of hunger Ratty's pantry kept human beings alive. During droughts and famines, the hungry people used to raid the pack rats' nests for the stores of seeds and jojoba nuts, dried cactus buds and fruits and any baby rats they might find.

Pampered and well fed, we might gag at the thought of sharing Ratty's stores of mesquite and palo verde beans and dried cactus buds. But Allen Ginsberg had a story from a Buddhist monk during the Cultural Revolution in China. He told the story to us in 1984 in China as our delegation of U.S writers invited by the Chinese Writers Association visited Buddhist shrines. The story was about hunger. One of the

Buddhist priests told Ginsberg that during the Cultural Revolution, after starving for weeks, he was so hungry that when he saw an undigested leaf of mustard greens in the shit of another priest, he picked the mustard leaf out of the shit, rinsed it off in a stream and ate it.

The huge toad that guards the front doorstep came out from her nest under the porch bricks, and sat awhile with us too. I like to think it is the same big toad I rescued from the cave-in of bricks under the front porch last year.

CHAPTER 52

At night before I fall asleep I read as many Emily Dickinson poems as I can. Her poems are full of surprises—their rhyme schemes unpredictable and brilliant as are her uses of the colloquial with the classic. The themes of the poems cover a vast range and are filled with ineffable and mysterious glimpses of transcendence and eternity. How sensuous and joyous this poem is:

> A Route of Evanescence
> With a Revolving Wheel—
> A Resonance of Emerald—
> A Rush of Cochineal—
> And every Blossom on the Bush
> Adjusts its tumbled Head—
> The mail from Tunis, probably,
> An easy Morning's Ride—

Emily Dickinson was famously reclusive, but how else to get the solitude and time to compose more than a thousand poems in one lifetime? She wrote many of her finest poems about bees or flies; her images of the sun and the light, of flowers and birds came to her in her garden. She wrote a wonderful poem about snakes that goes:

A narrow Fellow in the Grass
Occasionally rides—
You may have met Him—did you not
His notice sudden is—
The Grass divides as with a Comb—
A spotted shaft is seen—
And then it closes at your feet
And opens further on—
He likes a Boggy Acre
A floor too cool for Corn—
Yet when a boy, and Barefoot—
I more than once, at Noon
Have passed, I thought, a Whip lash
Unbraiding in the Sun
When stooping to secure it
It wrinkled, and was gone—
Several of Nature's People
I know, and they know me—
I feel for them a transport
Of cordiality—
But never met this Fellow
Attended, or alone
Without a tighter breathing
And Zero at the Bone—

Great thick whorled clouds fold over themselves bubbling up rising like silvery yucca soap suds. Veils of white rain soften and smear into pastel blues of towering sky dragons and cloud bears fishing in a fast river of wind.

Giant vertical clouds behind the Black Mountain take on the form of revenant warriors descending to Earth in swirling fog and mist. In the distance a faint rumble of thunder from the southwest, and the huge cloud flattens as it empties a deluge behind the mountains.

As the raindrops begin to fall from the cloud overhead the outline of the cloud begins to lose its edges, feathering into thin air. What lovely blue violet hues on the clouds along the west horizon.

This morning was too dry for rain, and the mist from the clouds evaporated before it reached the ground; it rose and once again became clouds.

CHAPTER 53

Yesterday, September 6, the dogs in back were barking, so I went out. I found a Gila monster lizard outside the fence, and outside the reach of the mastiffs. Beaded in jet black and coral, the big lizard was breathtaking in his beauty and a blessing to see.

The next day, Chapulin's in-laws and their relatives were all here for a visit in my front yard. Lord Chapulin and his wife must have told them I am a friend.

The grasshoppers prefer the white rain flowers over the pink flowers this summer. The foliage is what they like. They work unseen from the bottom of the stalks in the pot so the rain lily leaves get shorter quite rapidly.

Black—obsidian black, coal black—Chapulin wants another portrait this year. As soon as I complete the manuscript, I will do it.

Lord Chapulin's kinfolk stayed for another day. They didn't touch the four o'clock or jessamine; I don't trust them with the datura. I lifted off any grasshoppers I saw in the daturas; otherwise I won't have any datura flowers this winter. I am a little concerned by the number of Chapulin's entourage.

A pale green rain comes with a warm breeze out of the southeast. I hear thunder now, and more raindrops fall. Delicate threads of rain swirl into thick white draperies that fold across the dark hills.

Two thunderstorms this afternoon and evening—thunder and lightning and good but not huge rain. I brought the dogs indoors early tonight because the tarantulas and big toads come out after the rain, and of course rattlesnakes and Gila monster lizards. The dogs can't resist harassing them, and I don't want my dogs to harm them.

We haven't seen Godzilla lizard for about two weeks. There are baby lizards in the front yard now, and on the south-facing wall, a baby lizard no longer than my thumbnail. All the good rain we got nearly every afternoon in July and August may mean plenty of roaches and other insects off in the aloe patch or under the greasewood bushes. No need to show oneself to the predators in the front yard if the weeds are full of bugs. However we are beginning to worry that the largest and boldest of the mesquite lizards met an unfortunate end.

Again the following day as we sat out on the front porch, we wondered about the Godzilla lizard and what became of him. Just then I noticed motion in the top of the big mesquite tree and heard the characteristic rapid beak rattle of a roadrunner. Speak of a likely suspect in Godzilla's disappearance—there was Roadrunner, that cuckoo bird, clown and thief, death on snakes, lizards, baby tortoises, baby birds and rodents. Our suspicions grew after Roadrunner's visit.

A clan of roadrunners was already living here when I moved in. They built one of their nests inside the impenetrable arms of a six foot tall cholla cactus with spines so thick and sharp few predators ever try to rob their nests.

All the rain this summer brought many sorts of insects. There are a great many very large butterflies this year—mostly shades of gold and bright yellows because the wild flowers late in the summer are mostly hues of yellow or white.

I welcomed Lord Chapulin and his wife last year and invited their return. But the grasshoppers' visit this year gave me quite a surprise.

Chapulin's entourage glutted themselves on the leaves of the white rain lilies and moved into the pink lilies and to the four o'clocks which they don't eat but use for their siestas. The grasshoppers are so gorged they can't fly.

These grasshoppers are sneaky and crafty and quickly take cover when humans come around. Lord Chapulin and his wife were entirely different—so gracious and regal at all times. What a disappointment.

Today the grasshoppers in their wild celebration ate the white rain lilies flat to the dirt in the pot; luckily the lilies don't mind as long as there is plenty of water. I picked the revelers off the white four o'clock plant and the geraniums although they didn't really eat those plants, they merely rested on them.

I didn't take any chances after I'd seen what the black grasshoppers did to the rain lilies so I tossed the hoppers over the fence. I didn't realize one of the mastiffs was on the other side of the fence catching and eating the grasshoppers until that evening when the mastiff threw up a pile of black grasshopper legs and red wings all over the doggy bed.

Early the other morning after a night of an apparent grasshopper fiesta, I saw one big grasshopper eat the thorax of a fallen companion.

I remember that when I first read the web site reports about the black grasshoppers I thought they must be referring to "black grasshoppers" and not my beautiful green Chapulin with rosy magenta wings.

But now that I've had the entourage here for a few weeks, I am beginning to understand. The black grasshoppers, unlike their Lord, are furtive, sly guests. I had no idea Chapulin would have so many followers this year. Still I haven't killed any of the grasshoppers out of regard for Lord Chapulin.

Were the stories about black grasshoppers that I read on the Internet the reason for Lord Chapulin and his wife's sudden departure, and for the other grasshoppers to behave so boorishly? They hadn't done me any harm in the past—because of their majesty and beauty I invited them to eat the rain lilies. But after I'd read the infestation reports on the Internet, each time I saw a black grasshopper I recalled the stories of havoc, instead of seeing their majesty and beauty as I had at first. The negative energy of these stories must have touched Lord Chapulin, and his wife; they must have felt a change in me when I recalled what I'd learned on the Internet. So they did not visit for long. They did not feel I was their friend anymore.

CHAPTER 54

About two weeks ago in one of the rainstorms a big saguaro
fell, and shattered into five or six large pieces about ten feet
from the odd knob of basalt above the Gila Monster Mine.
The big segments of the cactus blocked the trail so that horses had to
detour around them. Within a few days the heat began to ferment the
cactus, which gave off a strong wine odor.

The saguaro was part of a small grove of the same size—sister
plants ten feet tall with many long branching arms which marked their
age at one hundred fifty years or more. I took a close look at the rocky
ledge where the fallen cactus once stood but could see no apparent
cause for its demise. Its companions in the grove appeared untouched
by the wind and other forces that had taken down their sister.

Years ago during an evening thunderstorm a saguaro fell across the
road, and a friend who'd just left our house returned to get help to
move the big saguaro so his car could get by. The toppled saguaro had
broken into five or six sections in its fall. Most of the sections were
at least two feet in diameter, and weighed hundreds of pounds each
because saguaros store water in their tissue and weigh more than a ton.
Many cacti are able to regenerate from severed branches or pads, but
not the saguaro.

I went to help roll the sections of broken saguaro out of the middle
of the road. After the rain the evening air was cool so I was surprised,

even shocked at the body heat that radiated from the broken pieces of the giant cactus, just as the body of any dead thing remains warm for a while.

By daylight, the saguaros are spectacular enough with their towering strange presence. But the first time my younger son saw them he was six years old and it was dark. He saw them in the car headlights and he asked me why there were so many telephone poles here.

After dark, especially in the moonlight, the saguaros come to life. You can feel a subtle energy as from the gathering of a large clan. They move gracefully, and sway in the wind.

The fallen saguaro becomes a home and resource to a great many beings—insects, rodents and birds that help devour the moist fermented cactus pulp, and later take up residence in the wooden ribs of its skeleton. Over the years the skeleton turns to a grayish white dust that leaves a white outline or "shadow" of the cactus on the ground where it fell.

The saguaros are mighty beings who are linked to life and death for all living creatures in this desert. From the saguaro fruit the Tohono O'Odom brewed the sacred wine that put them in the presence of their beloved ancestors during the summer ceremonies to welcome the rain clouds back again.

In the big arroyo near the rusted steel culvert half buried in sand, I glanced to my left and there was a turquoise rock on the ridge of freshly washed sand and pebbles. I found another smaller turquoise rock near the place of the sound of air rushing out.

One of Godzilla's heirs, a tiny mesquite lizard about an inch and a half long, was out under the mesquite tree eating tiny golden cockroaches after I moved my rain lily pots to try to discourage the grasshoppers.

If Godzilla lizard were still alive he'd never allow the baby lizard to eat any roaches. Now the territory under the tree and the aloe patch belongs to the two or three baby lizards that recently appeared. They are so tiny they are nearly impossible for a predator at some distance to see.

Godzilla the mesquite lizard reached a critical size—once he got so big and able to chase off rivals and to eat even more cockroaches and grow even larger, he became much too visible. On the ground or the wall or a branch of the mesquite tree, Godzilla became an easy target for roadrunners and racer snakes.

My most vivid memory of the Godzilla lizard is the morning I was watering, and moved a pot of red geraniums on the porch. Out came the most beautiful golden scorpion the size of my thumb. The sunlight made her glitter like solid gold and on her back, perfectly formed and curled in perfect rows, were dozens of golden translucent babies too young to leave their mother.

How beautiful they were in the sunlight, I thought, and an instant later Godzilla lizard raced up, fearless of me, and in two gulps ate the mother scorpion and the babies on her back, just like that. So we eat and then one day some hungry creature eats us.

Last night the local TV news reported that baby rattlesnakes are being born now, and the mothers protecting the babies "seem more aggressive" than usual. Despised and maligned since the Europeans invaded, rattlesnakes were thought to abandon their babies at birth. Two or three years ago researchers found that mother rattlesnakes remain close by to protect their newborn babies for at least ten days.

The eradication of ignorance about rattlesnakes moves slowly in Tucson. People here still believe that "relocating" a rattlesnake found in their yard does no harm to the rattlesnake. The fire department dumps the snakes out in the middle of nowhere in the heat of the day with no shade or shelter from the burning sun, in unfamiliar territory. Most of the relocated snakes will die.

My neighbors dump "relocated" rattlesnakes in the big arroyo below my house because they've heard I am a friend of snakes. I keep the area around the old corrals hospitable with a water trough and places for snakes to hide and to find rodents, but it is difficult to say if any of the snakes that were relocated here survived. The resident rattlesnakes stake out their territory and don't easily accept refugees because the overpopulation of an area will bring starvation for everyone. Then the relocated snakes have to deal with the roadrunners that live here, and with the great horned owls that kill and eat whatever they please. The odds for survival even at my place aren't good.

Last year Lyon and Snapper together managed to smash and tear to pieces a huge rattlesnake that lived under the dog house. The two mastiffs worked together, and while both were bitten, they had little swelling or pain. Lyon was emboldened by their success and became very aggressive with snakes. I found myself on alert and whenever I heard the mastiffs barking out back, I'd run out to make sure they were not killing a rattlesnake or other reptile.

Last Thursday evening I went for a swim. While I was away, Lyon tried to smash a big rattlesnake that had come into the dog yard. Maybe Snapper had learned her lesson last year because this time she apparently didn't participate in the attack. Last year she had helped divert the snake's attention, so Lyon could kill it without danger to himself. But this time he met the snake alone; most likely Lyon had brought down his huge right front paw to smash the big snake's head, but the snake had struck first. Ordinarily a snakebite into muscle is far more dangerous to a dog than a bite to the dog's head or neck. Luckily Lyon had developed enough immunity from previous bites to the skin on his head and neck that a bite into the muscle wasn't life-threatening.

But Lyon's front paw swelled up as big as a catcher's mitt. I gave him antihistamines and pain pills prescribed by Dr. Christo the veterinarian. By the following morning the swelling had gone down and he seemed fine. I was curious to see whether the dog had managed to kill the snake that bit him, so I searched the dog yard but found nothing.

By Saturday night Lyon had developed a secondary infection in his right paw and leg, and by Sunday morning, the veterinarian had to come to the house.

The site of the fang holes sloughed off necrotic tissue, and I wondered if Lyon was going to have further damage to his leg. Humans who get snakebitten on their limbs often suffer permanent withering of the muscle and nerve tissue; but they would not have previously built up as much resistance to the snake venom as Lyon has. The vet left antibiotics and antioxidant vitamins, and I let Lyon sleep on the floor in the bedroom because sleeping near their master helps mastiffs to heal. Monday morning the swelling had decreased dramatically, and Lyon wanted to return to the dog yard with the other three mastiffs who know enough to leave snakes alone. Will he stop attacking rattlesnakes? Time will tell.

Lyon is the smartest most beautiful dog I've ever lived with. He is black, silver and apricot brindle. He came from a renowned breeder and a great lineage created by Mrs. Greco, after World War Two when the English mastiff and other mastiff breeds were in danger of extinction in Europe due to the war.

So few old English mastiffs remained there was danger of degeneration from inbreeding unless a radical step was taken. The old English mastiff registry in England gave Mrs. Greco a one-time permit to breed a German mastiff to one of her English mastiffs, and the offspring were registered as old English mastiffs. This step gave the Greco dogs enough genetic diversity to be intelligent, gentle, free of hip or other problems and they are very beautiful—especially the brindles.

My English mastiffs learn human routines quickly; they dislike interruptions of these patterns. Once a house-sitter took Lyon with him while he fed the horses. The house-sitter forgot to turn off the faucet at the water trough. As he began to walk back up the hill to the house, Lyon stood next to the water faucet and barked until the house-sitter came back and shut off the water. Lyon knew the routine of feeding and watering the horses because he accompanied the humans, and he knew the last thing he and the humans always did was walk over to the water faucet to turn it off before they went up the hill.

Lyon has a strange routine with the long dry fronds of the potted pony tail palm by the clothesline. He slowly walks under the fronds so that they drag over the entire length of his head, back and tail, lightly touching, tickling him. He slips into a trance of quiet ecstasy, and continues to move back and forth under the dry palm fronds for minutes on end. Once or twice he's caught me spying on him but he maintains his dignity as he continues to let the dry fronds flutter down his spine.

Through circumstances beyond my control, I ended up with six of these wonderful mastiffs—all of them related to one another. I was the midwife for all of the pups Lyon and Thelma had, including the births of Macho and Osa. Snapper and Rosie are Lyon's daughters but from Xena, also a Greco dog.

CHAPTER 55

I only walked three times in September. Yesterday, October 6, I walked for the first time in weeks. The dirt and the stones of the trail welcomed me back. I felt it through the soles of my walking shoes; a softness, a giving way, a gentleness that welcomed me like an old friend. I suppose the trail and I are old friends after thirty years of my horseback rides and walks. For years I wasn't sure I'd be able to keep the old house or the acreage so I tried not to become too attached to the place. But now I've lived with these black basalt peaks green with saguaro and palo verde years longer than I lived in my beloved birthplace of sandstone, lava hills and juniper. All along I've been blessed.

The morning was cool and cloudy so I put on my Arizona Cardinals hat and I didn't bother to wear sunglasses. The sun came out as I started up the hill and passed the ant palace of stone. I wished then that I'd worn my sunglasses. But I felt so good to be walking on the trail I didn't mind the bright sun.

As I approached the side trail to the entrance of the Thunderbird Mine I saw something on the ground—trash of some sort. From my front porch off in the distance I'd seen two people at the mine entrance earlier in the morning. I went to remove the trash on the side trail but as I got closer I saw it was a pair of sunglasses. They fit.

The trail turned toward the east and I was glad for the sunglasses, and I felt such happiness for the generosity of the world. As I approached the Gila Monster Mine I was watchful for the two light beige rattle-snakes, one small, one larger, who like to nap in the middle of the trail where the sand is soft and fine.

At the Gila Monster Mine the broken limbs and trunk of the great saguaro still lay across the trail where the windstorm felled it weeks before. Shod hoof-prints showed that riders made their horses step over the broken cactus arms and start a new path to the left of another piece of an arm.

I passed the dance plaza of the javelinas and the deer where soft sand gets deposited from a small arroyo. Nearby I noticed a very elegant ant palace all in the base of an outcrop of orange pink granite. The coolness of the morning brought out the ants; their motion caught my attention. I forgot to look for the bright orange round rock on the hillside to the north-northeast.

I came upon the spot where I had earlier found the opalescent tumbled glass in the arroyo sand near the trail crossing. I always look for the reflection of the sun off other fragments of arroyo-tumbled glass in the sand. From there the trail goes up the hill where I must not look or I will see the two-story abomination. Then I had a premonition that the man and his machine had done more damage to the arroyo.

As I stepped around the mesquite at the edge of the big arroyo, I saw that the man and his machine had removed more large boulders and further destroyed the habitat on the bottom of the big arroyo. He left behind a reddish basalt boulder broken open in the middle of the arroyo as if he planned to take it next.

All the good energy I'd felt from the walk on the trail suddenly vanished. I felt sick. I'd really hoped that the tons of boulders and rocks the man and his machine had already removed would complete the landscaping of his gargantuan yard. But alas! He intended to turn the big arroyo into his own personal rock quarry.

Here is the catch with karma, or curses and witchcraft: they often don't take effect fast enough. Karma may not even things until your next life.

The Celtic curse, which the British poet Kathleen Raine had pronounced under the old tree by the sea against Gavin Maxwell, her ex-lover, took effect almost at once. Within three months Maxwell's beloved sea otter was killed while under Raine's care; then Maxwell's cottage by the sea mysteriously burned to the ground. Within twelve months of Raine's curse Maxwell developed brain cancer and was dead six months later.

I could have called again to complain that the man was operating a sand and gravel pit in violation of the county zoning laws but I wasn't hopeful. This is the old West and private property rights are absolute here; there's no such thing as the common good. I'd already had two county officials from different departments tell me they couldn't stop the man and his machine.

I lost all my walking momentum at the site of the damaged boulders, but a short distance past I found a turquoise rock, triangular in shape and the size of my thumb. I hadn't walked since the last rainstorm. I found another piece of turquoise stone the size and shape of a butterfly on a sandbar near the hidden place where I hear the air rush out of the Earth. The big arroyo was no less generous with its turquoise stones despite the new damage and new loss of boulders.

This machine man strikes me as the sort who will gouge more boulders from the big arroyo each time the county contacts him, to show his contempt for the government and environmental laws.

Each time I walk, I notice I feel better as I get farther away from the gouges and holes where the boulders were removed. The next big rainstorm and flood down the big arroyo would erode the bank and hill beneath the huge ugly house; the holes would fill in with rocks and sand. Eventually a five hundred year rain would come and carry down boulders from the slopes of the Black Mountain to jam the big arroyo at that place once again.

CHAPTER 56

Good news. The bees returned today to swarm in clusters over the hummingbird feeders. The hummingbirds also began to show up a few days ago. The cold spell from the north had sent the hummingbirds and bees down from the mountains where they avoided the big heat of summer.

I wondered if the great horned owls spent the summer in the mountains as well. They might spend the days in the mountains asleep high in the tops of pine trees at nine thousand feet where it is cool. Then after dark they might glide back down into the valley to hunt for heat-dazed rodents and lost house pets.

I think about the great horned owls frequently since the terrible attack on my military macaws in January. A week or so before the attack, I'd seen a great horned owl one morning on a power pole not far from the big arroyo. I was concerned the owl might harm itself in the power line, and made a note to call the power company to have them install a device on the pole which deters birds of prey from electrocuting themselves.

The power pole where the owl was perched is only a short distance across the arroyo from the site of the ancestors' place where I found the carved quartz crystal owl and the white quartz knife.

I bought a book on owls to learn more about them; perhaps, I thought, more knowledge would give me peace of mind and more power to protect my beloved parrots from the great horned owls by night and the red-tail hawks by day. I learned a great deal about owls, and great horned owls in particular, but the knowledge did nothing to abate my awe or my fear for any being that might face a great horned owl in combat.

The great horned owl is one of the few owl species that is not endangered. Great horned owls prey on smaller species of owls and will kill red-tail hawks and peregrine falcons. They may live twenty-eight years, far longer than other owl species.

Hidden under their feathers, the great horned owls have long necks, so that their skeletons most resemble that of a pterodactyl. With their long sharp claws and powerful beaks, they are capable of inflicting grave injury or even death on human beings.

The owl book noted that the great horned owl may become so fixated on its intended prey that it will dive in front of traffic and get hit. A writer friend tells of a rich gentleman from Virginia who saw a dead horned owl beside the highway a few days before Thanksgiving, and told his chauffeur to stop and pick up the owl. When they got home the man instructed the chauffeur to take the owl to the kitchen for the cook to prepare for Thanksgiving dinner. The meat was so tough and stringy that my friend managed to swallow only one bite.

I take no chances with the owls and my remaining macaws. Every night we plug in a light and a radio tuned to a right wing talk radio station; my theory is the great horned owls won't be able to concentrate on predations against the macaws in the octagon aviary if they hear the ugliness of the human voices from the radio and see a bright light.

The Gila woodpecker is drinking from the big hummingbird feeder. The bees laid claim to the two smaller feeders. Somehow the bees manage to drink from the hummingbird feeders—I'm not sure how— unless bees have long tongues like the butterflies and hummingbirds.

I saw a large mesquite lizard on the south-facing stucco wall of the house this morning. He seemed to be finding tiny insects in the rough surface of the stucco wall. His tail was fat. He might be a relative of the Godzilla lizard we used to watch in the front yard. Only the tiny lizards roam the front yard now; their small size makes them difficult for the roadrunner to spot.

Today the bees are fewer and not swarming on one another nor are they as excited as the bees that came yesterday. They are from a different hive and are not as numerous as yesterday's bees. These bees recognize me; they fly up around my face as yesterday's bees did. Some of them landed on my legs and arms as if they also recognize me by the scent of my skin.

CHAPTER 57

I f you focus on a certain point in the foothills on the north slope of the peak that is many hundreds of yards away, it is possible in certain light to see objects—rocks or cactus or a person—magnified or as if you were very close. More than once, when I looked west toward the peak I noticed something very odd: all light, all that is visible emanating from that point appears much larger than the surrounding terrain. A magic circle of telescopic vision which could only mean some sort of discontinuity of space-time due to a hidden mass or density with a strong gravitational pull within the volcanic peak or ridge of basalt.

The gravity of a parallel universe very near to ours might cause refractions of the sunlight so that objects would appear oddly different in certain spots on the peak's north-facing slope.

Or perhaps the gravity source is a tiny black hole smaller than the smallest subatomic particle, "a Hawking hole" exerting awesome gravity on all matter or energy that strays too close and falls into its gravity, one so powerful that light slows down noticeably from that point, and everything appears much larger.

After a rainstorm on the slopes of the peak, I've seen the walls of stone palaces built into the sheer sides of the mountain shimmer golden in the late afternoon light as the sun descends into the west. I glanced in the direction of that place on the slope of the mountain peak where things appear much larger than the surroundings, and for an instant that point expanded so everything in it appeared much larger in the golden light.

The small mesquite lizards are almost black; the darkest brown striated with dark gray that mimics the rough dark bark of the mesquite. They stay close to the mesquite tree this time of year. Perhaps this is because the gnats and other tiny insects that reach maturity now remain close to the mesquite leaves for moisture.

Inside the bottle of hummingbird sugar water are many small flying bugs of a metallic iridescent emerald gold. The Gila woodpeckers wait for these gold bugs to soak up the sugar before the woodpeckers gobble up the candied delicacies. I always think of Edgar Allan Poe's short story "The Gold-Bug" whenever I see these little flying gold bugs although Poe's bug resembled a scarab beetle.

Here is my new favorite Dickinson poem:

> Bee! I'm expecting you!
> Was saying Yesterday
> To Somebody you know
> That you were due—
> The Frogs got Home last Week—
> Are settled, and at work—
> Birds, mostly back—
> The Clover warm and thick—
> You'll get my Letter by
> The seventeenth; Reply
> Or better, be with me—
> Yours, Fly.

Halloween. The first day of the Celtic New Year. Yesterday morning the bees came for water and suddenly died. The wind was blowing the filthy dust from Tucson all across the valley, high into the sky.

Once the wind stopped blowing, the bees stopped dying. Later the local TV news reported that dozens of people went to hospital emergency rooms and urgent care centers for respiratory ailments.

Years ago in the mid-nineties, a mining supply company that sold chemicals used in smelting copper illegally dumped toxic wastes into the city sewers. The sewage treatment plant at Roger Road released a cloud of toxic gas that traveled six miles, into the Tucson Mountains, and woke me up at four in the morning.

It knocked Sandino to the floor of the aviary and required an emergency visit to the vet for cortisone to save him. The four baby military macaws in the nest with Sandino and Paco were killed.

Over a hundred people from the area around the mining supply company were rushed to hospitals. People were outraged and demanded the county shut the company down, but instead the company cleverly filed for Chapter Eleven bankruptcy which prevents company shut-downs even for environmental reasons. Copper is big business in Arizona, the Copper State.

My small red plastic writing table barely has space for the notebook or the manuscript because it is covered with pieces of crystal quartz I picked up here and there. The crystals range from opaque to translucent, even in a single piece. I noticed all the pieces of crystal quartz I found at the ancestors' place were translucent. The figure of the owl carved out of crystal quartz has a translucent head and wings.

I spotted the bits of crystal quartz easily because they were surrounded by darker jaspers and cherts that formed a half-moon pattern around the crystals. The crystals were in the same area, within a few feet of one another, among the chips and pieces of white quartz and flint struck off for arrow points and knives. The flints, cherts and jaspers the ancestors gathered to chip stood out plainly on the pale gray volcanic soil. I found the white quartz knife not far from there.

The first quartz crystal I picked up was unlike any other stone in the area; it was so bright next to the darker rocks. Clearly it was carried to this spot by human beings. The quartz crystal is the size and shape of my thumb. One end is white quartz with many many tiny crystals amassed so they can't be seen individually; this mass of crystals is called a "massive specimen."

Before I saw a photograph of a massive specimen, I mistook the patterns of the quartz crystals as fractures caused by pressure or explosion. However the reason the quartz crystals grow in a mass may be due to pressure or an explosion that occurs during the crystals' formation.

I imagine the crystals on full moon nights would catch the light and glitter—hence their value to medicine people, and to sorcerers.

CHAPTER 58

On my walk this morning I could see the machine man's intentions for the other boulders and rocks. He'd already removed the sand and smaller rocks around them that held them in place. I feel sick when I think about it because nothing can be done to stop the harm.

Once past that place I felt better. The arroyo is undiminished in spirit. I found a turquoise rock that fits in my palm. It is a light sienna orange, an iron oxide stone with delicate outlines in chrysocolla that accentuate the rock's trapezoidal shape. The warm orange red and yellow oxides show off the chrysocolla's beauty. It is one of the loveliest turquoise rocks I've found in a while.

A short distance later I bent over to pick up a fragment of brown bottle glass and I spotted a tiny spot of blue so intense I thought it might be a bit of plastic or more spent bubblegum the color of turquoise.

It was a nugget of chrysocolla the size of the end of my little finger though thinner than my finger. It is very solid and hard, though I don't think it has chalcedony with it. When I licked its surface, it seemed almost impermeable but very soon the moisture on the surface of the nugget was gone, absorbed by the chrysocolla and the dry air in the room.

I happened to turn on National Public Radio while Irene Pepperberg was a guest, talking about her new book, *Alex and Me*.

I had followed her research into animal intelligence with the famous African gray parrot Alex. I bought the book she published with Harvard University Press in 2000 on her laboratory research work over twenty years with Alex. She compared the results of her work with the gray parrot to that done on language acquisition by the great apes, dolphins and human infants. Alex had the same level of ability to communicate as the great apes and the dolphins.

Today on NPR, Pepperberg talked about her time in Tucson when she was at the University of Arizona. She lived west of Tucson in the desert. One afternoon she brought Alex home with her from the lab where he usually spent the night. She'd gotten a nice cage and stocked it with Alex's favorite foods and toys. But once in the cage, Alex looked out the window where two tiny desert screech owls were nesting in a mesquite tree. Pepperberg said Alex immediately started to say "I wanna go back! I wanna go back!" Pepperberg pulled the curtains shut so the parrot couldn't see the nesting owls, but Alex knew they were still there, and Alex kept saying he wanted to go back until finally Pepperberg drove the parrot back to the lab and his cage.

Her work with Alex inspired me to raise my African gray parrot as if she were a parrot child and not a bird. Pepperberg had to follow strict protocols to be able to call her research "hard science." I had no such impediments. I wanted my parrot child to learn language as a human child does, in the context of a household, and here that means big dogs and other parrots.

Two of my old English mastiffs, Rosie and Macho, spend nights and most days in the summer in the same room with Gray Bird. She knows their names and calls them just as I do.

Gray Bird watches children's educational television every morning. This season there are a number of children's cartoons with dogs in them including Clifford the Big Red Dog and Martha the Talking Dog.

The cartoons with the dogs seem to interest her more because she knows what the words "dog" and "dogs" mean. She also knows the dogs have individual names. She never makes a mistake with the names of the six mastiffs, even when I sometimes confuse the two silver fawn mastiffs; Gray Bird always knows which is Thelma and which is Osa.

Gray Bird makes up nicknames for herself. She heard me sing a song about a little gray bird with a little black beak and a little red tail, and she started repeating "Black Beak" and responded to it when I said it; so "Black Beak" became Gray Bird's first but not last nickname. She also goes by "Chippy Bird Song," and of course terms of endearment like Gray Baby and Baby Bird.

But just recently Gray Bird called herself "Gray-bee," her contraction of Gray Baby. If she wants to be called Gray-bee or Black Beak we are happy to oblige to encourage her inventions with names and other words.

Gray Bird is a big fan of Elmo. She knows the names of the other *Sesame Street* puppets as well, and she knows what time the program is broadcast. She can sing the *Sesame Street* theme song, and she sings other songs that I sing to her, songs I made up so that Gray Bird is *always* the subject of the songs.

I enjoy *Sesame Street* sometimes, so I watched it with Gray Bird which helped reinforce her attention to the program. She likes to watch the Barney program, but I let her do that by herself.

In Africa where the gray parrots live, the tribal people revere them as sacred beings, and their red tail feathers which they shed from time to time are used in prayer bundles and other objects of spiritual power.

CHAPTER 59

I thought about the owl attack on my macaws in January. The man and machine and the violence he committed against the arroyo had disrupted the area, and must have driven the nesting owls to great lengths. To have three large macaws attacked in two separate aviaries on the same night seems strange and out of proportion.

At first I wondered: Was it the Owl Being, angered by the portraits of the other Lords of the Night and his portrait not yet begun by me? Or did I give someone macaw feathers that somehow found their way to a ritual that costs the macaw's life in order to heal the human?

No. It was the dust and noise that disrupted that part of the arroyo; it was the damage done to the great horned owls' habitat by the machine which was just as ferocious and out of proportion as the attack on my beautiful macaws.

I'd already sent county authorities out to survey the private sand and gravel pit; I'd sent letters with photographs I'd made of the progression of the damage; I'd made phone calls to people who could see nothing wrong with gouging boulders from the big arroyo.

The idea had been developing for a while. I mulled it over as I practiced walking past the broken boulders and gouged earth without reacting, averting my gaze, taking deep breaths, not allowing myself to be upset by the widening pit of broken rock and torn up sand. I tried not to notice the new damage, the smashed limestone that once formed part of the bank.

I had to do something. At least I had to try. I recalled many years ago, a group of animal rights activists tried to protect the helpless pure white baby seals from bludgeoning by hunters. The animal rights people stained the baby seals' white coats with a non-toxic dye. The stain lasted until the baby seals got older, and their coats darkened naturally and became less valuable to the hunters.

What if I painted the emblem of the Star Beings on the rocks that the machine man was about to rip out of the arroyo? This thought crossed my mind and I knew who sent it.

My initial reaction was what good would the paint on the boulders do? Did the dye on the white coats of the baby seals save them? The Star Beings reminded me it might take years before the boulders crushed the man on his machine; if I wanted to speed things up I must do something.

But I was directed by the Star Beings to act: to use children's washable white tempera to paint the boulders and rocks in danger. It was a long shot, a last try because the man clearly intended to damage and remove more boulders that he'd already begun to excavate.

The Star Beings directed me to paint their glyph, the white cross figure of the star, on all sides of the boulders, and especially on the scars left by the metal claw of the machine or cracks or other damaged inflicted by the machine.

What if the machine man didn't care about small white crosses painted on the boulders, and he and his machine ripped the boulders out of the arroyo anyway?

Then I realized: once the Star Beings' small white crosses were painted on the boulders and rocks in the arroyo they worked a kind of magic. All human beings were put on notice that the boulders were under the protection of the Star Beings and must not be disturbed or damaged; all violators would pay terrible consequences.

The ancient petroglyph the ancestors incised into the boulder in the big arroyo was done only for the most important spiritual purposes.

I carried a small day pack with the paint, a jar of clean water, a rag and a paintbrush. I was on a mission for the Star Beings so I didn't take along my camera.

The sun was very warm for early November. I hoped not to be interrupted while I painted because a number of hikers and horseback riders use the public right-of-way corridor the arroyo provides.

I worked for more than an hour to paint the small white crosses on the boulders and the rocks the man had already started to excavate. Then I went to work on the others nearby. There were a lot of boulders and rocks to paint star symbols on. In the bright sun and the heat, I wore myself out. When I got finished the place looked as if there had been a great meteorite shower of small white crosses on the boulders and rocks in the damaged area.

If others mistook them for Christian crosses, it would be fitting, because Jesus Christ was also known as the Morning Star or Venus among indigenous worshippers in the Americas.

I was hot and tired when I finally packed up the paintbrush and the leftover white poster paint. But before I headed home I surveyed and savored the white crosses on the rocks and boulders; the scattered white stars transformed the gouged earth and shattered rocks just as the Star Beings intended. Now instead of dread filling my heart when I walked up the arroyo past the gravel pit, I'll see the constellation of white crosses, the sign, the warning from the Star Beings, and my heart will be filled with happiness and hope.

I realized the notice I painted to him from the Star Beings might set off the man's mania. But he intended to destroy those rocks before the small white crosses appeared, so it was worth a try.

Later it came to me (from the Star Beings again) each cross represents a fracture, a broken bone in the body of the man who dares to harm the boulders and rocks. It doesn't have to happen here in the big arroyo with a boulder that crushes him and his machine—the broken bones—as many fractures as there are painted stars—could easily come to him in a car crash in Tucson traffic.

On my way home from my mission for the Star Beings I found a chrysocolla nugget the size of a bean, and a piece of turquoise rock the size and shape of an apple wedge.

Mid-November now. I went to photograph the rocks I painted yesterday. I took a different path over the new open space land the old neighbors gave to the county. I never realized a smaller arroyo parallels the big arroyo for a short distance. I crossed it to get back to the big arroyo and in the brushy deep shady bottom I found the skull, spine, ribs and feet of a large javelina with long curved incisors. Dried meat bits remained on the bones, enough that I knew some large predator would be back to chew the bones clean.

The large size of the javelina and its tusks made me realize only a pack of coyotes or a powerful large predator would have dared attack such a big javelina. Mountain lion, I'd guess, because the coyotes are pack animals and in a matter of hours, they would have eaten or carried away all trace of the javelina. Mountain lions are solitary beings, except in mating season. The rest of the year they live and hunt alone and stash their kills so they can return and feed on them.

It occurred to me the ancestors might not have passed up those bones, especially not in lean times when the marrow in the bones would have sustained the people another day, enough time to find something else to eat. Boil those bones a long time with some chilitipines, some palo verde beans and cactus buds and you'd have a tasty stew.

Sometimes, at odd moments—such as tonight as I shut the refrigerator door—I hear what sounds like Dolly barking in her yard. All the other dogs were indoors bedded down for the night, and they remained quiet. The one year anniversary of her death is this week.

My noble Thelma dog has another infection in her foot—the same foot that we treated with high-powered antibiotics a few months ago. We took her to the vet office to x-ray her sore paw. She got up on the waiting room bench and stared out the window at the parking lot. She knew which vehicle brought her to the vet office and she looked at the old white car longingly; she knows if she can just get back to it, she will be able to return home.

Thelma weighs two hundred twenty pounds, too heavy for Dr. Christo, his assistant and me to lift onto the x-ray table. But I recalled that back in the waiting room Thelma had the bad manners to get up on the shaky bench intended for people. I told the vet Thelma would get up on the bench, so he dragged the wooden bench into the x-ray room. Thelma seemed to understand we were trying to do something important so when I asked her, she climbed up onto the bench which we pushed up against the x-ray table. She graciously allowed us to lift her huge left front paw onto the x-ray table. Not once did Thelma try to move her paw or get off the bench, although she is strong enough to do anything she wants.

The vet and I agreed we'd postpone antibiotics, and instead give Thelma medicine for the pain while we tried to boost her immune system with supplements and herbs. I soaked her foot in a strong tea made from dried greasewood leaves.

Greasewood, or chaparral, is a mighty plant, a powerful medicine that repels harmful organisms. It protects against insects including the dreaded assassin beetles that suck blood and trigger allergic reactions. But it also heals insect bites and skin inflammations, wounds, and pre-cancerous skin lesions, and even dries up warts and moles. A caution too: I once managed to use greasewood salve too frequently on myself and got mild itching and redness in the area, which went away as soon as I stopped using it.

Thelma got sick all over the place during the night. This morning she refused to eat. The vet prescribed soft salty food with pumpkin for bulk but she refuses to touch it.

Thelma is a silver fawn "classic" old English mastiff with a short wide head, and broad chest and rib cage; she is robust but not fat. She is full of only good energy and good will toward all humans, and toward other dogs and other living beings. When she is happy her whole body wags along with her tail. She is eight years old which is the beginning of old age for a mastiff.

One day later. Thelma refused to spend the night in the house last night. It was a warm night in the high fifties, but I worried she was getting ready to die. During the night I heard her bark and I wondered if the ghost dogs had come to prepare her to go with them to Paradise.

I got up at dawn to go out to check on her. I expected to find her dead, but raindrops were falling and she was up and wagging her tail, ready to come indoors out of the rain. Later she ate all her food and I knew she wasn't going to die. What a relief!

One of the cockatoo sisters, Mrs. Rambo, died this morning, November 25. I felt so badly. I felt I might have noticed something was wrong if I'd been doing the feeding and watering of the cockatoos instead of working every available moment on this manuscript. So I took back the feeding and watering of the parrots. I enjoy the time I spend caring for them a great deal.

The fall has been warm so I've put the fine mist sprayer on the hose to give the military macaws in the octagon aviary a treat. The misting gets them excited about bathing and they go to the stainless steel soup caldron after I fill it with clean water and they begin to dip their beaks and heads into the water while perched on the rim of the pan. Then they dip their wings to skim the water and flick their wings back on themselves so the water showers their head and back. Gracefully at first then exuberant and joyous as they sprinkle more water on themselves, macaws at their bath are one of my glimpses of Paradise.

Four days later. A warm rain out of the southeast fell gently all night. The rain barrel overflowed.

Tomorrow I will hike to the round rusty orange rock on the hillside that faces the dance plaza of the deer and javelinas. This seems like a good way to end the year of walks along the trail. I want to visit the little white crosses on the rocks to see what effects all the rain had on the washable paint.

The last day of November. I decided to make a new walking trail—off the back of the ridge and down to the small arroyo which the wild things, mostly the javelina, use for travel and as a sanctuary.

My plan was to walk to the rusty orange rock on the side of the hill, just a short distance on the old burro trail from the Gila Monster Mine pit. Although I was going north from my house, the ridge is very steep and rocky and I didn't want to fall, so I took my time. I stopped or detoured to take a look at odd rocks or strange formations that caught my eye.

After thirty years here I know this area a little, but the earth is constantly changing, rocks that move, pebbles that roll out from under the sole of your shoe and throw you down, shifts and changes that are new to me because they were not here, not yet visible when I last hiked here with Dolly Dog and her brother, Banana, thirteen years ago.

I noticed a small area at the foot of the ridge where I saw a soft grainy whitish rock, a soda stone, a chalky calcite in a thin layer like petrified pancake batter. With the toe of my shoe I tipped over the thin broken piece of the light soft stone. The odd deposit of chalky calcite appeared to come from a single source. I detoured to look more closely; the thin layer of whitish stone had a somewhat circular shape as if a stone in water made ripples from a center point. I looked where I thought the center might be and lo and behold I saw a narrow crack in the ground; it appeared to be the remnant of an ancient steam spout or mud geyser. Warm water still comes out of neighborhood wells. It is "fossil water" from volcanic steam that was trapped a million years ago in pockets of lava and basalt five hundred feet below.

I hadn't walked very far in the small arroyo when I disturbed a small herd of javelinas. They stampeded into the thickets of catsclaw mesquite and greasewood on the bank. I caught a glimpse of a baby javelina so I knew I had to be careful because the entire herd of javelina may charge a predator if they feel a threat to one of their babies. I hurried away, down the small arroyo, but to my left, to the north I could make out a game trail out of the arroyo that led to the old jeep trail about fifty yards away.

I crossed the jeep trail and headed for the small orange hill that lies east of the Gila Monster Mine. On my way to the small orange hill I encountered an odd patch of large round orange stones that looked as if they'd been molten then dropped in cold water. They appeared to be a large family of round orange stones like no others anywhere. They were all sizes and variations of round or egg-shaped forms; the largest were the size of sofas.

They looked so beautiful on the ridge above a little gulley, a great saguaro two hundred years old had grown up from between the largest round stones and towered over them.

How strange the round rusty orange rock on the hillside looked as I got closer to it, very different than it looked from the distance of the trail. With all the rain the desert shrubs and trees had grown mightily all summer and it had become difficult for me to see the rusty orange rock which I always thought appeared to be the image of a war shield, one of the Pueblo war shields that protected supernaturally. Yet on closer examination, the rock seemed a darker shade of red brown and less orange; it did not look at all like the round rust orange rock I'd seen from the trail whenever I walked. This rock had a brown iron ore deposit in the shape of an egg, not a circle or war shield like the orange rock had. On further reflection, I decided I hadn't reached the rock I intended but another similar rock with a dark rust center.

From the orange hill I returned exactly the way I'd come, by intuition, not by any conscious effort, so once again I got to pass close by a clan or tribe of round rocks. I got back on the trail and continued my walk. As I neared the big arroyo, high on the ridge above it, I saw the man on his machine enclosed by the high wall that surrounds his penitentiary style structure. I had a bad feeling at once about the boulders in the arroyo.

When I reached the arroyo I saw the machine tracks, and three of the large boulders I'd painted with white crosses had been toppled and parts broken off; then the machine had pushed them to the middle of the arroyo as if to block it. Now the man and machine were blocked from reaching the other boulders he'd partially excavated to remove. I wasn't sure what this signaled.

I had done as the Star Beings directed. Now life would become dangerous for that man with the machine. He was on notice the boulders and sand of the big arroyo were under the protection of the Star Beings. Now the Star Beings would show him no mercy. The Star Beings disliked human beings as it was, but they especially despised and destroyed his kind.

The big arroyo itself is space, open space, empty space, carved for eons through the rocks by floodwater as it descends toward the sea. Slowly but relentlessly the erosion will work so the bank of the arroyo will be undermined and in a flood it will collapse, and the wall around the house will topple into floodwaters with it. The boulders and rocks taken to landscape the yard will roll into the floodwater plop! plop! They always were travelers; the detour the man and machine took them on mattered less than a molecule. They will be on their way once more to the Santa Cruz River on its way to join the Salt River then on to the Colorado at Yuma and finally the sea.

Again to the sea. The boulders and rocks of limestone and quartzite originated in the Great Sea. As the stones from millions of years reckon it, man and machine are no more than a shadow of a mote of dust.

CHAPTER 60

My dear friend Mei-Mei came to Tucson the first week of December 2008. She gave seminars and performed a wonderful reading of her new work last night. Later Mei-Mei and I took a walk along the trail. I told her about the orange red rock that appears to be round on the hillside, but when I hiked up to it I felt I'd somehow gotten to a similar rock but not the round rock I'd seen from the trail. Distance and light affect the appearances of rocks, but the rock just looked too different to be the right one.

A short distance past the pit of the Gila Monster Mine, at the east end of the deer and javelina dance plaza, I stopped and pointed out the round red orange iron oxide rock. The old-time people used iron oxides for pottery, face paint and for cliff murals and sand paintings.

We left the trail and hiked cross-country from past the tribe of large round rocks at the edge of a small arroyo; then we took the old burro trail that passes at the foot of the small orange hill.

The hillside was steep but not too rocky to scale. We reached the orange red rock which looked entirely different than the rock I remembered from my recent visit. There must be two similar red orange iron oxide rocks in the same area of the orange hillside.

Yet when I looked I didn't see another such round orange rock. I need to make a more thorough survey. Today the sun was almost behind the hills so we needed to get back to the main trail.

We passed the place populated by the round rocks, and took the trail past the ant palaces with the star patterns of stones around their entrances. Then we came up the last rise before the big arroyo.

I braced myself for what I might see next, but the man and his machine had not returned since he'd pushed the two boulders across the trail. Some of the paint on the small white stars got scraped off when he toppled the boulders and pushed them across the trail, but a few of the crosses were still visible. The white crosses on the other rocks made a pictograph of a constellation fallen to Earth.

Now I realized the boulders the man pushed over were his attempt to block the trail in the bottom of the arroyo to discourage hikers and horseback riders who would have to squeeze by the rocks. He also blocked his own access to the fragile rock along the north side of the arroyo and the boulders which he'd begun to excavate before I painted them. Of course he could always use the machine to push the boulders aside if he wanted to go after the rocks and boulders painted with the white crosses, but I got the feeling the man didn't want those rocks for his yard, so maybe the painting worked after all.

We continued up the big arroyo homeward. We met a woman with her two dogs. She asked if we'd seen the "gang graffiti" painted on the rocks. The woman said she'd had a break-in and sent the sheriff's deputies who were investigating to see the "gang graffiti" on the rocks. Clearly she connected her burglary with the "gang graffiti."

Gangs spray-paint their graffiti all over Tucson but none of it looks anything like the small crosses painted with a brush and tempera. In Tucson "gang" and "gang graffiti" are code words white people use to indicate young brown or black men who they consider to be "aliens" even if they were born in Arizona.

How interesting that the small white crosses were interpreted as "gang graffiti" and not connected somehow with Christianity. Apparently the emblem of the Star Beings penetrated the psyches of the newcomers who got the message: indigenous forces are present to oppose you.

The woman concluded by saying that now she and her neighbors had to install an expensive gate on their private driveway. She and her neighbors are newcomers to Tucson—early retirees with enough money to build "dream houses" in the desert despite the financial crash.

The woman's reaction gave me an insight into the boulders toppled across the trail. Apparently the machine man had a similar response to the appearance of the white crosses of the Star Beings and thought an urban gang had driven miles out of town to the big arroyo to paint "gang graffiti" on the rocks he was excavating. The boulders he pushed over with the machine were intended to block the arroyo from further visits by gang members.

New Year's Day, 2009. The hikers' parking lot was nearly full when I left for my walk this morning. The holiday and the lovely warm weather brought out a great many visitors to the national park, but I only met one couple on the trail after I left the parking lot. Most park visitors come to hike the Sweetwater Trail that overlooks the city.

I found the tracks of a lone deer that danced last night at the sandy dance plaza. The ground is still damp in the low places like the dance plaza. I paused there to look at the orange hillside and to study the round orange rock. I wanted to make sure there wasn't a second, similar orange red rock on the hillside.

I didn't see another orange red iron oxide rock, but above and to the left of the round red orange rock on a prominent outcrop of the hill, I thought I saw petroglyphs in a lighter stone where the dark stone was pecked away. It might have been the angle of the morning light and nothing more.

It was a year ago today that I found the second attack by the man and the machine on the beautiful boulders and sandbars in the big arroyo. But this morning the place was very still, and felt at peace. The boulders with the crosses, even the ones the man flipped over, were beginning to lose the appearance of sudden violence; the machine tracks were smoothed by the rain. A number of the small white crosses already looked old and faded; they recede into the basalt and quartzite with every raindrop.

Gentle warm rains from the south have already graced us. Venus is a night sun brighter and larger each night. This is a good place to end. Gratitude to all of you beings of the stars.